The Classic Guide to
STILL LIFE AND FIGURE DRAWING
RETRO RESTORED EDITION

by
EDMUND KOLLER

**The Classic Guide to Still Life and Figure Drawing:
Retro Restored Edition**

Originally printed in 1926

Written by Edmund Koller
Cover design by Mark Bussler

Copyright © 2021 Inecom, LLC.
All Rights Reserved

No parts of this book may be reproduced or broadcast in any
way without written permission from Inecom, LLC.

www.CGRpublishing.com

The Complete Book of Birds:
Illustrated Enlarged Special
Edition

Robot Kitten Factory #1

The Complete Butterfly Book:
Enlarged Illustrated Special
Edition

International Library of Technology

159B

Still-Life and Figure Drawing

271 ILLUSTRATIONS

By

E. L. KOLLER

DIRECTOR OF ART SCHOOLS
INTERNATIONAL CORRESPONDENCE SCHOOLS
MEMBER OF THE AMERICAN FEDERATION OF ARTS

LINE DRAWING
MODEL DRAWING
LIGHT AND SHADE
THE HUMAN FIGURE
THE FIGURE IN REPOSE
THE FIGURE IN ACTION

1926

CONTENTS

Note.—This volume is made up of a number of separate Sections, the page numbers of which usually begin with 1. To enable the reader to distinguish between the different Sections, each one is designated by a number preceded by a Section mark (§), which appears at the top of each page, opposite the page number. In this list of contents, the Section number is given following the title of the Section, and under each title appears a full synopsis of the subjects treated. This table of contents will enable the reader to find readily any topic covered.

LINE DRAWING, § 1

	Pages
Purpose	9
Materials and Methods of Work	11
Drawing Exercises	16

Preliminary practice work; General information; Plates 1–6.

MODEL DRAWING, § 2

Purpose	87
Materials and Methods of Work	90

Blocking in and proportioning; Foreshortening of cube, pyramid, hexagonal prism, cylinder, cone, sphere, hemisphere, vase.

Drawing Exercises	139

General information; Plates 1–4.

LIGHT AND SHADE, § 3

Purpose	146
Light, Shade, and Shadow	147
Sources and Kinds of Illumination	147

Main sources of light; Diffused lighting; Front lighting; Rear lighting; Overhead lighting; Conventional lighting.

CONTENTS

LIGHT AND SHADE—(Continued)

	Pages
Light and Shade................................	154

 Direction of the rays of light; Angle of light rays in conventional lighting; High light and half light; Half shade; Deep shade; Formation of shadows; A shadow cast on a horizontal surface; A shadow cast on to a vertical plane; A shadow cast on to neighboring planes or objects not vertical; A shadow cast on to a curved surface; The shadow of an object having curved contours.

Demonstrations With the Wooden Models...........	168
Materials and Methods of Work....................	194

 Preliminary practice; Rendering from the model; Rendering in charcoal.

Drawing Exercises................................	204

 General information; Plates 1–10.

THE HUMAN FIGURE, § 4

Purpose	216

 Proper foundation for figure drawing; Foundation for caricaturing and cartooning.

Proportions of Human Figure......................	218

 Frame work of figure; Methods of proportioning entire figure; Methods of proportioning parts of figure; The face and its features.

Drawing Exercises................................	271

 General information; Plates 1–4.

THE FIGURE IN REPOSE, § 5

Drawings from Special Studies and Photographs......	274
Studies from Charcoal Drawings and Photographs....	275
Examples of Charcoal Studies and Photographs......	288
Drawings from Casts.............................	314

 Function of cast; Suggestions for practice study; Studies made direct from casts.

Drawings from Living Models......................	336

 Function of living models; Suggestions for practice work; Studies made direct from living models.

Figure-Drawing Exercises.........................	340

 General information; Plates 1–10.

CONTENTS

THE FIGURE IN ACTION, §6

	Pages
Action	347
Drawing from Photographs	354
Use of camera; Specimen photographs of action; Making sketches from photographs.	
Drawing from Living Models	366
Making time sketches; Making rapid-action sketches; Making sketches from memory.	
Drawing Expressions and Drapery	388
Facial expressions; Portraiture; Gesture; Drapery.	
Figure Drawing Exercises	413
General information; Plates 1–8.	

PREFACE

This volume, which is made up of Instruction Papers, or Sections, used in the Art Courses of the International Correspondence Schools, is the first one of a series on practical illustrating; and the subjects covered in it are intended to serve as a foundation for the more advanced and technical subjects that are treated in volumes that are to follow. The volume itself, however, will serve as a complete treatise on drawing, if the reader does not care to go into illustrating.

The subjects treated are progressively arranged to lead from the simplest forms of drawing to those that are more difficult. First of all, instruction is given on the methods of limbering up the hand and muscles to give the flexibility required in drawing freehand. Then follow exercises with straight lines and curved lines. Next, the drawing direct from simple objects, such as geometric models, is taken up; first, in outline only, where foreshortening is taught, and then in charcoal-rendered tones and masses, where light, shade, and the accurate casting of shadows are explained. Such work is considered still-life drawing. When the student has learned the freehand drawing of simple still-life objects, he is prepared to take up figure drawing. First, the blocking in and proportioning of the male and the female figure (adult and child) are taught, then the drawing of the figure in repose and in action. This is accomplished by having the student work, first, from progressively-arranged charcoal studies of the human figure; second, from plaster casts of the figure and its parts; and third, from actual living models (friends, acquaintances, etc.) posed according to directions.

PREFACE

The system of detailed explanations for home study, as used here, thus lacks none of the characteristics or advantages possessed by the best resident art schools. Those familiar with the subject will see at a glance that the methods of still-life and figure drawing presented here are somewhat unique and differ in some respects from those usually described in textbooks on these subjects. It is a fact, however, that the systems and methods of teaching here used are not mere theories, but are the result of years of experiment and periodical reshaping and improvement, and have stood the test of actual training of hundreds of students for practical illustrating work.

From the very nature of the subjects treated, it must be evident that a mere reading of the text and an inspection of the pictures, without actual working out of the drawing exercises, will accomplish little for the reader. To obtain the benefits of the instruction here given, the student-reader must actually do the drawing work described in order that he may get the understanding that comes from practice. If he is a student of a school using this text, he will, of course, submit his drawings to his teachers for criticism; in any case he will find much advantage in doing the work and criticising it as best he can. The reader will probably want to extend the knowledge of drawing he obtains from this volume. He is, therefore, advised to procure the four succeeding volumes of the series, which have the following titles: Black-and-White Technique, Color Technique and Composition, Drawing for Process Reproduction, and Commercial Illustrating and Cartooning.

E. L. KOLLER.

Scranton, Pa.

I L T 159B

LINE DRAWING

PURPOSE

1. Foundation for an Art Training.—The proper foundation for successful work in any line of practical art, illustrative or decorative, is the *ability to draw well*. To acquire such ability must therefore be the first concern of the beginner. Ability to draw does not mean ability to copy lines and pictures made by other artists; it means, rather, training the eye to see accurately, and the hand to delineate properly what is seen, so that original compositions and designs may be made.

Unfortunately, the tendency of the age is to seek short cuts to proficiency. Just as the young music pupil is eager to play composition pieces before mastering finger exercises and the scales, so the beginner in the study of practical art work is eager to draw pictures and to make designs before ever his eye has been trained to see intelligently, and his hand to draw properly, even the simplest forms. Coupled with this idea of short cuts to excellence is the equally fallacious idea that there is such a thing as an "inborn talent" for drawing, and that one who possesses such "talent" needs no systematic foundation training in drawing.

The sooner the beginner realizes that there are no short cuts to proficiency in practical art work, and that there is no such thing as being born with an ability for drawing, the better he will be prepared to undertake a serious course of art training. One is no more born with an ability for drawing than he is born with an ability for story writing or for surgical work. It is true that one may have an inborn sense of beauty, of proportion, of humor, etc., and, through inheritance and early training, may have had his powers of observation, memory, judgment, imagination, etc. well developed. All these powers must be developed in the young artist who wants to be successful, but their development does not fall within the province of the art instructor. It is a common thing to have the beginner in the study of practical art say to his instructor: "I can copy pictures and designs perfectly, but I cannot originate them; I want you to teach me originality." This shows an entirely wrong conception of the whole matter. These mental qualities must be acquired and developed by the beginner himself. No art instructor can give to the student originality, a sense of humor, keen powers of observation and memory, business enterprise, etc., and those who profess to do so are deceiving the beginner. The province of the art instructor, is therefore, first of all, to train the beginner *to draw;* and such is the purpose of this Section.

2. First Stage in Learning to Draw.—First of all, in learning to draw, the beginner must become familiar with the materials with which the drawings are to be made. Next, it will be necessary for him to limber up the muscles of the arm, wrist, hand, and fingers by special exercises, so as to get the stiffness out of these muscles and to enable him to become accustomed to holding the pencil as an instrument for drawing. When the muscles have been properly limbered up, simple exercises in drawing lines with a lead pencil may be attempted. Next, these practice lines may be made to take definite directions, straight and curved, and eye measurement may be brought to bear, so that simple geometric figures can be drawn with accented lines. After these preliminary exercises, the drawing of simple household objects—represented as "flat" drawings—can be attempted.

Work of the kind just described is known as **line drawing**, because it comprises exercises in drawing lines, as such, preliminary to undertaking more advanced drawing work later. This is the first stage in learning to draw; and is the extent of the work covered in this Section.

3. Importance of First Stage.—The training given in this first stage in learning to draw is such as is needed not only by the novice, but also by those who may have had training or experience elsewhere. For this reason it will be expected that each student will proceed with this Section as arranged, and that he will not request permission to omit this preliminary work because it may appear simple and elementary.

However, persons who have had systematic training and practical experience elsewhere may submit specimens of their drawings, and, if these meet with the approval of the instructors at the Schools, may then proceed with the advanced work.

Such test drawings must be in the nature of regular training-school drawings, giving evidence of a regular course of study elsewhere, or published reproductions of commercial drawings prepared and sold by the student. Drawings such as copies of magazine covers, lithographs, pictures of girls' heads, cartoons, etc., must not be submitted for they will not be considered. Further, no such copy work as just described should be submitted for criticism, for such criticism cannot be given at this early stage of the Course. The correct procedure is to go ahead with the present Section, and those that follow, and to do the work as directed.

MATERIALS AND METHODS OF WORK

MATERIALS REQUIRED

4. Board, Paper, Pencils, Etc.—To prevent the student from being delayed in starting the work of his Course, the proper drawing materials for this Section, Line Drawing, are provided as follows:

One **drawing board**, size about 16 in. × 22 in. This size of board is best for this work, as well as for future work. It can be conveniently rested on the knees, and will accommodate not only a plate-size sheet (15 in. × 10 in.) but also a full-size sheet of drawing paper, which is 15 in. × 20 in. or thereabouts.

Twelve sheets of **drawing paper**, size 15 in. × 20 in. This paper is known as cold-pressed white drawing paper, and is entirely suitable for line drawing.

LINE DRAWING

Four **drawing pencils**—one H, one HH, one B, and one HB. These pencils, if properly cared for, will be sufficient for the work called for in this Section.

In addition to the foregoing materials, **thumbtacks, erasers, a sandpaper pencil pointer,** and a **pencil holder** are supplied. The use of each one of these articles will be self-evident, and will be fully understood as the drawing work progresses.

METHODS OF WORK

5. Getting the Paper Ready for Use.—For use in the exercises that follow later, each of the twelve sheets of drawing paper just mentioned should be cut into two equal parts across

Fig. 1

the shorter dimension, so as to make twenty-four 15″ × 10″ sheets, and if, for any reason, the sheet is somewhat larger, it should be trimmed to the 15″ × 10″ size.

The manner in which to place and fasten a sheet of paper of this size on the drawing board is shown in Fig. 1. The 15″ × 10″ sheet is laid at the upper left corner of the drawing board so that its longest dimension is horizontal with the longest dimension of the drawing board. It is secured to the board by sticking a thumbtack through each corner of the paper and forcing the tack into the wood. The paper is placed in this position so as to leave plenty of room at the right and the lower part of the drawing board on which to rest the wrist and the elbow when drawing various kinds of lines.

6. Method of Sharpening Pencils.—All the pencils mentioned for use in this work are sharpened in the following manner: First, with a sharp knife, the wood of the pencil,

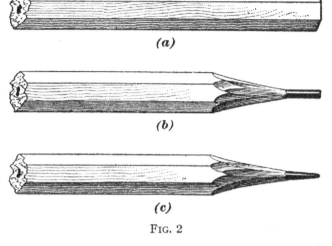

Fig. 2

Fig. 2 (*a*), is cut away to a point, allowing about $\frac{1}{4}$ inch of the lead to project, as shown in (*b*). Next, the lead is rubbed

Fig. 3

on the sandpaper pad to bring it to a round point, as shown in (*c*). A needle point is not desired.

LINE DRAWING

The purpose of Fig. 2 is simply to show the stages of sharpening the pencil, and has no reference whatever to the *length* of the pencil. The illustration, of necessity, shows only a short section of the pencil—apparently broken off. The beginner must understand, however, that he is to use the pencil full length (as shown in Figs. 3 to 7, inclusive); that is, about 6 or 7 inches long, and never less than 4 inches.

7. Correct Position for Drawing.—The correct position to assume in making drawings is illustrated in Fig. 3. As will be observed, the lower edge of the drawing board rests on the lap, or on the knees, and the upper edge against the edge of a table, the board being slightly inclined. The table should be located near a window and so arranged that the light will come over the left shoulder and from above. In this way, no shadows are cast upon the drawing board, provided the right hand is used in drawing. If the left hand is used, the light must, of course, come over the right shoulder.

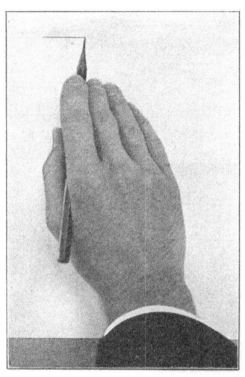

Fig. 4

The remarks about the direction in which the light should come apply as well if artificial light, such as an incandescent bulb, a bracket or a portable gas light, or an oil lamp, must be used. If a lamp must be placed on the table against which the drawing board is usually made to rest, another table or even a chair should be used to help support the drawing board. In no case should the light be placed so that it will shine into the eyes.

8. Methods of Holding the Pencil.—For drawing *horizontal lines* and *horizontal curves*, that is, lines and curves that run in the same direction as the top edge of the drawing

LINE DRAWING

board when it is held in its correct position, the pencil is held somewhat as it is held in writing. In other words, it is held lightly between the thumb and the first and second fingers, with its upper end resting slightly above the hollow where the thumb joins the back of the hand. The pencil is held as nearly parallel to the surface of the paper as possible, the hand being partly flattened, as shown in Fig. 4.

For drawing *vertical lines* and *vertical curves*, that is, lines and curves

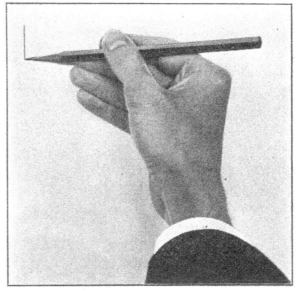

Fig. 5

that run in the same direction as the side edge of the drawing board, the pencil should be supported in a horizontal direction in the hollow between the outstretched first and second fingers by means of pressure from the tip of the thumb placed over it, as is shown in Fig. 5.

For drawing *right oblique lines* and *right oblique curves*, that is, lines and curves running from upper right to lower left, the pencil is held in the manner shown in Fig. 6; and for drawing *left oblique lines* and *left oblique curves*, that is, lines and curves running from upper left to lower right, it is held in the manner illustrated in Fig. 7. Both of these methods, Figs. 6 and 7, are simply variations of the method shown in Fig. 5.

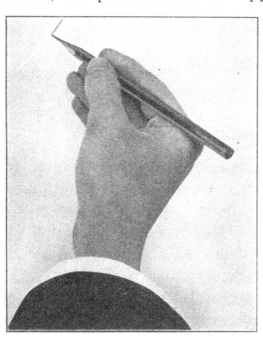

Fig. 6

LINE DRAWING

It may be said in connection with the methods of holding the pencil that only a long pencil should be used. When the pencil gets to be less than 4 inches in length, it should be placed in the pencil holder provided for this purpose

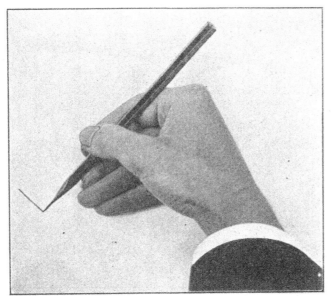
Fig. 7

These methods of holding the pencil when drawing various kinds of lines are suggested because actual practice has proven them to be good methods. The beginner need not feel bound to follow these methods if he can get equally good results by holding the pencil in some other manner.

DRAWING EXERCISES

PRELIMINARY PRACTICE WORK

9. Limbering Up the Muscles.—No matter how familiar a person may be with handling the lead pencil in ordinary handwriting, he usually handles it in an awkward manner when beginning to draw. This awkwardness, of course, is due to the fact that, in drawing, many finger, hand, and arm muscles not used in handwriting are brought into play to delineate lines that run in many different directions and vary in length from the lines in handwriting. It is necessary, therefore, before attempting to draw, to "limber up," or make pliant, these muscles, and this may be done by practicing repeatedly the exercises here outlined. These exercises will do no good if the directions are simply read and then passed over. They

LINE DRAWING

should be practiced faithfully, not only before taking up the drawing exercises, but at odd times as the work progresses. As has been said, the success of the present work, as well as that of the advanced work, will depend on having the muscles of the fingers, arm, and hand supple. Should any of these muscles get tired in practicing these limbering-up exercises, the arm should be permitted to drop loosely to the side of the body or to rest easily on the table or the drawing board.

10. Exercises With the Bare Hand.—The following exercises are for the bare hand; that is, the hand without the pencil:

1. Lay the right hand flat on the table with the palm downwards, and the fingers outstretched but close together. Shut the hand slowly, making a fist, and then open it out flat. Do this about ten times, slowly at first and rapidly toward the last.

2. Lay the hand flat on the table, palm downwards and the fingers straight outstretched. Spread them apart fanwise as far as possible, and then bring them together again. Repeat this about ten times.

3. Lay the hand flat on the table, palm downwards. Then slowly raise the wrist and whole arm free from the table, lifting them about 4 or 5 inches, but keep the finger tips pressed upon the table, so firmly that the fingers bend slightly. Then let the hand and arm down slowly, still keeping up the pressure on the finger tips. Repeat this about five or six times.

4. Follow the same exercise as that in paragraph 3, but press upon one finger tip at a time, until each one of the four fingers has been so exercised five or six times.

5. With the forearm, wrist, and hand lying flat upon the table and the wrist acting as a hinge, alternately raise and lower the outstretched hand eight or ten times; then swing the hand alternately from left to right and right to left eight or ten times, keeping the forearm rigid on the table as the palm of the hand lightly glides from side to side.

6. Rest the finger tips lightly on the table, keeping the arm, elbow, and wrist entirely free from the table. Now move

LINE DRAWING

the bent arm backwards and forwards over the table, permitting it to be supported by the gliding finger tips and using the shoulder as a hinge. Repeat eight or ten times.

7. Repeat the motion called for in paragraph 6, swinging the arm from right to left, instead of backwards and forwards.

11. Exercises With the Pencil.—The following exercises are to be performed with the pencil properly held and on the inclined drawing board, a piece of drawing paper being pinned to the drawing board.

1. Hold the pencil as shown in Fig. 4, with the hand, wrist, and arm either entirely free from the board or steadied by the little finger. Swing the pencil from left to right and back, alternating about ten times, keeping the fingers and wrist unbending and using the shoulder as a hinge.

Repeat, using the elbow resting on the board as a hinge.

Repeat, using the wrist as a hinge.

Repeat, using the wrist and finger movements.

If necessary, raise the lower end of the drawing board for the last three movements.

2. Hold the pencil as in the exercise called for in paragraph 1, and, with the same full-arm movement, make a

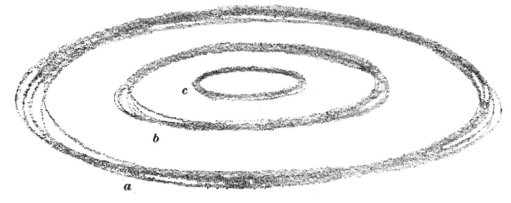

Fig. 8

long ellipse, as shown at *a*, Fig. 8, going from right to left for upper curves and from left to right for lower curves. Go over the ellipse eight or ten times. Raise the lower end of the drawing board if necessary to give the hand and arm more room for the swinging motion.

LINE DRAWING

Repeat, using the elbow as a hinge and also a slight finger movement. The ellipse in this case will be smaller, as shown at *b*.

Repeat, using the wrist as a hinge and also a slight finger

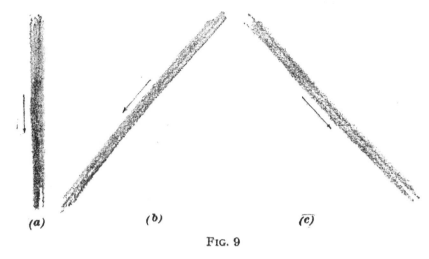

Fig. 9

movement. This ellipse will be still smaller, as shown at *c*.

3. With the pencil held as shown in Fig. 5, and with the wrist and arm either entirely free from the board or steadied by the side of the hand, draw the pencil up and down vertically

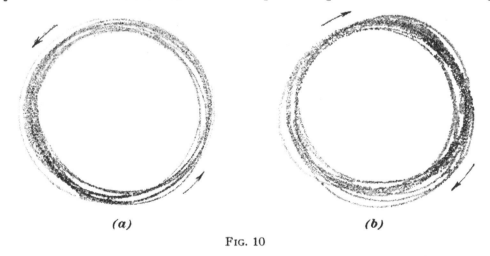

Fig. 10

so as to make lines like those shown in Fig. 9 (*a*), using the shoulder as a hinge. Repeat about ten times.

With the pencil held as in Fig. 6, repeat, making right oblique lines, as shown in Fig. 9 (*b*).

With the pencil held as in Fig. 7, repeat, making left oblique lines, as shown in Fig. 9 (*c*).

LINE DRAWING

4. With the pencil held as shown in Fig. 5, and with the same full-arm movement, as before, make circles of various sizes, as shown in Fig. 10, going over each one about ten times, first in one direction and then in the other.

GENERAL INFORMATION

12. Drawing cannot be learned merely by reading the text, nor can the proper training be received by simply preparing drawings. Comments and helpful advice from a capable instructor are also needed. Accordingly, this Section and those which follow contain properly graded exercises in the form of *plates* that must be actually prepared by the student and submitted to the Schools for criticism.

This Section contains six drawing plates, each of which is divided into eight drawing exercises. Each plate is numbered, as Plate 1, Plate 2, etc., and each exercise on each plate is lettered, as A, B, C, etc., so that there will be no difficulty in referring to them.

The drawings submitted for criticism must represent the very best efforts of the student. The directions for the whole plate about to be drawn should be carefully read; then, the directions for each exercise should be taken up in order and the preliminary practice work called for in connection with each exercise carefully done before drawing the plate to be submitted. It is not the practice work that is to be sent in, but the *result* of the practice work, properly arranged on the drawing paper. Although it is not necessary to send in a mechanically exact drawing, yet the best efforts of the student are desired, not some hastily drawn first attempts.

The twenty-four sheets of 15″×10″ drawing paper already described are sufficient for this work. Six of these sheets are to be used for the final drawing plates to be sent to the Schools; twelve may be used for preliminary practice work, two sheets for each plate; and the remaining six sheets are to be reserved for any work that may have to be redrawn. Thus, a generous supply of paper is on hand for practice work, and it should be so utilized.

LINE DRAWING

The drawing plates, when completed, are to be mailed to the Schools in mailing tubes, at first-class postage rates. The number of plates to be mailed at a time is mentioned in connection with the directions for each drawing plate.

PLATE 1

13. Purpose.—In keeping with the object of this entire Section, the exercises for Plate 1, which is shown greatly reduced in Fig. 11, are intended to give preliminary training in the control of the muscles used in drawing and to use eye measurement as a guide thereto; in other words, to teach the drawing of lines within a definite space and to use the eye in laying out measurements. Up to this point, it has been necessary to practice only movements with the pencil that require no particular control or restraint of the muscles. The exercises on Plate 1 are therefore a step forward in learning to draw.

14. Subdivision of the Drawing Sheet.—The first work in connection with Plate 1 consists in subdividing the sheet of drawing paper, which is 15 inches wide by 10 inches high, into eight spaces, each of which should be $3\frac{3}{4}$ inches wide and 5 inches high, so as to accommodate the eight drawing exercises, which are to be arranged in the manner shown in Fig. 11. The drawing paper is subdivided in the following manner, the student of course being properly seated in front of the drawing board and the paper being secured to it with thumbtacks, as previously explained:

First, divide the space into two large rectangles by drawing a vertical line down through the center of the paper, or plate. Next, divide these two vertical rectangles, in turn, by a vertical center line, when there will be four vertical strips all of the same width. Next, divide the 10-inch height on each side into two parts and draw a horizontal line connecting the two points of subdivision. This line will cut each one of the four vertical strips into two equal parts, thus making the required eight equal rectangles—two horizontal rows of four rectangles

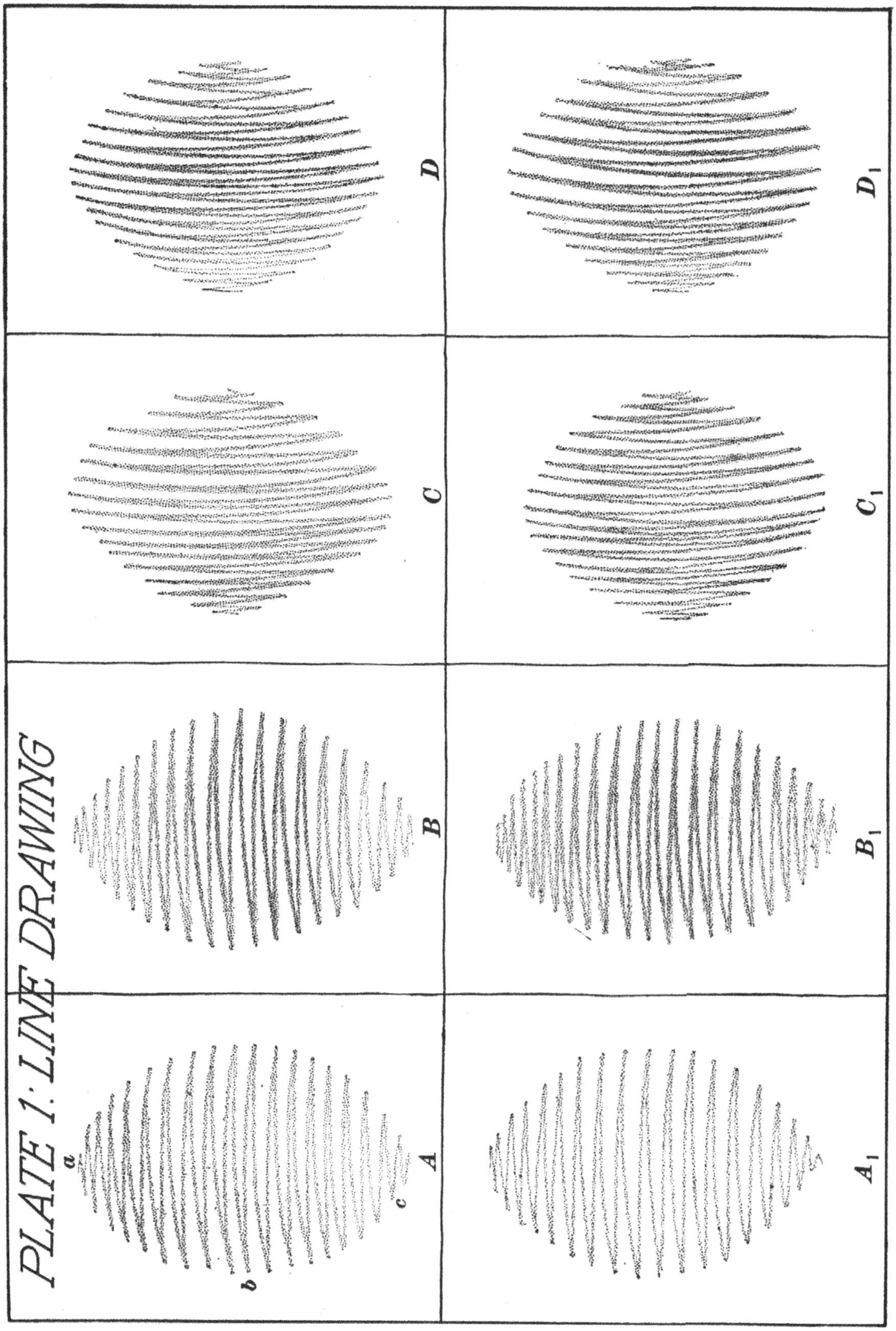
PLATE 1: LINE DRAWING
a
b
c
A
B
C
D
A1
B1
C1
D1

FIG. 11

LINE DRAWING

each. This method of subdividing the plate into eight equal rectangles is to be applied in the case of all the plates in this Section; therefore, it is well to practice the method here outlined until it can be done well and quickly.

In subdividing the drawing plate, it is earnestly urged that eye measurement only be used, for this will lead to an inde-

Fig. 12

pendence of mechanical aids in future work. The subdivision of the plate in this manner should be supplemented by preliminary practicing, testing, repracticing, and retesting until it can be done accurately. Of course, it may be impossible for some to divide the plate accurately by eye measurement. In such cases, a foot rule or a yardstick may be used to lay off the distances. Thus, the vertical height may be divided on each side, starting at the top, into spaces of 5 inches, and the dimension points connected by a long horizontal line. The horizontal width may then be divided into two spaces having a width of 7½ inches, and each of these into two other spaces having a width of 3¾ inches, and three vertical lines drawn down through the plate. Each rectangle will then be 3¾ inches wide and 5 inches high.

15. Exercise A, Plate 1.—Exercise A of Plate 1, as shown reduced in the first upper rectangle of Fig. 11 and in full size in Fig. 12, consists simply of **practice lines.** These lines are not to be copied slavishly from Fig. 12; they are shown there simply to give a good idea of the kind of line practice that is expected to appear on the plate to be submitted for criticism. This exercise is to be done in the following manner, but no attempt should be made to put it on the drawing plate until it has been practiced repeatedly:

With a B pencil sharpened as previously directed and held in the manner indicated in Fig. 4, make the strokes as shown in Fig. 12, starting at the top with short strokes and working toward the bottom, lengthening the strokes at the middle of the rectangle and shortening them again at the bottom. This simple series of curving zigzag lines should be practiced repeatedly until it is possible to increase and decrease the sweeping motions of the pencil with a degree of uniformity that will cause the outline formed by the sharp turns of the curving zigzag lines to form evenly graded curves. To do this, the pencil is carried with an easy swinging motion from right to left and back, the hand and arm swinging from the shoulder, or from the elbow, as a hinge. Either method will give freedom of line. The same amount of pressure on the pencil is to be used throughout the length of the line, with the attempt to keep the line of uniform weight. The weight may vary slightly on account of the softness of the lead, but if the pressure is kept even the desired result will be secured.

Work such as that shown in Fig. 13 is crude and uneven, and does not conform to what is required to train the hand

LINE DRAWING

so that its motions will go no farther than is necessary. If Exercise A on the drawing plate submitted for criticism resembles such work, it will not be satisfactory.

16. Exercise B, Plate 1.—After Exercise A has been completed, the drawing of Exercise B, shown small in the second upper rectangle of Plate 1, Fig. 11, and in full size in

Fig. 13

Fig. 14, should be faithfully practiced and then drawn on the plate to be submitted for criticism. For this exercise, the pencil is held in the same manner as for Exercise A. The direction and sweep of the lines are also the same as before, but the pressure exerted on the pencil should vary. As the pencil descends in these zigzag curves toward the widest part at the middle, the pressure should be increased so as to

LINE DRAWING

produce heavier and darker strokes. Then, as the pencil descends toward the narrow part at the bottom, the pressure should be gradually decreased, so as to make the lines light and even, as at the top.

17. Exercise C, Plate 1.—Exercise C, as shown in the third rectangle of upper row of Plate 1, Fig. 11, is similar to

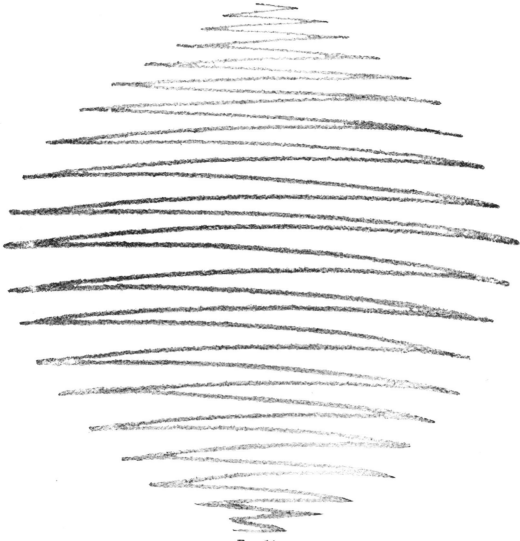

Fig. 14

Exercise A, except that the strokes run in a general vertical direction instead of in a horizontal direction. The strokes are to be of the same weight throughout as those of Exercise A. To make the strokes called for in Exercise C, the pencil must be held in the manner shown in Fig. 5, and the lines must be

LINE DRAWING

drawn by swinging the fingers, the pencil being held in such a way that they move as if hinged at the place where they join the palm of the hand. Such a motion is required to give the proper curve to the line. If the lines were straight, the motion could be from either the elbow or the shoulder.

As in the case of the two preceding exercises, Exercise C should be practiced until it is possible to make lines suitable for the drawing plate.

18. Exercise D, Plate 1.—The lines called for in Exercise D have the same sweep and direction as those of Exercise C, as is shown in the fourth rectangle of upper row, Plate 1, Fig. 11. However, they are strengthened by gradually increasing the pressure on the pencil as it moves toward the middle of the figure and decreasing the pressure from that point on. This exercise should receive the same care and attention as the preceding ones. When it is completed, the upper row of rectangles on the drawing plate to be submitted will be full.

19. Additional Exercises for Plate 1.—The lower four rectangles of the drawing plate should be used for additional attempts at demonstrating the proficiency attained in drawing the lines called for in Exercises A to D, and they may be called Exercise A_1, Exercise B_1, Exercise C_1, and Exercise D_1, as shown in Fig. 11. Thus, Exercise A_1 will be another attempt at Exercise A, and will be placed in the rectangle below Exercise A; exercise B_1 will be placed below Exercise B; and so on.

Although these exercises may appear simple, they should be practiced over and over, because the success of the drawings that follow will depend on the faithfulness with which these exercises are practiced.

20. Final Work on Plate 1.—After the exercises have been properly drawn in their respective places on the drawing plate, it is necessary to letter or to write the title, Plate 1: Line Drawing, at the top of the drawing plate, as shown in Fig. 11, so that the plate may be readily identified. No specified size is given for the lettering of the title, but it is advisable to proportion the letters in the manner shown in

LINE DRAWING

the illustration, drawing light parallel horizontal guide lines to assist in keeping the lettering uniform in height.

Next, on the back of the plate, in the lower left corner, must be placed the student's class letters and number, his name and address, and the date on which the plate was completed. This information is absolutely necessary, for without it there would be no means of telling by whom the work was executed, or when it was finished. To make the identification doubly sure, it will be advisable, also, to use the gummed identification label provided for this purpose.

The drawing plate prepared by the student should next be rolled and placed in a mailing tube, which, after being properly addressed, should be mailed to the Schools at first-class postage rates.

It is now in order to proceed with the work required on Plate 2.

21. Additional Practice on Line Movements.—The line movements of Plate 1 are not to serve merely as plate exercises to be submitted to the Schools for criticism. They are to be practiced repeatedly. No day should go by without practice being done. At first such practice may seem irksome and monotonous, but after a while it becomes a natural thing to do; and when the results of this faithful practice work begin to show in the ease and facility with which the hand grasps and uses the pencil for drawing, then the practice work will become a pleasure.

The preliminary exercises for limbering up the finger, hand, wrist, and arm muscles, also should be practiced daily. In fact, experienced artists working commercially find it necessary to keep their muscles in proper trim, just as professional vocalists devote hours each day to the simple practice of running the scales. If these professionals see the advantage of such simple practice exercises, it is very evident that the beginner needs them in even greater measure. To slight them will mean inability to do good work later.

LINE DRAWING

PLATE 2

22. Purpose.—The exercises on Plate 2, which is shown in a reduced size in Fig. 15, are intended as additional training in limbering up the muscles of the fingers, hand, and arm, and in enabling the eye and the hand to work in harmony and with accuracy. Although these exercises in drawing straight and curved lines are apparently simple, they are more difficult than they at first appear. Mastering them successfully forms the only firm foundation for correct drawing. Once the art of properly drawing straight lines and curved lines and their combinations is mastered, it is possible to make a correct outline drawing of anything. The very first requirement that directors of commercial art departments specify, in the case of applicants for positions as artists is that they must be able to *draw well*. The fact that the applicant may know the technical details and office practices of process reproduction work, or may be familiar with certain artistic "short cuts" and "tricks of the trade," will of course be to his advantage, but this theoretical knowledge will be of little avail unless he can draw accurately; and the foundation of such proficiency is the ability to draw straight lines, curved lines, and their combinations.

For the reasons previously mentioned, the exercises on Plate 2 should be thoroughly practiced before preparing the plate to be submitted for criticism. The work on the plate submitted must not be practice work, but must represent the best efforts of the student after thorough practicing has been done.

23. General Directions.—As was done in connection with the preparation of Plate 1, the sheet for Plate 2 should be divided into eight $3\frac{3}{4}'' \times 5''$ rectangles by means of one long horizontal bisecting line and three equally spaced vertical lines, as is shown in Fig. 15, the work being done in the manner already explained. This illustration serves to show clearly how the exercises, six in number, are to be arranged on the drawing plate, and Fig. 16, which shows Exercise A drawn

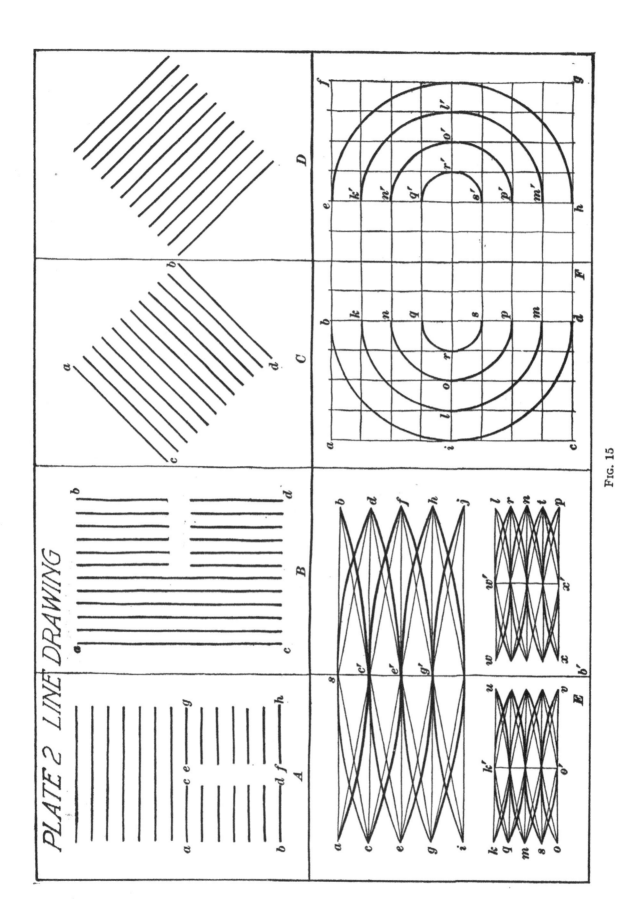

Fig. 15

LINE DRAWING

full size, gives a good idea of the weight and character of line to be used in preparing the exercises. These exercises are not to be copied from the illustrations here shown; rather, they are to be drawn according to the directions set forth in the text. Neither are the reference letters in the illustrations to appear on the plate submitted for criticism. The descriptions of the exercises call for lines of certain length that are to be spaced definite distances apart. These dimensions need not be adhered

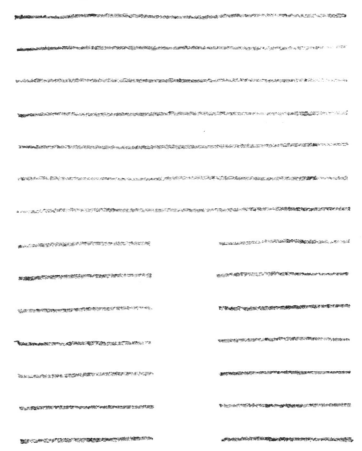

Fig. 16

to strictly, for just as much practice will be secured if there are more or fewer lines and if they are spaced farther apart or closer together. The chief requirements are to place the practice lines in their appropriate rectangles, to have the spacing uniform, and to allow a reasonable margin around each exercise, so as not to crowd or overlap the exercises on the plate.

It will be noticed that the lines in the small chart, or guide plate, shown in Fig. 15 are very sharp, black, and distinct,

LINE DRAWING

and do not resemble the soft delicacy of pencil lines. This chart is purposely printed with sharp lines to serve as a clear guide to the student in laying out the exercises on the plate, and is not intended to show quality or character of the pencil lines to be used on the plate. Fig. 16 shows the weight and quality of pencil line to be used. This information should be borne in mind also when drawing Plates 3, 4, 5, and 6.

24. Exercise A, Plate 2.—As is shown in Figs. 15 and 16, Exercise A of Plate 2 consists of seven $2\frac{1}{2}$-inch horizontal lines, and fourteen 1-inch horizontal lines arranged in columns, the long lines being placed above the two columns of short lines. All the lines are spaced $\frac{1}{4}$ inch apart, and a space of $\frac{1}{2}$ inch occurs between the two columns of short lines. This exercise is drawn in the following manner:

The B drawing pencil is held in the manner shown in Fig. 4, and, first, the long strokes are made in the upper part of the first upper rectangle of the drawing plate. The hand must *not* be moved from the wrist as a hinge, for such a motion would result in curved or arched lines, whereas perfectly straight lines are desired. The hand, wrist, and entire arm should move together from the shoulder as a hinge, the hand being supported, as it glides from left to right along the paper, by the third finger and the little finger resting on the paper. First draw, carefully, from left to right, the seven lines, making long deliberate sweeps. Perhaps the first line will not be straight, but by trying again and again a straight line can be drawn easily and freely without any particular effort. As an aid to getting a perfectly straight horizontal line, try to keep it parallel with the upper edge of the paper. To assist in getting the lines of the proper length, place dots at the positions that are to be the beginning and the ending points of the lines. In this way draw all the long horizontal lines.

The same method should be followed in drawing the shorter lines of the exercise. Care should be observed to keep them all the same length, so that the contours $a\,b$, $c\,d$, $e\,f$, $g\,h$, etc., as shown in Fig. 15 A, form straight vertical lines and not jagged curves. The work on this exercise should be as even and

LINE DRAWING

regular, approximately, as that shown in Fig. 16. Uneven, hastily executed work, such as is shown in Fig. 17, will not be accepted. The lines called for in this exercise should be practiced with great frequency, even after the drawing plate has been completed.

25. Exercise B, Plate 2.—The lines of Exercise B, as is shown in the second rectangle in top row, Fig. 15, are like those

Fig. 17

of the preceding exercise, except that they are vertical and are somewhat longer, the long lines being 3½ inches and the short ones 1½ inches. To draw them, the pencil must be held as shown in Fig. 5, so that it will be at right angles at all times to the line that is being drawn. The movement should be from the shoulder as a hinge, although a little movement of the fingers and wrist may help as the lines are being drawn toward the bottom of the space. Try to have all the lines exactly vertical, by keeping them parallel to the right and left ends of the sheet; also, preserve uniformity of lengths in the lines so that the contours *a b* and *c d* are straight, an aid to which will be the placing of preliminary dots at the proposed extremities of the lines, as is explained in connection with the drawing of Exercise A.

Exercise B presents no great difficulty; nevertheless its simplicity does not mean that it is not important. These vertical lines should be practiced frequently, just as is advised for the horizontal lines.

26. Exercise C, Plate 2.—The lines to be drawn in Exercise C, third rectangle in top row, Plate 1, are known as right oblique lines, because, as has been mentioned before, they are drawn from the upper right-hand corner to the lower left-hand corner. They are not difficult to draw because their slant is similar to the slant of ordinary handwriting. The pencil should be held as shown in Fig. 6, with the elbow drawn close to the body and the hand placed on the lower right-hand corner of the sheet, the pencil being at right angles to the line about to be drawn. Each line should be about $2\frac{1}{2}$ inches long, and there should be a space of $\frac{1}{4}$ inch between the lines, which should be kept parallel. Also, each line should run at a 45° slant; that is, at such a slant that it will divide a right angle into two parts.

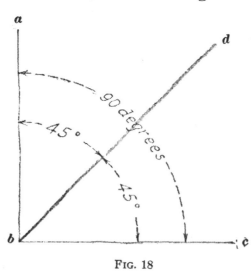

Fig. 18

The meaning of 45° slant will become clear on referring to Fig. 18, the angle *a b c* of which is a *right angle*, or an angle of 90°. Thus, the line *d b*, which cuts this right angle into two 45° parts, is called a *45° slant* or a *45° line*.

In drawing Exercise C the contours *a b* and *c d* formed by the ends of the lines must be kept perfectly straight, as in the case of preceding exercises.

LINE DRAWING

27. Exercise D, Plate 2.—The lines to be drawn in Exercise D of Plate 2, shown in the fourth rectangle in top row, Fig. 15, are the opposite of those required in Exercise C; that is, they are **left oblique lines,** or lines that extend from the upper left-hand corner to the lower right-hand corner, as has already been explained. These lines are perhaps the most difficult of all straight lines to draw unless the pencil is held properly. The pencil should be held as shown in Fig. 7, the elbow being held some distance from the body and up along the right-hand end of the drawing board, so that the hand will rest to the right of and above the exercises, the pencil being at right angles to the line as it is being drawn. Otherwise, the directions for drawing the preceding exercise apply.

28. Exercise E, Plate 2.—Exercise E of Plate 2 serves to introduce **curved lines.** As shown in Fig. 15, left half of lower row, it is to occupy the first two rectangles of the lower row on the plate, thus giving a space $7\frac{1}{2}$ inches wide and 5 inches high in which to work.

The training up to this point has been entirely in the drawing of straight lines. This training has a direct bearing on the drawing of curved lines, and will assist the beginner in drawing them. The reason for this is that the correct portrayal of a curved line must be based on his perception of the manner and degree of its variation from a straight line. No curved line can be drawn correctly unless it is considered in relation to a straight line. While a curved line of no specified extent or shape may be drawn easily and naturally, the curve cannot be duplicated unless it is considered in relation to a straight line or a series of straight lines. This fact can be easily proved by making such an attempt.

For the reason just laid down, this exercise in the drawing of curved lines is based on a series of straight lines, and the curves are drawn in relation to them. The method of drawing Exercise E is as follows: First lay off freehand, in the $7\frac{1}{2}''\times 5''$ space, eight parallel horizontal lines, as $a\,b$, $c\,d$, $e\,f$, etc., each about 6 inches long and spaced about $\frac{1}{2}$ inch apart, as

LINE DRAWING

shown in Fig. 15. Then draw line sb', which is really the original line separating the first and second rectangles of the lower row. Having done this, draw straight oblique lines from c to s, s to d, e to c', c' to f, g to e', e' to h, i to g', g' to j, etc. All these guide lines must be drawn faintly, but distinctly, with a hard pencil, but the actual lines of the curves, which are to be drawn later, must be made with a softer pencil so as to be good and strong. It is now a simple matter to draw the curves cs and sd, so that they join at s, thus making one continuous sweep, or arc. Similarly, the long curves ef, gh and ij are drawn. The pencil is held as shown in Fig. 4, and the hand and forearm work from the elbow, resting on the board, as a pivot. Some added motion may be needed from the wrist and fingers to make a graceful curve. To keep both sides of the long curve symmetrical, the two shorter curves must swell away from the straight line to exactly the same distance.

In drawing the long reversed curves ab, cd, ef, and gh, the same principle of corresponding relation to the straight line must be observed, but a different movement of the hand is needed. These long reversed curves may be drawn in either of two ways. First, the pencil may be held as shown in Fig. 4 and, keeping the wrist and elbow free from the board and using the shoulder as a pivot or hinge, the hand may glide along the surface of the paper, being steadied by the little finger as it moves. Second, the pencil may be held as before, and the fleshy or muscular under part of the forearm may be allowed to rest on the paper, in which case the arm will have sufficient play to guide the pencil as it moves over the desired curve.

After the large curves are drawn, the smaller ones should be made in the same way. Draw the parallel lines qr and st midway between kl and mn, and mn and op, and then draw verticals from u to v, w to x, k' to o', and w' to x'. The small curves are then drawn in the same way as the large ones. It is best to avoid wrist and finger movements and to work entirely by full-arm movement; that is, from the shoulder as a hinge, or pivot. However, if the beginner finds it absolutely impossible to use the arm movement, the finger-and-wrist movement may be resorted to.

LINE DRAWING

The beginner may be helped in making curves by drawing them in sections. For instance, the smaller curves at the bottom of the exercise may be drawn with a series of shorter curves, as in Fig. 19, making the "break" in the curve at the point where the curve is

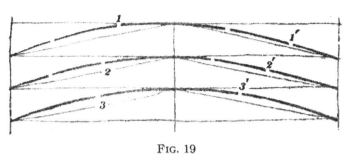

FIG. 19

farthest above the straight line, as *1*, *1'*, *2*, *2'*, *3* and *3'*, Fig. 19. This method avoids pointed or sunken curves, such as are shown at *a*, *b*, and *c*, Fig. 20.

29. Exercise F, Plate 2.—In Exercise F, as is shown in Fig. 15, right-hand half of lower row, the training in drawing curved lines is continued. As in the preceding exercise, the preliminary guide lines must be drawn in lightly but accurately. First, draw nine horizontal guide lines about 6 inches long and ½ inch apart. Then cross these by thirteen vertical lines, separated at distances of ½ inch; that is, six lines on each side of the vertical center line that marks off the two spaces this exercise occupies. This network of guide lines will then be twelve squares wide and eight squares high. It is important that this network be drawn with considerable accuracy in order that the curves may be drawn properly. As will be seen in the illustration, the rectangles *a b d c* and *e f g h* are the ones in which the curved-line work is to be laid out.

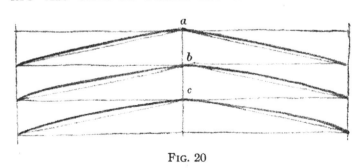

FIG. 20

First, with the pencil held as shown in Fig. 5, and using the motion from the shoulder as a hinge, or from the wrist as a hinge in combination with the finger movement, get the sweep of the quarter arc, or curve, *b i*. At first, simply go through the movement without

LINE DRAWING

actually touching the pencil point to the paper, gliding it along in a quarter circle to "feel" the way. Then let the pencil glide along lightly, and, finally, let it make the full-strength mark. The direction of the stroke may be from b to i, or from i to b, as preferred. Proceed in the same manner with the lower quarter circle $i\,d$. Then draw the other curves, $k\,l\,m$, $n\,o\,p$ and $q\,r\,s$, working in quarter circles. The plan of using short curves with a small "break" at each end may be helpful.

The series of semicircles in rectangle $e\,f\,g\,h$ should be drawn with the pencil held as before—that is, in the manner shown in Fig. 5, or in Fig. 6 and Fig. 7, if desired—and the hand and arm working from the shoulder as a hinge. The direction of the curves will of course be different from those in rectangle $a\,b\,d\,c$. The same preliminary method should be employed here, however; namely, first gliding the hand and pencil along the direction of the curve, without touching the point to the paper, and then later drawing the curve full strength.

It may be well to mention again that the foundation network of lines should be drawn very faintly, preferably with a hard, sharp pencil, used lightly; whereas, the curves themselves should be good and strong, but not in blurred, wide lines. A sharp point should be constantly kept on the B pencil when making the curved lines.

30. Final Work on Plate 2.—The drawing of Exercise F on Plate 2 completes the regular exercises for this plate. The identifying data should now be put on the plate in the manner previously described, lettering or writing the title, Plate 2: Line Drawing, at the top of the sheet, and placing the class letters and number, the name and address, and the date of completion on the back of the sheet in the lower left-hand corner. The sheet should then be rolled and placed in a mailing tube, and sent to the Schools for examination.

If by this time Plate 1 has not been returned, the additional practice work on straight and curved lines that follows should be given attention, after which the drawing of Plate 3 may be taken up. However, if Plate 1 has been returned, the criticisms on it should be carefully observed and all redrawn work

LINE DRAWING

called for should be done before proceeding with the additional practice work on straight and curved lines or with Plate 3. Much profit will be gained by observing carefully the criticisms on the plates as they are returned and by redrawing any work called for.

31. Additional Practice on Straight and Curved Lines.—The practice work in drawing straight and curved lines called for in Plate 2 must not be lost sight of after the plate has been finished, as it is a very easy matter to become "rusty." Therefore, the exercises of this plate should be drawn at odd moments on paper of any kind, and it will be found by the beginner that the more practicing he does the better able will he be to draw correctly.

By remembering that any curve may be considered as consisting of an infinite number of

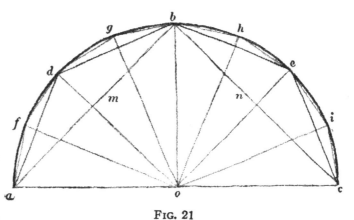

FIG. 21

straight lines, the drawing of curves will be simplified. This fact is further demonstrated in Fig. 21. Thus, the semicircular curve shown in this illustration is really based on two lines ab and bc of equal lengths and at right angles. Nevertheless, the drawing of this arc can be further simplified by marking out still other straight lines of equal lengths, as ad and db, and be and ec, keeping the distances do and eo equal to ao, bo, and co, respectively. Similarly, additional straight lines af, fd, dg, gb, etc. may be built up; and if these straight lines were increased indefinitely a regular curve would result. Thus it is seen that, to draw a graceful curve freehand, particularly to duplicate a curve already drawn, dependence must not be placed on mere accidents of motion from the swinging arm, wrist, or hand, although these help in the actual delineation of the curve; rather, the curved line must be considered as being related to a

LINE DRAWING

straight line or a series of straight lines. This matter will be considered further when the drawing of simple line figures and other advanced work is taken up.

PLATE 3

32. Purpose.—Up to this point, the aim has been simply to limber up the muscles required in drawing and to teach the drawing of straight lines and curves; that is, figures having only one dimension, namely, *length*. The purpose of the exercises called for on Plate 3, in addition to continuing along the same lines as the preceding exercises, is to give training, by means of combinations of these lines, in the drawing of figures having two dimensions, namely, *length* and *breadth*. Thus, the beginner in drawing will receive training that will enable him to draw lines of given lengths, and figures of given sizes and proportions, entirely freehand and by eye measurement.

As is shown in Fig. 22, the exercises used in giving this training are the simple *geometrical figures*, which include the *square*, the *triangle*, the *hexagon*, the *octagon*, etc. The beginner must not imagine that shapes of this kind are too simple for him to practice on. The figures selected are ones that form the governing shapes of models from which, later on, the principles of model drawing and of portraying light, shade, and shadow will be taught. Thus, it will be seen that mastering the drawing of these simple geometrical figures is a step nearer the advanced work that is to come.

It must, of course, be admitted that the beginner's desire in most cases is to draw pictures or designs; yet, as has been mentioned before, there are no short cuts in learning to draw and the best results are secured by gradually working up from simple things to such difficult things as figures, decorative work, and so on. By bearing this in mind, there should be no shirking in following out the requirements at this point; rather, there should be a keen desire to advance by performing this preliminary work well.

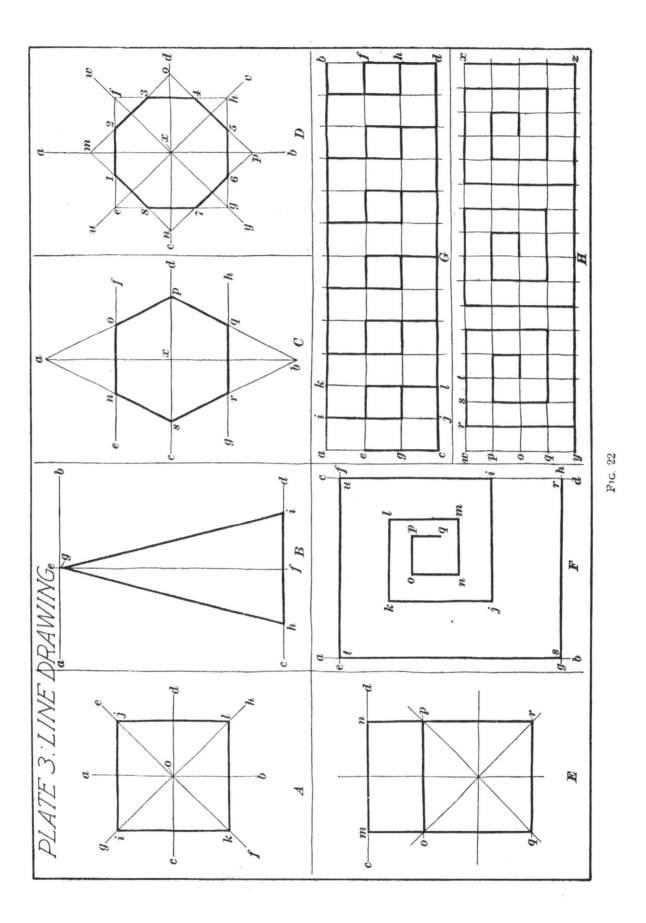

Fig. 22

LINE DRAWING

33. General Directions.—As before, the 15″ × 10″ sheet of drawing paper should be divided into eight rectangles 3¾ inches wide and 5 inches high by means of a horizontal center line and three equally spaced vertical lines. The exercises are to be arranged on the plate in the manner shown in Fig. 22, and the weight and character of the lines to be made

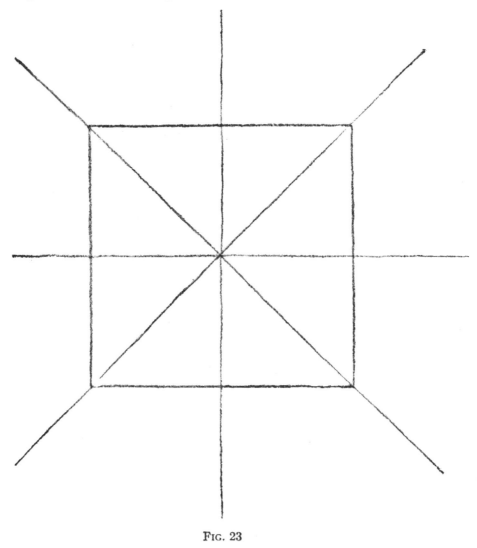

Fig. 23

are as shown in Fig. 23, which illustrates the full-size drawing of Exercise A, Plate 3. As in the preceding plate, no reference letters are to appear on the plate that is to be submitted for criticism.

34. Exercise A, Plate 3.—Exercise A of Plate 3, as shown in Fig. 22, first rectangle, top row, and also in Fig. 23,

LINE DRAWING

consists in drawing a simple **square,** which will form the governing shape of the cube, to be studied later. A square consists of four straight lines of exactly equal length, two of them horizontal and the other two vertical, which, of course, makes all the interior angles of the square right angles.

The drawing of any symmetrical geometrical polygon is always simplified by first lightly plotting out guide lines with a hard pencil having a sharp point, and then drawing the figure itself with a softer pencil. Therefore, to draw the square, first draw freehand with a hard pencil a vertical line ab, Fig. 22 A, bisecting the $3\frac{3}{4}$-inch width of the first $3\frac{3}{4}'' \times 5''$ rectangle in the upper row. Then draw a horizontal line cd bisecting the 5-inch height of the rectangle. Next, draw a right oblique line ef and a left oblique line gh, at exact angles of 45° with line cd. All these lines, of course, pass through point o. No difficulty should be met in drawing these lines, because ample practice in making such lines has already been called for.

Next, through the vertical line ab, and at a point 1 inch above o, draw with a sharp B pencil a line ij. This line, if properly drawn, will be 2 inches long. Similarly, draw a horizontal line kl, 1 inch below o and two vertical lines ik, and jl 1 inch to the left and the right, respectively, of o. Then, each line will be 2 inches long, the angles will be right angles, and $ijlk$ will be a perfect square.

35. Dimensions by Eye Measurement.—The success met in drawing Exercise A, as well as the exercises that follow it, will depend considerably on how well measurements can be estimated with the eye. It is advisable, therefore, to practice the making of lines, both vertical and horizontal, that are estimated to be 1 inch long and $\frac{1}{4}$ inch apart and then test the lengths and distances by means of the proper divisions on a rule or a yardstick to see how nearly accurate they are. Additional attempts should be made at drawing such lines freehand until it is possible to make lines 1, 2, or 3 inches long and to space them $\frac{1}{4}$, $\frac{1}{2}$, etc. inches apart purely by eye measurement. This practice of dimensions by eye measurement and verification by actual rule measurement is very important. Therefore, it should be kept up day after day until the laying out of dimensions by eye measurement becomes a natural and simple matter.

36. Exercise B, Plate 3.—As shown in Fig. 22, second rectangle, top row, Exercise B consists in drawing freehand an **isosceles triangle;** that is, a triangle with two of its sides equal. The drawing of this triangle is of value, in that it forms the governing shape of the pyramid and the cone, to be studied later. It is to be 4 inches high and 2 inches wide at the base, but the important point is to get it symmetrical, or evenly balanced on each side of a center line, so that the sides gh and gi will be of the same length. This triangle should be drawn as follows:

With a hard, sharp-pointed pencil, draw lightly a horizontal guide line ab $\frac{1}{2}$ inch below the upper edge of the second rectangle in the top row and a line cd $\frac{1}{2}$ inch above the lower edge of the rectangle. Next, draw a vertical guide line ef exactly bisecting the $3\frac{3}{4}$-inch width of the rectangle, and locate points h and i 1 inch to the left and the right, respectively, of line ef, on line cd. With a softer pencil, either the B or the HB, connect points g and h, g and i, and h and i with right oblique, left oblique, and horizontal lines, respectively, and the triangle will be completed. The erection of a *vertical line*, that is, a line perpendicular to the middle point of the base line, is the surest guide in drawing freehand a symmetrical triangle.

37. Exercise C, Plate 3.—Exercise C, as shown in Fig. 22, third rectangle, top row, calls for the drawing of another combination of horizontal and oblique lines, namely, a **hexagon,** which is so called because it has six equal sides. The object in this case is not to draw a regular hexagon geometrically, for which there are definite rules, but to draw one with approximate regularity by eye measurement and freehand. To do so proceed as follows:

Draw lightly a vertical center line ab so as to bisect the $3\frac{3}{4}$-inch width of the third rectangle in the upper row on the drawing plate, the point a being $\frac{3}{8}$ inch below top **edge of sheet**

LINE DRAWING

and the point b $\frac{3}{8}$ inch above bottom edge of rectangle. Next, draw a horizontal guide line cd, bisecting the 5-inch height of the rectangle and cutting the line ab at the point x. Through points $1\frac{1}{8}$ inches above x and $1\frac{1}{8}$ inches below x draw the horizontal lines ef and gh, respectively, of indefinite extent. Lay off points s and p $1\frac{1}{4}$ inches to the left and to the right, respectively, of point x, and through these points draw the right oblique lines as and pb, and the left oblique lines ap and sb, thus establishing points n, o, q, and r where the horizontals ef and gh are cut. Finally, form the hexagon by connecting the points n, o, p, q, r, and s with straight lines, drawn with a sharp B pencil.

This figure must be drawn with considerable care, and each line forming a side of the hexagon should be $1\frac{1}{4}$ inches long, or the least bit less. Several attempts may have to be made before an accurate and symmetrical figure is secured.

38. Exercise D, Plate 3.—Exercise D of Plate 3, as shown in Fig. 22, fourth rectangle, top row, requires the drawing freehand, of an **octagon,** so called because it has eight equal sides. This figure may be considered as the governing form upon which the circle will later be constructed when that figure is studied. The octagon is drawn freehand as follows:

First, as shown in D of Fig. 22, draw bisecting vertical and horizontal guide lines ab and cd in the manner already explained. Then draw right and left oblique lines uv and wy at 45° angles so as to intersect the point x. Next, 1 inch above and 1 inch below x, draw horizontal lines that will intersect the oblique lines at the points e, f, h, and g, and at 1 inch to the left and 1 inch to the right of x draw vertical lines connecting e and g and f and h, respectively, forming the square $efhg$. Next, considering the oblique lines uv and wy as the basis, draw another large square, similar to the one just drawn, but at a 45° angle with it, as follows: First, draw right oblique lines mn and op exactly parallel to wy and 1 inch from it each way. Then draw left oblique lines np and mo parallel to uv and 1 inch from it each way, thus forming the diagonal square $mopn$. This second square drawn upon the first square, will form an eight-pointed star, and the points *1, 2, 3, 4, 5, 6, 7,* and *8* will be established. Finally, with an HB or a B pencil, connect points *1* to *8* with straight lines, and the octagon will be formed.

If carefully drawn, each side of the octagon will be a little more than $\frac{3}{4}$ inch long, or what is known as $\frac{3}{4}$-inch "strong."

The principle of drawing an octagon by having two squares, centered on the same point, make a 45° angle with each other, should be remembered for future application.

39. Exercise E, Plate 3.—Exercise E, which occupies the first lower rectangle of Plate 3, as is shown in Fig. 22, calls for the drawing of a **rectangle** composed of part of a 2-inch square—that is, a rectangle *m n p o* 2 inches wide and 1 inch high—and a 2-inch square *o p r q*. The horizontal line *c d* forming the top of the figure is to be 1 inch below the upper edge of the $3\frac{3}{4}''\times5''$ rectangle. The drawing of this figure introduces nothing that has not already been taken up; it is merely a combination of parts of figures that have already been drawn. It should therefore be laid out and drawn without further directions. This figure serves as a basis for the oval that will be studied and drawn later.

40. Exercise F, Plate 3.—Exercise F, as shown in Fig. 22, second rectangle, lower row, takes up the drawing of one style of **fret ornament** much used in Greek art. This design consists entirely of vertical and horizontal lines; therefore, in drawing it, the greatest requirement is the ability to judge properly, by eye measurement, the lengths of the various lines and their distances from neighboring parallel lines. It is advisable before beginning this exercise to do additional practice work in drawing, freehand, and by eye measurement only, lines of various lengths and in spacing these lines various distances apart. Special attention, also, should be given to dividing, by eye measurement, certain lines into three equal parts, so as to become accustomed to ascertaining easily what distance would be one-third or two-thirds of any given line. To draw this fret, or key design, proceed as follows:

First, draw vertical lines *a b* and *c d* $\frac{1}{4}$ inch from the left and right edges, respectively, of the $3\frac{3}{4}'' \times 5''$ rectangle and

LINE DRAWING

horizontal lines ef and gh ½ inch below the upper edge and above the lower edge, respectively, of the rectangle, thus forming a rectangle $turs$. Next, lay off on line ur a distance ui, equal to two-thirds the length of ur, adding a little to it so as to make it two-thirds "strong," and thus determining the vertical distance ui. Next, lay off the horizontal distance ij equal to a little more than two-thirds of line rs; then, vertical distance jk equal to a little more than two-thirds of line iu; then, horizontal distance kl a little greater than two-thirds of line ji; then, lm a little more than two-thirds of line kj; then, mn a little more than two-thirds of lk; no a little more than two-thirds of ml; op a little more than two-thirds of nm; and, finally, pq a little more than two-thirds of on. Strengthen in with a B pencil having a sharp point the lines as laid out, and the fret $rstuijklmnopq$ will be completed in its proper proportions.

This fret forms the basis of the spiral or volute that is taken up later.

41. Exercise G, Plate 3.—Exercise G differs from any of those already given on Plate 3 in that it is to extend across the upper halves of the last two rectangles of Plate 3, which, as shown in Fig. 22, are divided by a horizontal line. Thus, it will be contained within a space 7½ inches wide and 2½ inches high. This exercise, as will be observed, is in straight-line work, and it forms the basis for the guilloche ornament, which is to be drawn later. Exercise G may be executed in the following manner:

Draw lightly, with a hard pencil, the rectangle $abdc$, making it about 2 inches high and 7 inches long, so as to allow a margin of about ¼ inch all around it. Next, divide the rectangle vertically into three equal parts by the horizontal lines ef and gh. Then divide each of the lines ab and cd into twelve equal parts and draw the vertical lines ij, kl, etc. A simple method of dividing a line into twelve equal parts consists first, in bisecting it; then, in bisecting each half so as to get four equal parts; and then, in dividing each of the four parts into three equal parts. Thus, the rectangle will

LINE DRAWING

be divided into a network of smaller rectangles almost square, twelve long and three high. Finally, with a B pencil, strengthen the lines, that are shown heavy and black in Fig. 22 G, thus forming the repeating straight-line figure of the fret pattern.

42. Exercise H, Plate 3.—Exercise H, the last to appear on Plate 3, as shown in Fig. 22, is to extend across the lower halves of the last two rectangles, directly under Exercise G. The design to be worked out is a **running fret,** or **key pattern,** and it forms the basis of the running scroll pattern to be drawn later. This exercise should be done as follows:

First, draw the rectangle $w\,x\,z\,y$ the same size and in the same manner as directed for that of Exercise G. Then divide the vertical line $w\,y$ into four equal parts by first bisecting the line and then bisecting each half thus obtained, thus locating the points o, p, and q. Then, extend horizontal lines across the rectangle from these points. Next, divide the horizontal line $w\,x$ into sixteen equal parts, and locate the points r, s, t, etc., by first bisecting the line; then by bisecting each half, which will give four parts; then by bisecting each one of the four parts, which will give eight equal parts; and, finally, by bisecting each one of the eight parts. Then draw vertical lines from the points r, s, t, etc. across the rectangle, so as to divide it into a network of smaller rectangles sixteen wide and four high. Then, as in the preceding exercise, complete this exercise by strengthening the lines that are to appear prominent and show the outline of the running fret.

43. Final Work on Plate 3.—After the last regular exercise on Plate 3 is completed, it is necessary, as in the preceding exercises, to insert the identifying data. Thus, the title, Plate 3: Line Drawing, should be lettered or written at the top of the sheet, and on the back of the sheet, in the lower left-hand corner, should be placed the class letters and number, the name and address, and the date on which the plate was completed.

Plate 3, however, should not be sent to the Schools for criticism at this time, because it contains the underlying forms of the exercises of Plate 4, and will therefore be needed as a guide and for reference in executing the exercises on Plate 4.

LINE DRAWING

Before the drawing of Plate 4 is taken up, the comments and criticisms on plates that have been returned to the student should be carefully noted. If he is requested to redraw any of the exercises, he should do the work at once—only those exercises being redrawn for which new attempts were requested —and send this redrawn work in to the Schools for further criticism. Whether or not redrawn work is requested, the student should endeavor to profit by the comments and suggestions given in the instructors' criticisms and should do the additional practicing advised.

PLATE 4

44. Purpose.—The purpose of the exercises of Plate 4, which is shown in reduced size in Fig. 24, is to bring curved lines into use for making figures, some of which have two dimensions. The object at this stage is not to give training in drawing anything simply for its own sake, that is, to produce a piece of work for exhibition purposes; the idea, rather, is simply to continue training exercises that will assist in limbering up the finger, wrist, and arm muscles, and in cultivating the use of eye measurement and freehand work for judging distances and dimensions.

It has been shown that all curved lines are based on straight lines and can be drawn correctly only when considered in relation to straight lines. Similarly, curved-line figures are based on straight-line figures, and can be drawn accurately only with such straight-line figures as their construction lines; Plate 4, therefore, is to be drawn according to this principle.

45. General Directions.—The first work in executing Plate 4 consists in subdividing the $15'' \times 10''$ sheet of drawing paper into eight equal rectangles, just as was done in beginning the preceding plates. The exercises for these plates, as well as the manner in which they are to appear on it, are shown in Fig. 24, and the quality of the lines to be used for guide lines and full lines of the figures of the exercises is shown in Fig. 25. Neither of these illustrations is to be copied slavishly

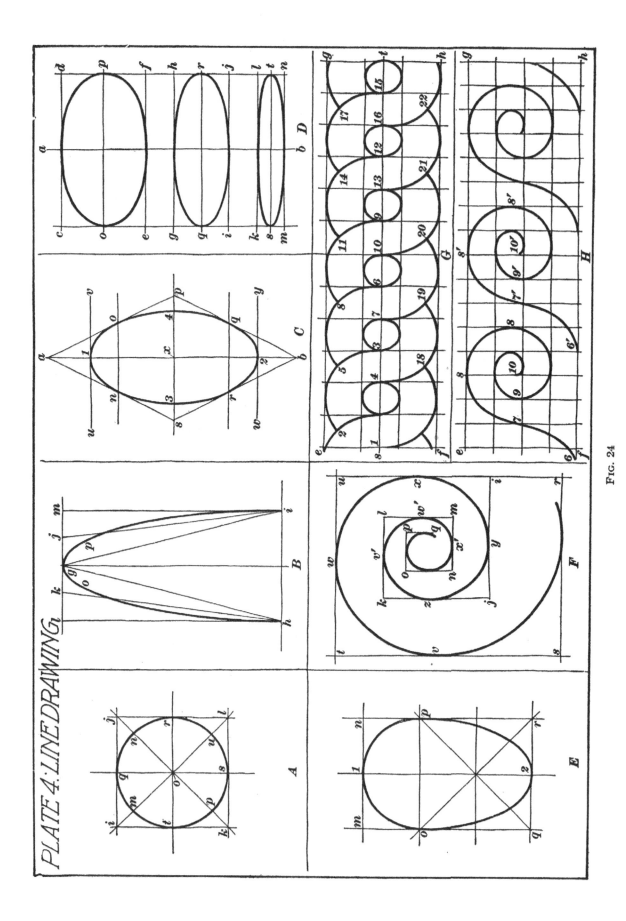

FIG. 24

LINE DRAWING

nor are any of the reference letters to appear on the plate; as in connection with the preceding plates, the illustrations are to serve merely as guides to the proper laying out of the work.

Material assistance in drawing Plate 4 will be had by keeping in sight for reference purposes the drawing of Plate 3 that was just finished, as both the guide and structural lines on it are

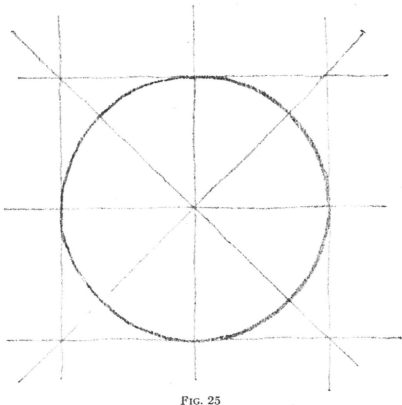

FIG. 25

the same as the guide lines in which the curved figures of Plate 4 are to be laid out.

46. Exercise A, Plate 4.—As shown on reduced scale in Fig. 24, first rectangle, top row, and full size in Fig. 25, Exercise A of Plate 4 calls for the drawing of a **circle**. This exercise may be executed as follows:

First, lay out a simple square in the manner explained in connection with the drawing of Exercise A of Plate 3. However, do not strengthen in any lines with the soft pencil; consider them all as guide lines and draw them lightly with the hard pencil. Next, within the square $i\,j\,l\,k$, Fig. 24 A, thus made,

LINE DRAWING

draw the circle in the following manner: As the lines $o\,t$, $o\,q$, $o\,r$, and $o\,s$, are known to be 1 inch long, lay off on the diagonals of the square $o\,m$, $o\,n$, $o\,u$, and $o\,p$, each 1 inch in length, thus obtaining points q, n, r, u, s, p, t, and m, all equal distances from the center o. Next, draw curves through these points as was done in Exercise F of Plate 2, and the required circle will be formed.

If it is desired, straight lines may first be drawn so as to connect t and m, m and q, q and n, etc., thus forming an octagon, and the short curves forming sections of the circle may be drawn in relation to these short lines, according to the method used in making the curved lines in Exercise E of Plate 2.

After the preceding methods of drawing a circle have been mastered, the following additional methods will perhaps simplify the work:

1. First, draw simply a vertical and a horizontal line that intersect each other and then draw a 45° right oblique and a 45° left oblique line, through the point of intersection. Then lay off points on these lines at equal distances from the point of intersection, any desired radius being used, and, finally, draw curves through the points to form the circle.

2. In still another method, the actual vertical, horizontal, and oblique lines need not be drawn. Simply place a dot to show the center of the circle; then around this dot place other dots equal distances from the center dot; and, finally, draw the connecting curves, as before.

3. First draw a perfect square by means of two vertical and two horizontal lines; then form the circle by rounding off the corners with quarter circles.

The methods of drawing circles just described should be practiced repeatedly. The more the beginner practices them the better able will he be to draw not only circles, but curved forms of all kinds. It is necessary at this time to use the guide lines here described to insure accuracy.

47. Exercise B, Plate 4.—Exercise B, as shown in Fig. 24, second rectangle, top row, consists in drawing a long, sweeping curve combined with a short one, a combination

LINE DRAWING

that is used very often in drawing vases, drapery, and even the human figure. It is advisable, therefore, to become accustomed to curves of this kind in their elementary forms. This double curve is drawn in the following manner:

First draw lightly the isosceles triangle $h\,g\,i$, proceeding in the manner explained in connection with drawing Exercise B, Plate 3. Then draw vertical lines $l\,h$ and $m\,i$, and bisect lines $l\,g$ and $g\,m$, thus locating points k and j. Next, draw two oblique lines $k\,h$ and $j\,i$, and, with the pencil held as shown in Fig. 5, draw the long sweeping curve $h\,g\,i$, using lines $k\,k$ and $j\,i$ as guides. This curve really consists of three separate curves $h\,o$, $o\,g\,p$, and $p\,i$, and should be made in such sections. Be careful to avoid getting the curve pointed at g. Curve $o\,g\,p$ should be almost a semicircle.

48. Exercise C, Plate 4.—Exercise C, as shown in Fig. 24, third rectangle, top row, calls for the drawing of an **ellipse** freehand and entirely by eye measurement. Of course, the ellipse, as well as other figures composed of regular curves, may be formed with drawing instruments or other mechanical aids, but these methods are not to be considered at present. To execute Exercise C, proceed as follows:

First, draw lightly all the construction lines and the hexagon based on them, following the directions for drawing Exercise C of Plate 3. Further, draw the short horizontal lines $u\,v$ and $w\,y$, of indefinite extent, about one-third of the distance down from point a to line $s\,p$ and about one-third of the distance up from point b to line $s\,p$ respectively. Thus, points 1 and 2 will be determined. Next, determine points 3 and 4, by making $s\,3$ and $p\,4$ a little less than one-third the lengths of $s\,x$ and $p\,x$, respectively. Finally, through the points 1, o, 4, q, 2, r, 3, and n thus obtained draw curved lines to form the ellipse.

The actual drawing of the curves involves nothing new, and may be done as described in connection with Exercise B. Care, however, must be observed to get the two sides of the ellipse symmetrical. A lack of symmetry may be detected in several ways. For instance, the sheet may be twisted around and the figure looked at from various angles; in this way, any variation in the symmetry of the two sides can be detected. Another method of testing and securing symmetry consists in placing one straight edge of a piece of mirror, unframed, along the vertical center line of the ellipse so that the mirror is perpendicular. If it is assumed that the right-hand side of the ellipse has been drawn correctly, the mirror will then reflect and reverse the correctly drawn right-hand side so that it appears as the left-hand side of the ellipse. If the perpendicular mirror is now quickly lifted away so that the actual drawing of the left-hand side can be seen, and then quickly replaced again perpendicularly on the center line so that the correct image can be seen, and then lifted away again, the correct image and the (possibly) faulty drawing of the left side can be compared. In this way the desired corrections in the drawing of the left-hand side of the ellipse can be made to conform to the image seen in the perpendicular mirror.

In drawing the curves comprising the ellipse, care must be taken to avoid the formation of "pointed" curves at positions *1, 4, 2, 3*, etc. The individual curves must join one another properly so as to make one continuous sweep to form the ellipse.

The elliptical forms shown in this and the following exercise must be practiced frequently, for they are used constantly in practical work, not only as decorative or ornamental forms, but particularly in the drawing of perspective views of circular shapes, such as wheels seen in part profile, circular archways and window tops, and the bases of cones, cylinders, and vases seen in perspective. Ease and familiarity in drawing such shapes correctly will therefore make simple the drawing of many forms and contours of models that might otherwise be very difficult.

49. Exercise D, Plate 4.—Exercise D provides for additional practice in ellipse drawing. As shown in Fig. 24, fourth rectangle, top row, three ellipses of uniform length and of different heights are to be drawn in a horizontal position. The application of ellipses so drawn is shown later.

As guide lines for these ellipses, first draw a vertical center line *a b* and then two horizontal lines, one *c d* $\frac{1}{2}$ inch below the upper edge of the sheet and the other $m\,n$ $\frac{1}{2}$ inch above the lower edge of the rectangle. Next, draw vertical lines $c\,m$ and $d\,n$ $\frac{1}{2}$ inch from the left border and right edge of the sheet, respectively, as shown. Then draw the following horizontal lines: $e\,f$, $1\frac{1}{2}$ inch below $c\,d$; $g\,h$, $\frac{1}{2}$ inch below $e\,f$; $i\,j$, 1 inch below $g\,h$; and $k\,l$, $\frac{1}{2}$ inch below $i\,j$. The line $m\,n$ will then be about $\frac{1}{2}$ inch below $k\,l$. These lines form three rectangles $c\,d\,f\,e$, $g\,h\,j\,i$, and $k\,l\,n\,m$. Next, draw the horizontal bisecting lines $o\,p$, $q\,r$, and $s\,t$. Within these rectangles draw the horizontal ellipses as shown, holding the pencil in the manner indicated in Fig. 4, and taking care to avoid pointed curves at the places where the ellipses touch the sides of the rectangles.

50. Exercise E, Plate 4.—Exercise E gives practice as shown in Fig. 24, first rectangle, lower row, in drawing the **oval,** or *egg-shaped figure*, which has for its upper part a semicircle, and for its lower part a semiellipse. In order to draw this exercise freehand, the half square $m\,n\,p\,o$ and the square $o\,p\,r\,q$ are constructed as directed for Exercise E of Plate 3. Then, it simply remains to draw in with a sharp B pencil the curve of the semicircle o–1–p, and the curve of the semiellipse o–2–p. The semicircle is drawn in the manner explained in the preceding exercises, and the semiellipse in the manner explained in connection with drawing Exercises B, C, and D of this plate.

51. Exercise F, Plate 4.—Exercise F, Plate 4, serves to combine practice in drawing curves with practice in eye measurement of decreasing distances. The figure to be drawn in this exercise is shown in Fig. 24, second rectangle, lower row, and is known as a **scroll,** or *volute*. It consists of a continuous curve that winds more tightly as it approaches the center, or eye. This curve is based on the fret drawn in Exercise F, Plate 3, and before attempting to draw the scroll, this same fret should be constructed, in the manner previously directed.

In drawing the curves of the scroll, they should be laid out as quarter circles, not semicircles. First, bisect the lines $s\,t$, $t\,u$, $u\,i$, $i\,j$, $j\,k$, $k\,l$, $l\,m$, $m\,n$, $n\,o$, $o\,p$, and $p\,q$, thus locating the points v, w, x, y, z, v', etc. Next, draw quarter circles,

LINE DRAWING

first from line *r s* to point *v*, then *v w*, *w x*, *x y*, *y z*, *z v'*, etc., being careful to make the places of joining of the neighboring quarter circles smooth, that is, not pointed or sharply marked in any way. This can be accomplished by extending each quarter circle for about ¼ inch beyond its proper stopping place, and then starting the next quarter circle by first drawing over this ¼-inch extension. In this way, a continuous curve to form the volute can be drawn.

52. Exercise G, Plate 4.—Exercise G, as shown in Fig. 24, upper part of last two rectangles, provides for practice in duplicating symmetrical curves, based on large and small semicircles, to form a continuous border called a **guilloche**. The procedure in drawing this exercise is as follows:

First, draw the rectangle *e g h f* twelve smaller rectangles in width and three smaller rectangles in height, as directed for Exercise G, Plate 3, and then draw the horizontal center line *s t*. The larger semicircles to be drawn are all three spaces wide (that is, have a diameter of three spaces) and one and one-half spaces high (that is, have a radius of one and one-half spaces.) Each large semicircle will overlap the following semicircle to the extent of one space, as shown. Using a hard, sharp pencil, first draw very lightly the semicircles *1–2–5–3*, *4–5–8–6*, *7–8–11–9*, *10–11–14–12*, etc. Then, in a similar manner draw the semicircles *1–18–3*, *4–18–19–6*, *7–19–20–9*, etc. Next, draw the small circles occupying the second, fourth, sixth, eighth, tenth and twelfth rectangular spaces on the horizontal center line. Next, with the B pencil, well sharpened, strengthen in parts of each large semicircle, as shown. Upper semicircle *1–2–5–3* should be strengthened in from points *2* to *3*, semicircle *4–5–8–6*, from points *5* to *6*; and the rest of the upper semicircles treated similarly. Also, lower semicircle *1–18–3* should be strengthened in from points *1* to *18*, semicircle *4–18–19–6*, from points *4* to *19*; and the remaining lower semicircles treated in similar manner. Finally, strengthen in all the small circles around their entire circumferences, when the guilloche will be properly formed as shown by **the heavier** lines in Fig. 24, G.

LINE DRAWING

53. Exercise H, Plate 4.—Exercise H, as shown in Fig. 24, lower part of last two rectangles, consists of a **running scroll**, or *wave pattern*, that is based on the fret pattern drawn for Exercise H, Plate 3. Exercise H, Plate 4, should be done in the following manner:

First, draw a rectangle *e g h f* sixteen smaller rectangles wide and four smaller rectangles high, and construct thereon a fret pattern, following the directions given for drawing Exercise H, of Plate 3. Next draw the curves that form the scroll. The larger parts of the curves should be drawn as quarter circles, as in the case of the volute of Exercise F of this plate. Thus, curve *6–7* should be part of a quarter circle; curve *7–s*, a quarter circle; curve *s–8*, a somewhat smaller quarter circle; and the remaining curves *8–9* and *9–10*, continuous curves that are based on the combinations of quarter circles to complete the first member of the pattern. Similarly, curve *6'–7'* should be a quarter circle, as should also *7'–s'* and *s'–8'*; then *8'* to *9'* and *10'* should be drawn as continuous curves that are combinations of quarter circles. Finally, draw the remaining members of the wave pattern in the same manner, as shown by the heavier lines.

54. Final Work on Plate 4.—After completing all the exercises of Plate 4, the usual identifying data, namely, the title of the plate, Plate 4: Line Drawing, the class letters and number, the name and address, and the date of completion, should be placed at the proper places on the plate.

Plates 3 and 4 should then be rolled, placed in the mailing tube, and mailed to the Schools for examination.

If any redrawn work on the exercises of Plates 1 and 2 has by this time been asked for, all this work should be completed satisfactorily before going on with Plate 5. If, however, all previous work has been satisfactory, the work called for on Plate 5 should be started at once.

LINE DRAWING

PLATE 5

55. Purpose.—Up to this point, the training in line drawing has been confined to figures of one and of two dimensions; in Plate 5, and also in Plate 6, which is the last one of this Section, are given exercises that provide training in making outline drawings of the general appearance of objects having three dimensions, namely, *length*, *breadth*, and *thickness*. No attempt, however, is made at this stage to teach the drawing of any figure, pattern, or object for itself alone; nor is any attempt made at model drawing or at accurate foreshortening. These exercises, in keeping with those already studied, are introduced simply to train the eye to see and the hand to draw lines of various kinds as a foundation for the applied drawing that is to come later. In addition, they serve to introduce to the beginner the general appearance of the retreating sides or ends of such objects as the cube, pyramid, hexagonal prism, cylinder, cone, sphere, hemisphere, and vase, so that when the study of foreshortening is reached he will have a general idea of such solids. The solids called for on Plate 5 are based on the figures shown on Plate 3.

56. Accenting.—Before the drawing of Plates 5 and 6 is taken up, attention should be directed to the accenting of lines. By *accenting* is meant the gradual increase or decrease in the weight and thickness of lines as produced by the amount of pressure exerted on a pencil as it is drawn along the paper upon which an object is being drawn. Accenting, however, must be done according to certain well-understood principles, so that the lines accented with the soft pencil, which pencil is always used for accenting, are applied to the proper outlines of the object. Accenting must not be confused with what is called *shading;* that is, filling in with pencil strokes those parts of a model or an object that are in shade. It refers only to the accenting of the "outline" lines of the drawing. Furthermore, accenting should not be confused with the so-called "shade lines" that are used in mechanical drawing and in some systems of architectural drawing, where a wide black

LINE DRAWING

line of uniform width is ruled, always at the right hand and the lower edges of the drawing, to express shade in a conventional manner.

57. A few of the *general principles of accenting* that should be remembered are as follows:

1. The lines of that part of the object which is nearest the eye of the observer should be boldly accented with good, strong, black lines; and the lines showing parts of the object farthest from the eye should be left unaccented.

2. In any object, the different degrees of distance from the eye, of any part extending backwards or retreating, should be expressed by an accented line of differing weight and thickness in its various parts as it approaches or recedes from the eye.

3. When accents are placed, it is the object itself or parts of the object that must be accented, and not the edges of the background or pieces of background that may be seen between the various parts of the object.

4. The accenting lines of outline drawings of geometrical models, simple objects, etc. may be grouped mainly at, although not confined to, the right-hand side and at the bottom of the model, or object. This principle is based on the theory that, ordinarily, a conventionally lighted object is supposed to be illuminated from a point above and to the left.

The preceding principles are simply general considerations that must be borne in mind when accenting the drawings for the various exercises of Plates 5 and 6. However, there can be no hard-and-fast rule for doing it.

58. Accenting is not a difficult thing to do. In fact, an accented line can be drawn just as easily as a hard mechanical line—more easily, in fact. The chief thing is to cultivate *observation*, so as to be able to see the subtle differences of various parts of an object in outline. It is known, of course, that there are no such things as lines or outlines in nature, but there are edges or apparent edges, where one plane is separated from another plane, and it is these outlines that are now being considered.

LINE DRAWING

It is possible to express by outlines, without resorting to shading or rendering of any kind, characteristics of various kinds of objects or solids. For instance, it is known that a wooden geometric solid has hard, sharp edges; therefore, fairly sharp and distinct lines of accent will express the character of the texture and the surface of the wooden object. On the other hand, the curved side of an ordinary teapot, as it is silhouetted against a background, has no sharp edges, but a surface curved in silhouette and rounding away from the observer. Such a line would most appropriately be portrayed by a curved line of accent, starting rather narrow at the top and swelling out like a brush stroke, when pressure is exerted, as the stroke reaches the bottom. Again, the handle of the teapot may be made of woven wickerwork, not at all smooth, and nothing would be more appropriate than to portray the accented outline of the handle in wavelike accented strokes.

If the accenting lines are thus drawn with careful observance of just what lines are accented, and why they are accented, no difficulty should be encountered in doing this work properly.

59. Method Used in Accenting. In accenting, the lines are to be drawn with one touch, or stroke, of the B or 2B pencil, varying the pressure just enough to give proper character to the line. There should be no "patching up" or "teasing" of the line, as is done by certain professional penmen in making the broad down strokes of their ornamental capital letters. Neither should the accented line be heavy and of even width throughout its length. Avoid the appearance of a ruled line. Lines of accent placed with one touch or stroke of the well-sharpened soft pencil will, of course, be slightly irregular and varied; but these will not be inaccurate. This irregularity will, in fact, add to their artistic interest.

60. To illustrate the preceding points, a sheet of reproductions of outline pencil drawings properly accented is shown in Fig. 26. As will be observed, none of the lines in these examples are absolutely black, hard, or wiry. The strokes are either light gray or dark gray. This quality of line can be obtained only by using the softer grade of pencil, such as

FIG. 26

LINE DRAWING

the B or 2B. It will be seen, also, that the weight of the line varies somewhat according to the material or texture of the object. The vase, the glass, and the cup and saucer are composed of a hard, smooth material. Therefore, in order to suggest this quality of the surface, a sharper and finer line than is employed to express the softer and pliable surface of the pepper, the leaves, and the fruit is used. In drawing the leaves, the fruit, the pepper, etc. the softer material can be expressed better with a broader line than with a fine one, because the broad line possesses an elasticity and softness that is not visible in the finer and sharper line.

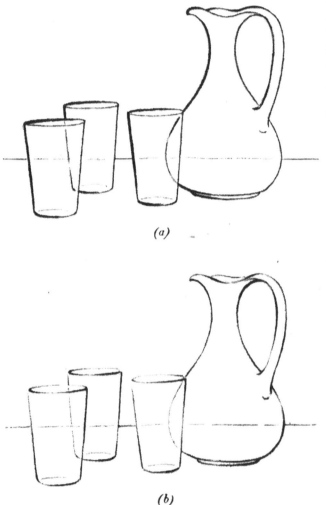

Fig. 27

It is evident from the variation of the weight of the lines that not all the contours or edges of the objects were equally distinct to the observer. Along some edges there possibly were reflections from other surfaces that rendered these edges almost invisible. This fact is conveyed to an onlooker by the faint pencil strokes used to portray these edges. Again, some edges were quite sharply defined, either because the background threw these edges into prominence or because they were nearest the eye of the observer. It was necessary, therefore, to use a more distinct and decided line to represent these contours as they actually appeared.

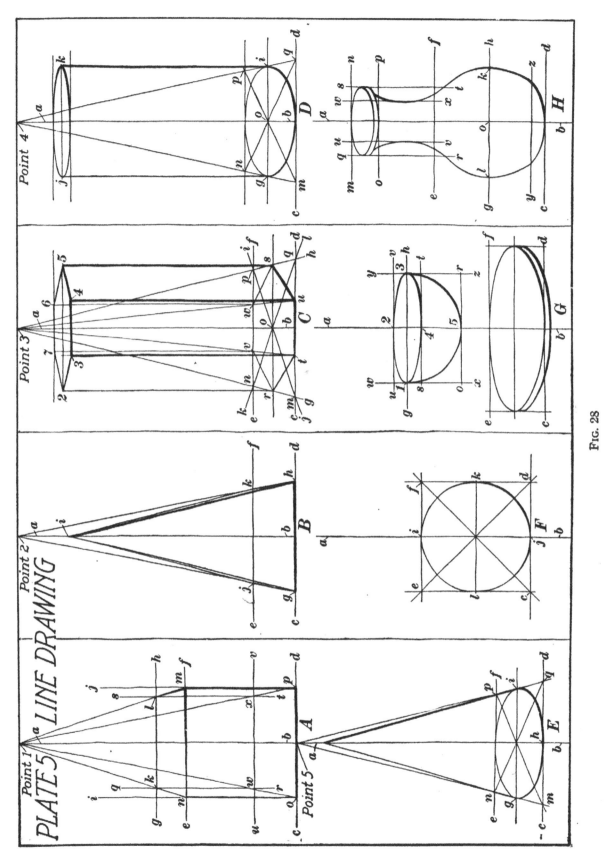

FIG. 28

LINE DRAWING

The companion illustrations in Fig. 27 will show clearly, without any necessary comment, what is faulty accenting and what is correct accenting. In (a) the accenting is improperly done because it does not succeed in portraying proper modeling or lighting and the heavy lines mean nothing at all, being placed at the upper left portions of the objects, where there is no occasion for accenting. In (b) the accenting is correctly done, as it conforms to the principles that have already been pointed out.

61. General Directions for Plate 5.—As was done in connection with the preceding drawing plates, the paper for Plate 5 should first be divided into eight equal rectangles. The way in which the exercises are to be arranged on this plate is illustrated in Fig. 28. No attempt must be made to copy the exercises as they appear here, because the weight of the lines, as well as the sizes of the figures themselves, are very much reduced. The quality of line and the system of accenting required for all the exercises of Plate 5 are plainly shown in Fig. 29, which is an illustration of Exercise A drawn to full size.

Each exercise of both Plates 5 and 6 should first be drawn with clear and distinct, but not hard and sharp, lines made with a fairly hard pencil, such as a 2H; that is, so that the outlines of each will be clearly defined, but not black. Then, each exercise should be accented by lines made with a well-sharpened B or 2B pencil and according to the directions just given for accenting. The appearance of the lines required is much the same as those called for in Exercise B and D, Plate 1.

62. Exercise A, Plate 5.—Exercise A of Plate 5, as shown on reduced scale in Fig. 28, first rectangle, top row and full size in Fig. 29, calls for a drawing that shows the outline appearance of the **cube,** which is a solid based on the square. This outline drawing of the cube shows it as it would appear full face and slightly below the level of the eye. While the rules and principles of foreshortening will not be fully discussed until a later Section is reached, the following general principle relating to the appearance of solids must be understood at this time:

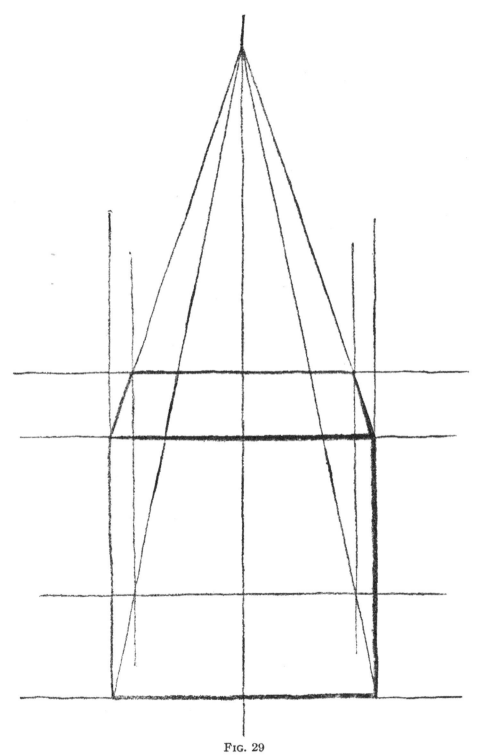

Fig. 29

LINE DRAWING

Principle of Foreshortening.—*The part of the solid nearest to the eye of the observer appears to be the largest, the part farthest from the eye appears to be the smallest, and those parts extending backwards and away from the eye appear to diminish in size and show lines retreating toward a point.*

Thus, while it is known that in an actual cube all the edges are equal in length, the upper rear edge $k\,l$ of the cube in Exercise A appears shorter than the edge $n\,m$ because it is farther from the eye. For this reason, also, the connecting sides $n\,k$ and $m\,l$ appear to retreat, and converge toward a point.

Drawing.—To make the outline drawing of the cube, proceed as follows: First draw the vertical center line $a\,b$, and let the lower front edge $c\,d$ of the cube rest on the lower line of the rectangle; that is, on the long horizontal line that divides the entire sheet into two rows of rectangles. Then draw $e\,f$ 2 inches above $c\,d$, and $g\,h$ $\frac{3}{8}$ or $\frac{1}{2}$ inch above $e\,f$. Next, draw vertical lines $i\,o$ and $j\,p$ 1 inch to the left and the right, respectively, of the vertical center line $a\,b$. Next, draw oblique lines from o to point *1* at the top edge of the sheet and from p to this same point and where these oblique lines cut horizontal line $u\,v$, drawn $\frac{3}{4}$ inch above $c\,d$, will determine points w and x. Thus, $w\,x\,p\,o$ becomes the bottom of the cube, although only the edge $o\,p$ shows. Next, draw vertical lines $q\,r$ and $s\,t$ through points w and x, and where these vertical lines cut the horizontal line $q\,h$ will determine points k and l. Next, with the same hard pencil, well sharpened, connect with straight lines that are clean, even, and not blurred the points k, l, m, and n and then points m, p, o, and n. This will complete the outline drawing of the cube, that is, of those sides or faces which show.

In drawing the cube, do not press hard on the pencil, nor draw a heavy line; simply make it distinct. The other sides and edges are faintly suggested by light lines to show what their positions would be, as might be determined if, for example, the cube were made of glass, and these sides and edges could be observed through it.

Accenting.—The next work in connection with the exercise is to accent it. With the B or the 2B pencil, accent the outline

LINE DRAWING

drawing of the cube, bearing in mind the foundation principles of accenting already explained. Note that lines mp and po are accented because they are the lines, at the right and at the bottom of the cube, that separate it from the background. Line lm is accented for a similar reason, but the accent decreases in weight and thickness as it goes back toward l. Line nm is accented because it separates a plane of the cube that receives the very brightest light from a plane that receives a less brilliant light. Lines separating planes lighted in different degrees are always accented.

63. Exercise B, Plate 5.—As shown in Fig. 28, second rectangle, top row, Exercise B consists in drawing and accenting a solid based on the isosceles triangle, namely, the **pyramid.** In this case, it will be a square pyramid, because its base will be a 2-inch square. This full-face view of the square pyramid shows it in the same position as the cube of Exercise A, and the sides of the base will, of course, retreat as in the case of the cube. The front edge of the 2-inch square base of the pyramid rests on the bottom line of the rectangle, thus bringing its base on a line with the base of the square in Exercise A. The pyramid is to be 4 inches high.

Drawing.—To draw the pyramid, proceed as follows: Lay out a space $jkhg$ in the same manner as space $wxpo$ of Exercise A was laid out; that is, by means of the horizontal line ef ¾ inch above cd and the retreating lines gj and hk formed by drawing oblique lines from points g and h to point 2 on the top edge of the sheet. Having done this, draw lines jg, gh, and hk to form the edges of the base that can be seen. Then establish point i on the line ab, 1 inch below the top of the sheet, and connect points j, g, h, and k with point i, thus forming the edges of the sides of the pyramid. Then complete the drawing of the pyramid by strengthening in these lines.

Care must be observed to not confuse point 2 at the top edge of the sheet, toward which the side edges of the base retreat, with point i, the top, or apex, of the pyramid.

Accenting.—With the B or the 2B pencil, accent the proper lines of the pyramid in the manner previously described.

LINE DRAWING

There is no full-sized drawing of the pyramid to serve as a guide; it is expected by this time that the principles of accenting are sufficiently well known to be applied to any figure that may have to be accented.

64. Exercise C, Plate 5.—For Exercise C, as shown in Fig. 28, third rectangle, top row, it is necessary to draw and to accent a symmetrical view of the solid known as a **hexagonal prism**; that is, a figure having a regular hexagon for its base and one for its top, the sides being rectangles and all vertical edges being parallel. The prism is to be 4 inches high.

Drawing.—The hexagonal prism should be drawn in the following manner: First draw the vertical center line $a\,b$ and then the horizontal line $c\,d$ resting on the lower line of the rectangle; that is, the horizontal bisecting line of the sheet. Then draw $e\,f$ in relation to $c\,d$, as in the case of Exercise B. Next, lay off points m and q $1\frac{1}{4}$ inches to the left and the right, respectively, of the vertical center line $a\,b$. Draw oblique (retreating) lines g–3 and h–3 through m and q to point 3 at the top edge of the sheet, thus establishing points n and p on line $e\,f$. Next, find the central point o of the shape $m\,n\,p\,q$ by drawing the diagonals $i\,j$ and $k\,l$ and noting their point of intersection. Through o draw a horizontal line intersecting the oblique lines, and thus establishing points r and s. Next, lay off points t and u on the horizontal line $c\,d$ $\frac{1}{2}$ inch to the left and the right, respectively, of the vertical center line, and then find points v and w by drawing oblique lines from t and u to point 3, which will intersect the horizontal line $e\,f$ at v and w. Next, connect v, w, s, u, t, r, and v, and the base of the hexagonal prism will be complete. Use very light lines in connecting points r, v, w and s, which represent the part of the contour of the base that would not be seen.

The top of the prism is drawn in a similar manner. First draw horizontal line $3, 4$, 1 inch below the top edge of the sheet, and lines $2, 5$, and $7, 6$, $\frac{1}{8}$ inch and $\frac{1}{4}$ inch respectively above line $3, 4$, and on these lines construct the top hexagon, as described. Establish points $7, 6, 5, 4, 3,$ and 2 directly

LINE DRAWING

above points *v, w, s, u, t*, and *r* of the base, and on the horizontal lines, as shown.

To form the long vertical sides of the hexagonal prism, simply connect the corresponding points in the top and in the base by vertical lines. Then draw clearly all the lines showing the edges of the top as were lines *r t, t u*, and *u s* of the base; which operation will complete the drawing of the hexagonal prism.

This hexagonal prism may be considered as the governing shape of the waste-paper basket that is to be drawn later.

Accenting.—The hexagonal prism just drawn should be accented according to the principles already laid down. As will be observed in the illustration, Fig. 28 C, the bottom and the right-hand vertical edges should receive the most attention.

65. Exercise D, Plate 5.—The solid known as the **cylinder** is the object to be drawn for Exercise D as shown in Fig. 28, fourth rectangle, top row. This solid consists of two circular forms—top and bottom—connected by a continually curving surface. The cylinder to be drawn for this exercise is based on the circle, which, in turn, is based on or is a development of the octagon, as has been shown. This cylinder consists simply of two ellipses connected by straight lines, as reference to the illustration will show.

Drawing.—To draw the cylinder, which is 2 inches wide and 4 inches high, the shape *n p q m*, which is really the perspective of a square, must be drawn first. Thus, draw the horizontal line *g i* a little less than ½ inch above the bottom of the rectangle, locating the points *g* and *i* 1 inch each side of the vertical center line *a b*. Then draw horizontal line *c d* in contact with the bottom of the rectangle, and draw lines through *g* and *i* to point *4* on the upper edge of the sheet, thus locating points *m* and *q*. As the point *o* has been located by the intersection of the line *g i* with *a b*, next, from points *m* and *q*, draw lines through *o*, locating points *p* and *n* on the retreating lines toward point *4*. Then draw line *n p*, completing the perspective square, within which the ellipse at the bottom of the cylinder can be lightly drawn. The top should

LINE DRAWING

next be drawn in a similar manner, placing the line $j\,k$ (the longer axis of the ellipse) $\frac{3}{4}$ inch below the top edge of sheet and making the ellipse 2 inches long and about $\frac{3}{8}$ inch high. The contours of this cylinder in outline should be completed by drawing the long vertical lines $j\,g$ and $k\,i$, connecting corresponding ends of the top ellipse and the bottom ellipse.

This cylinder will be considered the governing shape of the watering can that is to be drawn later.

Accenting.—The vertical line $k\,i$ of the ellipse may be accented as were the lines in previous exercises. The front curved lines $j\,k$ and $g\,b$, i, however, should start faintly at j and g, respectively, and gradually swell as they proceed toward the right. The most marked part of the accent should be about half way between b and i of the base, and also the corresponding place at the top, and then decrease somewhat as k and i are reached. The rear curve $j\,k$ at the top may be lightly accented as it approaches k.

66. Exercise E, Plate 5.—As shown in Fig. 28, first rectangle, lower row, Exercise E requires the drawing of a **cone,** which is a solid figure that tapers uniformly from a circular base upwards to a point called the apex. The general shape of the cone of this exercise is based on the isosceles triangle previously drawn, and its base is a circle, the drawing of the base being an ellipse; that is, a circle seen in perspective, or foreshortened.

Drawing.—The cone of Exercise E should be executed as follows: First draw the shape $n\,p\,q\,m$ by crossing the vertical center line $a\,b$ by the horizontal line $c\,d$ $\frac{1}{2}$ inch above the lower edge of the sheet, and the horizontal line $e\,f$ about $\frac{3}{4}$ inch above $c\,d$, cutting the oblique lines through g and i drawn to point 5 located at the middle of the top edge of the rectangle; points g and i having been located as before, 1 inch each side of $a\,b$, on the horizontal line midway between $n\,p$ and $m\,q$. Point a, the apex of the cone, is, of course, on the vertical center line, $\frac{1}{2}$ inch below the top edge of the rectangle. Complete the drawing of the cone, by drawing in clearly with the hard pencil that part of the elliptical base from g to h to i and also the lines $a\,g$ and $a\,i$.

LINE DRAWING

This cone will be the governing shape of the inverted funnel, that is to be drawn later.

Accenting.—The curved base line $g\,i$ of the cone should be accented just as the curved base line of the cylinder of Exercise D was accented, and the right side of the cone should be accented in the same manner as the line $i\,h$ of the pyramid in Exercise B.

67. Exercise F, Plate 5.—Exercise F, Fig. 28, second rectangle, lower row, serves to illustrate the method of drawing a **sphere,** but for the present no attempt will be made to show a sphere in its true foreshortening. This would require that the sphere be drawn within a cube, which can be done only after foreshortening, which is taken up later, has been learned.

Drawing.—To draw Exercise F as shown in Fig. 28, simply form a 2-inch circle within a square $e\,f\,d\,c$, the bottom line $c\,d$ of which is about ¾ inch above the lower edge of the sheet. The directions given for Exercise A of Plate 4 should be observed, and the curves of the circle should be drawn in clearly after being accurately determined.

The sphere thus drawn will be the governing shape of the teapot to be drawn later.

Accenting.—The accenting of the sphere can be done only conventionally. The pressure on the pencil should begin on the curve at the upper left, lightly through i, gradually increasing as it approaches k, keeping rather firm until its full strength is reached between k and j, and then decreasing as it comes around toward l.

68. Exercise G, Plate 5.—As shown in Fig. 28, third rectangle, lower row, Exercise G consists in drawing two objects, a **disk** and a **hemisphere.** These objects are the governing shapes of many well-known articles seen every day, such as a cup and saucer, etc.

The principle of drawing the disk shown at the bottom of the rectangle and the ellipse that shows the flat part of the hemisphere is exactly the same as was used in drawing the ellipses for the bases of the figures in Exercises D and E of this plate; that is, the horizontal limiting lines are located and then

LINE DRAWING

the sides of an imaginary enclosing square are located and retreated back toward a point, which operation gives, in perspective, the square in which the ellipse may then be drawn. To save time, however, this process of retreating sides may be dispensed with and simply the side limits of the ellipse plotted in with short vertical lines.

Drawing.—To draw the disk, therefore, first draw a horizontal line $c\,d$ $\frac{1}{2}$ inch above the bottom of the sheet and a line $e\,f$ 1 inch above $c\,d$. Then plot in an ellipse between these two horizontal lines, making it 3 inches long—that is, extending $1\frac{1}{2}$ inches to the left and the right, respectively, of the vertical center line $a\,b$—and using short vertical strokes $e\,c$ and $f\,d$ to limit and determine its ends. Next, show that the disk has thickness by drawing the front half of another ellipse, one about $\frac{1}{16}$ inch below the other, and connecting the corresponding ends by vertical lines, as shown. Draw in clearly the entire upper ellipse, the front half of the lower ellipse, and the short lengths ($\frac{1}{16}$ inch) of the short vertical lines, so as to show the thickness of the disk.

To draw the hemisphere in the upper part of the rectangle, draw a horizontal line $o\,r$ 2 inches above the bottom edge of the sheet, a line $g\,h$ 1 inch above $o\,r$, and lines $u\,v$ and $s\,t$ $\frac{1}{4}$ inch above and below, respectively, the line $g\,h$. Then draw vertical lines $w\,x$ and $y\,z$ 1 inch to the left and right, respectively, of vertical center line $a\,b$. Next, draw a full ellipse *1-2-3-4* and the semicircle *1-5-3*, and draw in the lines clearly, which operation will complete the drawing of the hemisphere.

This hemisphere and disk may be considered as the underlying form of the cup and saucer to be drawn later.

Accenting.—The elliptical top of the hemisphere is accented as was the ellipse $j\,k$ of Exercise D, the front part of the curve being more strongly accented than the rear part and the strongest accent being midway between *4* and *3*. The semicircular curve *1-5-3* is most strongly accented between 3 and 5.

The upper ellipse of the disk at the lower part of the rectangle is accented as were the ellipses in previous exercises, and the front half of the lower ellipse of the disk is accented similarly.

LINE DRAWING

69. Exercise H, Plate 5.—Exercise H, Plate 5, as is shown in Fig. 28, fourth rectangle, lower row, calls for the drawing of a **vase form.** The drawing of this form is not so difficult as it would appear, for it is based on geometrical solids that have already been taken up. The lower half is spherical, the top, in perspective, is elliptical; and the neck is simply formed by reverse curves that are themselves parts of semicircles.

Drawing.—To draw the vase, lay off horizontal lines as follows: $c\,d$, $\frac{1}{2}$ inch above the lower edge of the sheet; $y\,z$, $\frac{1}{4}$ inch above $c\,d$; $g\,h$ 1 inch above $c\,d$; $e\,f$, 2 inches above $c\,d$; $m\,n$, 1 inch below the top edge of the rectangle; and $o\,p$, $\frac{1}{2}$ inch below $m\,n$. Next, draw vertical lines as follows: $a\,b$, as the vertical center line of the rectangle; $u\,v$ and $w\,x$, $\frac{3}{8}$ inch to the left and right, respectively, of $a\,b$; $q\,r$, $\frac{1}{4}$ inch to the left of $u\,v$; and $s\,t$, $\frac{1}{4}$ inch to the right of $w\,x$. The points l and k are 2 inches apart because the vase is 2 inches wide. Next, draw lightly, but accurately, a 2-inch circle within the 2-inch square, of which o is the center. Strengthen in the circle until the points where the vertical lines $q\,r$ and $s\,t$ cut it; from those points upwards draw the reverse curves, curving them inwards to touch lines $u\,v$ and $w\,x$ and then outwards toward lines $q\,r$ and $s\,t$. Next lay out in the rectangle formed by $q\,r$, $s\,t$, $m\,n$, and $o\,p$ the ellipses to form the top edge and its thickness; and, finally, form the base by the front curve of a $1\frac{1}{2}$-inch ellipse laid out on the line $y\,z$ as its longer axis.

Accenting.—The ellipses of the top and the bottom of the vase form should be accented in the same manner as the previous ellipses, and the contour of the vase itself should be treated in the same way as the sphere in Exercise F of this plate.

70. Final Work on Plate 5.—After the drawing of Exercise H is completed, the proper identifying data should be placed on the plate. Thus, the title, Plate 5: Line Drawing, should be lettered or written at the top of the sheet, and the student's class letters and number, his name and address, and the date on which the work was completed should be put on the back of the sheet, in the lower left-hand corner.

I L T 159B—6

LINE DRAWING

Plate 5 should not be sent to the Schools at this time, however. It should be retained and used as a guide in drawing Plate 6.

It is now in order to proceed with the work on Plate 6.

PLATE 6

71. Purpose.—The purpose of Plate 6, which is shown on reduced scale in Fig. 30, is to demonstrate the fact that a knowledge of all the figures in the preceding exercises is absolutely essential to the person learning to draw. Any one who is familiar with the square, the triangle, the hexagon, the octagon, and the circle, and also with the cube, the pyramid, the hexagonal prism, the cylinder, the cone, the sphere, the hemisphere, and the vase form is at once able to see that these shapes are the foundations of various objects that come within his vision. For instance, a cigar humidor, a ring box, or any box that is as high as it is long and wide, at once suggests a cube. A metronome, a pyramidal bread toaster, or any other object whose four sides slope up to, or almost to, a point, suggests a pyramid. A waste basket with six long flat sides suggests a hexagonal prism; a watering can is simply a cylinder with a spout and a handle on it; an inverted funnel is a cone; a teapot, a baseball, an apple, etc., suggest a sphere; a teacup and saucer are simply the lower half of a hemisphere resting on a disk; and so on.

It must not be inferred, however, that the exercises of this plate are intended to give instruction in how to draw *directly* from such objects. Their purpose, rather, is simply to continue practice in eye measurement and freehand line drawing, and to show how all common objects, utensils, etc. are based on certain geometric solids, thus making possible drawing directly from such solids a much simpler matter, when that work is taken up later, than if it had not been led up to by easy steps.

An additional purpose of the exercises of Plate 6 is to provide training that will accustom the beginner to using clean, accurate,

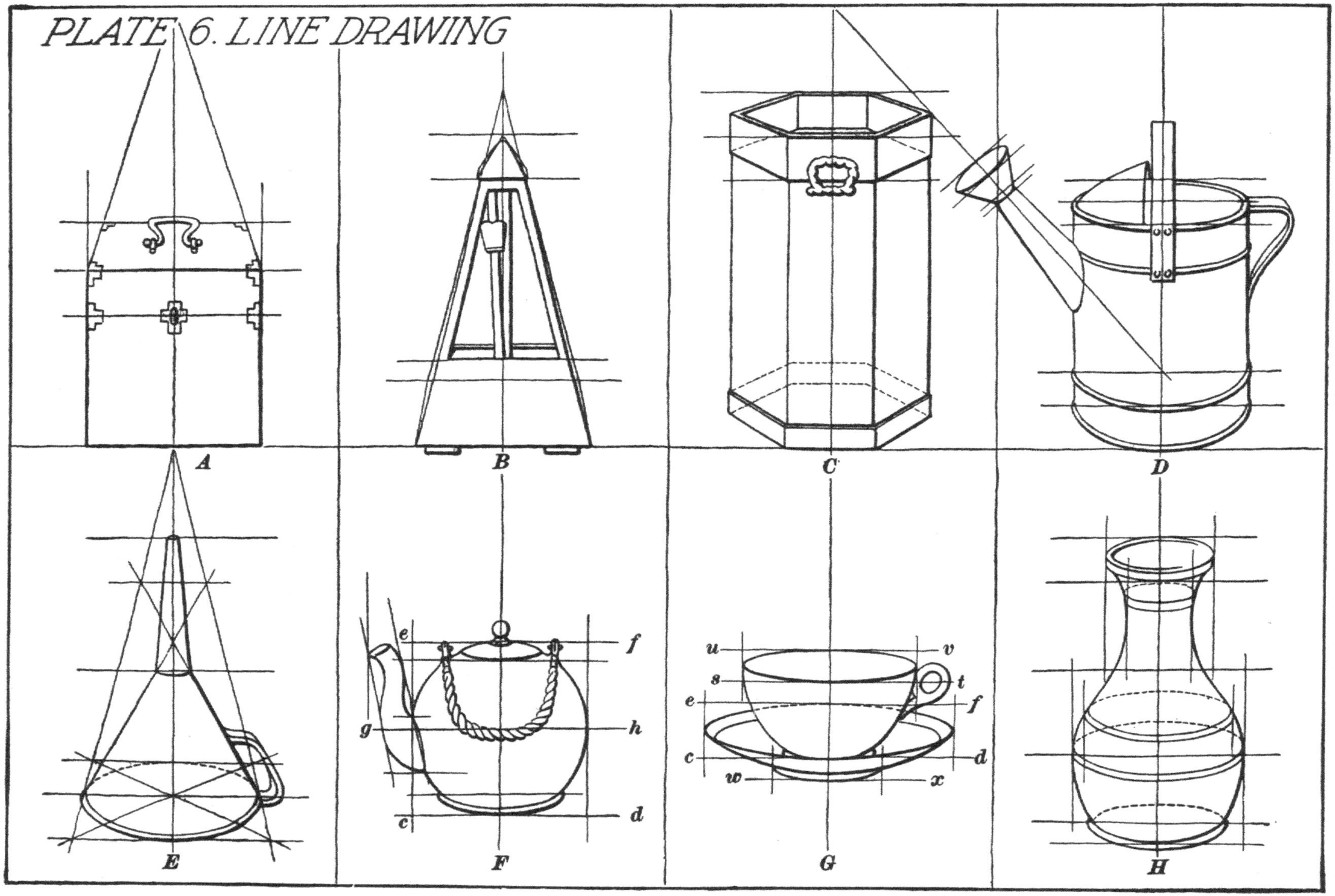
PLATE 6. LINE DRAWING
A
B
C
D
E
F
G
H
e
f
g
h
c
d
u
v
s
t
e
f
c
d
w
x

Fig. 30

LINE DRAWING

and sure lines. It should be borne in mind that all the exercises of this Section are to provide training for a definite kind of work in the industrial or commercial art field, in some photo-engraving plant, art department, studio, or designing room. In such places, the so-called artistic swing or dash to lines that are drawn has very little place; what is wanted are good, clean lines, each one of which serves a definite purpose.

72. General Directions.—Plate 6 is to be laid off into divisions as were the previous plates, namely, eight rectangles $3\frac{3}{4}$ inches wide and 5 inches high, formed by drawing one horizontal center line and three vertical lines within the $15'' \times 10''$ space. In Fig. 30 are shown on reduced scale the objects to be drawn and the way in which they are to appear on the drawing plate, and in Fig. 31 is shown a full-sized drawing of Exercise A that serves to give an idea of the quality of line to be used and the method of accenting. The objects and utensils on Plate 6 are to be drawn to the same size and scale as the geometrical forms on Plate 5, and should fit into their appropriate rectangles, as shown in Fig. 30.

73. Exercise A, Plate 6.—As shown on reduced scale in Fig. 30, first rectangle, top row, and full size in Fig. 31, Exercise A, Plate 6, requires the drawing of an ordinary **humidor,** which is an air-tight box used for keeping cigars and tobacco moist. The humidor is selected because of its cubical shape, although other types of objects illustrating the cube could be chosen.

Drawing.—To draw the humidor, a cube should first be constructed in the same manner as the cube of Exercise A, Plate 5; that is, by means of the plotting in lines there employed, the front face of the cube being about 2 inches square. To avoid confusion, the construction lines in Fig. 30 are not lettered; however, as will be observed, they are the same as those in Exercise A of Plate 5. When the cube is constructed, it simply remains to draw a horizontal line about $\frac{1}{2}$ inch below the top edge of the face of the cube, so as to show the place where the cover, or lid, joins the body of the box. The little ornamental corners and the top handle can then be put in

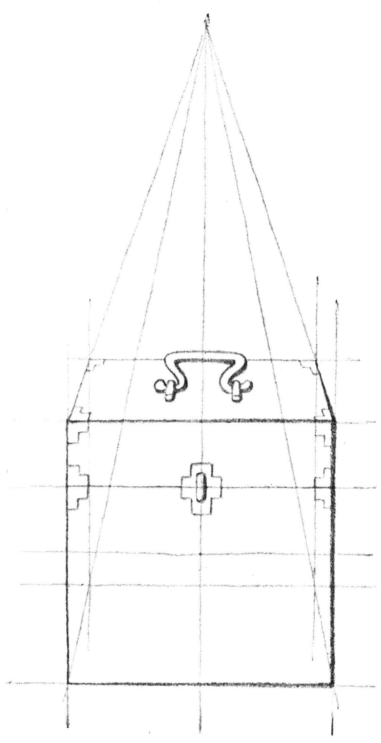

Fig. 31

LINE DRAWING

quite easily. All the work should be done with the hard pencil, 2H, well sharpened, using clean-cut lines. The lines should be of equal weight throughout the entire drawing and there should be no "fuzzy" or "sketchy" lines; that is, lines composed of little, uncertain vague strokes.

Accenting.—The outlines of the humidor should next be accented as were the outlines of the cube in Exercise A of Plate 5. Particular care should be given to accenting the drawing of the handle, so as to show the rounding of the metal parts. The full-size drawing in Fig. 31 shows clearly how this should be done. The metal corners, the lock plate, etc., are not to be accented, because they are not raised above the wooden surface of the box, but are level with it, and therefore do not make a sufficiently distinct line with it to need accenting. It should be borne in mind that only "outline" accenting is required; no "shading" is to be done at all.

74. Exercise B, Plate 6.—Exercise B, as shown in Fig. 30, second rectangle, top row, calls for the drawing of a regulation **metronome,** which is an instrument for indicating and marking time in music. It is selected for this exercise on account of its pyramidal shape, although, of course, other familiar objects of pyramidal shape would also be suitable.

Drawing.—To draw the metronome, proceed as follows: First, draw the pyramid, as described for Exercise B, Plate 5. Then, $\frac{1}{2}$ inch below the top of the pyramid draw a short horizontal line, and $\frac{1}{2}$ inch below this line draw another one. The upper one of these two lines will be the position of the rounded apex of the pyramidal top, or cap, of the metronome, and the lower one will establish the bottom of this pyramidal cap. Draw the outlines of the cap as shown, at first making all lines with the 2H pencil and of equal weight throughout. The four outer edges, and the lines of the base of the metronome correspond exactly with the edges and base of the pyramid. Next, draw the little rectangles, or feet, at their proper places, and then draw a horizontal guide line about $\frac{1}{4}$ inch above the guide line for the rear of the base—that is, about 1 inch above the base of the metronome—to establish the bottom of the

LINE DRAWING

opening through which the oscillating rod or pendulum is seen. Draw the sides and top of this opening as shown, with lines parallel to the outer edges and top of the body of the instrument, and, finally, draw the central rod and pendulum in the manner indicated.

Accenting.—The exterior of the metronome may be accented as was the pyramid. As noted, the cap slightly overhangs the body of the instrument, for which reason the line where it joins should be strongly accented. In accenting the edges of the opening, the upper and left-hand edges are accented because the inside edges of this opening are conventionally in shade. The details inside are of course accented in the usual way, as shown.

It must again be emphasized that no attempts should be made at what is ordinarily termed shading, or rendering the various parts in shades of black, white, and gray masses. These drawings are to be made in outline only; that is, accented outline.

75. Exercise C, Plate 6.—As shown in Fig. 30, third rectangle, top row, an ordinary **six-sided waste basket**, the shape of which is based on the regular hexagonal prism, is to be drawn for Exercise C of Plate 6.

Drawing.—The procedure in drawing this exercise is as follows: First draw a hexagonal prism as described for Exercise C, Plate 5. Then lower its top somewhat, in the following way: Draw a horizontal line 1 inch below the upper edge of the rectangle, and another one $\frac{1}{2}$ inch below this one. These two horizontal lines, intersecting the sides of the hexagonal prism, will form a rectangle in which a hexagon in perspective should be laid out, as was the top of the hexagon for Exercise C, Plate 5, except that this one is to be lower. Then place the raised bands at the top and the bottom, as shown, the upper one being about $\frac{1}{2}$ inch wide and the lower one a little less than $\frac{1}{4}$ inch wide. To do this properly, carefully drawn hexagons should first be dotted in lightly to show the upper and lower limits of the raised bands. The front three sides can then be strengthened in, in the case of each band. The end of each band will extend out slightly from the edge of the body of the basket, as indicated. Finally, draw the wickerwork handle, imitating as closely as possible the drawing in Fig. 30, except to make the drawing on the proper enlarged scale.

Accenting.—In accenting the lines of the waste basket, proceed as in the case of the prism in Exercise C of Plate 5. The interior edge and the short vertical interior lines that show at the top are accented as shown. The accenting of the handle and of the projecting parts of the upper band is accomplished by strengthening the lower and right-hand lines throughout.

76. Exercise D, Plate 6.—For Exercise D a **watering can** must be drawn. As shown in Fig. 30, fourth rectangle, top row, this can is simply a cylinder with a few accessories, namely, a spout, based on the cone; a nozzle, based on the circle and ellipse; and handles, based on simple curves, semicircular and others. So far, training has been given in the drawing of all these curves.

Drawing.—In the drawing of Exercise D, the full height of the cylinder will not be used, for it would throw the watering can out of proportion. Therefore, draw a horizontal line 2 inches below the upper edge of the rectangle and a second one $\frac{1}{2}$ inch below the upper one. Within the rectangle formed by the intersection of these horizontal lines with the edges of the cylinder, draw an ellipse to form the circular top. The shield that prevents the water from splashing out over the side can simply be shown by one long curve for its top and a short one for its profile at the left. The small handle at the side is not easily drawn; it should therefore be first studied carefully. Note that it is made of a flat strip of tin with a slightly rolled edge. At the top, where the handle joins the body of the can, it starts straight out at right angles to the can, and the top of the strip is seen until it starts to make the sharp downward curve. After the curve is made, only the rolled edge shows for a short section, and then gradually the under side of the strip comes into view, and appears to become the upper side. It then curves down again and joins flat to the side of the can, where again only the rolled edge of the strip shows. To get a good idea of its shape, bend a piece of flexible tin, or a strip of cardboard, or even a strip of paper,

LINE DRAWING

into the shape of this handle, and, looking at it from above, note how the curving strip or handle appears at its various parts. It will be well, also, to observe how long narrow leaves, such as those of the jonquil, the iris, the narcissus, the gladiolus, etc., bend over in this same graceful curve, and to note the direction of the edges as the curve occurs, and how first one side and then the other is seen. The carrying handle of the can consists simply of two long vertical lines about $\frac{1}{4}$ inch apart and two horizontal ones at top and bottom, with the four fastening rivets, as shown, the handle being centered on the vertical center line of the rectangle.

To draw the spout properly, its direction must first be determined. Locate the point where the upper horizontal line of the lower set, used to lay off the ellipse for the bottom of the can, crosses the vertical center line. Then locate the point where the vertical center line of Exercise C of this plate cuts the upper edge of the sheet. This corresponds to point *3* of Exercise C, Plate 5. Connect these two points by a long oblique line, and upon this line draw the spout. Where this long oblique line cuts the left side of the can, lay off a vertical ellipse about $\frac{3}{4}$ inch high and $\frac{1}{4}$ inch wide. Next, where the central one of the three horizontal lines used to locate the ellipse forming the top of the can cuts the long oblique line, draw a small ellipse, at a 45° slant, about $\frac{1}{4}$ inch long and $\frac{1}{16}$ inch wide. Connect by straight lines the corresponding ends of the two ellipses, when the body of the spout will be formed. It simply remains to draw another ellipse about $\frac{1}{4}$ or $\frac{1}{2}$ inch farther up along the oblique line; this should be about $\frac{3}{4}$ or $\frac{7}{8}$ inch long and $\frac{1}{4}$ inch wide, to form the "sprinkler," which, when connected by oblique lines with the smaller ellipse, will complete the drawing of the spout. The dimensions here stated need not be followed arbitrarily; they may be varied whenever it is necessary to secure better proportions.

The raised rings $\frac{1}{2}$ inch below the top of the body of the can consist of parallel curved lines based on horizontal ellipses. Similar double lines are used to indicate the raised ridges at the bottom of the can. The method of doing this is more clearly shown in Exercise H of this plate.

LINE DRAWING

All surface markings on a cylindrical object must always be drawn in the manner just described; that is, they must be based on the direction of the curving surface of the cylinder. Therefore, parallel rings must naturally be portrayed as semiellipses, but the entire ellipse must first be dotted in; otherwise, the curves will not properly join the vertical sides, but will be pointed, as previously explained.

Accenting.—Accenting the lines of the watering can offers excellent opportunity for the display of good judgment. However, it requires only to combine the practice already had in accenting the straight line, the ellipse, the cylinder, the cone, etc. to secure good results. The body of the can and its surface rings may be accented as was the waste basket of Exercise C. The lower and right-hand lines of the edge of the side handle should be treated as shown, the accenting lines varying in weight and quality. This applies also to the carrying handle. The joining of the spout with the body of the can, the spout itself, and the nozzle, or sprinkler, should all be accented as shown in Fig. 30, D.

It must be noted that practically every part of the can is a curving surface. The accenting lines must therefore differ from those used on figures with sharp edges. A certain variation of width and weight must be indicated, as practiced on the middle strokes of Exercises B and D, Plate 1. To secure such quality in the accent lines, continual practicing must be done, starting the line with a rather gentle pressure on the soft (B or 2B) pencil and gradually increasing the pressure until a line sufficiently strong is obtained. References should be made again to the examples of correct accenting shown in Fig. 26.

77. Exercise E, Plate 6.—The requirement of Exercise E, Plate 6, is to draw an **inverted funnel**, as is shown in Fig. 30, first rectangle, lower row. An inverted funnel is, of course, a cone, but in this case its sides do not follow exactly the direction of slant of the cone in Exercise E of Plate 5, although it is governed by it.

Drawing.—The drawing for Exercise E should be made as follows: First, draw the regular cone, as in Exercise E, Plate 5.

LINE DRAWING

Then draw a horizontal line 1 inch below the upper edge of the rectangle, and a second one ½ inch below the first. Where the lower one cuts the sides of the large cone, establish points. From the left-hand one of these points draw a right oblique line to the right-hand end of the ellipse at the base, and a left oblique line from the right-hand point to the left-hand end of the ellipse at the base. These two lines will determine the slant of the sides of the funnel. Next, draw a short horizontal line cutting the vertical center line about half way between the upper and the lower edges of the rectangle. Here locate the ⅜-inch ellipse for forming the wider part of the spout, and 1 inch below the upper edge of the rectangle, that is, where the top horizontal line cuts the center line, locate the small ⅛-inch ellipse to form the end of the spout. Next, draw straight lines to form the sides of the funnel and spout, and finally draw the handle. This handle is drawn according to the same principle as the side handle of the watering can of Exercise D of this plate. The part that joins the rim of the funnel is about 1 inch above the lower edge of the sheet, and the other joining part of the handle is about ¾ inch higher.

Accenting.—No new principle of accenting is brought out here. The funnel is accented as was the cone on Plate 5, and the handle is treated as was the handle of the watering can in Exercise D of this plate.

78. Exercise F, Plate 6.—As shown in Fig. 30, second rectangle, lower row, Exercise F consists in drawing a **teapot**. As will be observed, this teapot is not exactly spherical, the bottom being flattened considerably so that the teapot will be stable and not tip or roll over, but its general form is spherical. Therefore, in executing this exercise, it is first necessary to draw as guide lines a 2-inch sphere and its construction lines, following the directions given for Exercise F of Plate 5.

Drawing.—After the sphere and its construction lines have been drawn, the teapot should be executed as follows: First, draw a horizontal line about ¼ inch above line $c\,d$, which is located ¾ inch above the lower edge of the sheet; this will determine the major axis of the ellipse for the flat base of the teapot. Of course, a horizontal ellipse about $1\frac{1}{2}$ inches long must be constructed on this line, and the front half of it drawn in as a full line, to show properly the appearance of the base. Next draw ef 2 inches above cd and another horizontal line $\frac{1}{4}$ inch below ef so as to determine the lower limits of the semiellipse of the lid of the teapot. The knob of the lid extends about $\frac{1}{4}$ inch above the top curve of the lid. The contour of the teapot itself follows that of the original sphere. Next, the drawing of the spout is required. This work must be done very carefully. First, draw a vertical line $\frac{1}{2}$ inch to the left of the vertical line ec (the left edge of the enclosing square) to determine the extreme side extension of the nozzle of the spout. Then draw a short horizontal line, $\frac{1}{2}$ inch above c, to indicate the point where the lower part of the spout joins the teapot. The upper part of the spout joins the teapot at a point about $\frac{1}{8}$ inch above the horizontal line gh. The oblique guide lines, drawn as shown, will assist in drawing the curves of the spout. The handle, and its fastenings to the teapot should next be drawn as shown, using the horizontal line gh to aid in determining its position against the side of the teapot, and the ends of the ellipse of the lid to determine the points where the handle is fastened to the top of the teapot. Note that the thickness of the handle decreases as it approaches the fastenings.

Accenting.—The accenting of the outlines of the teapot requires no directions in addition to those already given for the previous exercises. The lid, because its edge is raised above the spherical surface of the teapot, should be accented as was the lower edge of the cap of the metronome in Exercise B of this plate. The spout may be treated as was the spout of the watering can in Exercise D, allowing, of course, for the curving of the contours. The handle is treated like the handle of the waste basket in Exercise C. The accenting lines of the body of the teapot are exactly like those of the sphere. A careful study of how the accenting for this exercise is done in Fig. 30, together with a conscientious effort to use similar accenting, will secure proper results.

LINE DRAWING

79. Exercise G, Plate 6.—The objects to be drawn for Exercise G are a **teacup** and a **saucer,** as reference to Fig. 30, third rectangle, lower row, will show. No difficulty will be experienced in drawing this exercise if it is remembered that the objects are simply combinations of several ellipses and some curved lines.

Drawing.—The principle of laying out the construction and guide lines for the cup and saucer is the same as that used for laying out the hemisphere and the disk of Exercise G, Plate 5. However, to portray the teacup properly resting in the saucer, the hemisphere is lowered and the disk is raised in the $3\frac{3}{4}'' \times 5''$ rectangle. Thus, draw $c\,d$ $1\frac{1}{2}$ inches above the lower edge of the sheet; $e\,f$, a little more than $\frac{1}{2}$ inch, say $\frac{5}{8}$ inch, above $c\,d$; $s\,t$, $\frac{1}{4}$ inch above $e\,f$; and $u\,v$, $\frac{3}{8}$ inch above $s\,t$. Then draw the short vertical lines as in the case of the hemisphere and the disk on Plate 5, thus completing the rectangles in which are to be drawn the ellipses forming the top of the cup and the top of the saucer. Next, draw in the ellipse for the top of the cup and the larger one for the top rim of the saucer, and also the semicircular curve that forms the body of the cup. To form the flat bottom of the saucer, a small ellipse, say about $1\frac{1}{4}$ inches long, should be drawn between the horizontal lines $c\,d$ and $w\,x$ —$w\,x$ is drawn $\frac{1}{4}$ inch below $c\,d$—and the front half strengthened in. The ends of the ellipses of the saucer can then be connected by curved lines, thus completing the drawing of the saucer. No special directions are needed for drawing the handle of the teacup, if the extreme side extension is not greater than $\frac{1}{4}$ or $\frac{3}{8}$ inch. Sufficient practice in drawing curves should be had by this time to enable the handle to be drawn without any trouble.

Accenting.—Nothing new in accenting is needed here. The ellipses are treated as they were those of the watering can, the funnel, and the teapot; and the hemispherical surface of the teacup is accented as was the teapot in Exercise F of this plate.

80. Exercise H, Plate 6.—As shown in Fig. 30, fourth rectangle, lower row, Exercise H, which is the last exercise of Plate 6, calls for the drawing of a **carafe,** or *water bottle.*

LINE DRAWING

Drawing.—This object is drawn in exactly the same way as the vase form of Exercise H, Plate 5. The only additions in this exercise are the indication of the hollow inside the water-bottle top, as shown, and the series of parallel rings around the body of the water bottle. These rings should be constructed as were previous ellipses, namely, within rectangles laid out as shown. Unless the full ellipses are always dotted in for such rings, the rings cannot be properly drawn as they curve around the receding sides of the object.

The greatest care must be taken to make the two sides of the object symmetrical. It is usually best to draw the left side first so that, when drawing the right side, the hand and pencil will not hide the contour to be duplicated. If the repeating mirror previously referred to is used, the right side of the figure should be drawn first, as previously explained. Similarly, care must be observed to get the two halves of all ellipses exactly alike.

Accenting.—The water bottle is accented in exactly the same manner as was the vase form in Exercise H, Plate 5. The ellipses of the top and the bottom of the water bottle should be accented by strengthening the right-hand parts of the fronts of the ellipses. The lower parts of the surface rings and the indication of the hollow portion at the top should also be accented as shown.

81. Final Work on Plate 6.—After the drawing and accenting of Exercise H are completed, the regular identifying data should be placed in the regular positions—the title, Plate 6: Line Drawing, at the top of the sheet, and the class letters and number, name and address, and date of completion, on the back of the sheet, in the lower left-hand corner. Plates 5 and 6 should then be mailed to the Schools in the usual way for examination.

If any redrawn work on any of the plates of this Section has been called for and has not yet been completed, it should be satisfactorily finished at this time. After all the required work on the plates of this Section has been completed, the work of the next Section should be taken up at once.

MODEL DRAWING

PURPOSE

1. Second Stage in Learning to Draw.—Up to this point only the first stage in learning to draw has been covered; namely, the drawing of lines and two-dimension forms in outline for the practice it gives in making arm, wrist, hand, and finger muscles pliant and supple. Such drawings were not made simply for the purpose of representing objects as such, but as a general introduction to the type forms or geometric solids. The chief purpose, aside from muscle practice, has been to give a training in the handling of the pencil, in eye measurement, and in the correct proportioning of lines and spaces.

The second stage in learning to draw is the drawing of objects, and the most effective method of learning to do this is to make drawings from the objects themselves. As these objects serve as models, this work is called **model drawing.** The instruction in model drawing that is given here extends the training that has already been given in line drawing.

2. Advantages of Drawing Direct from Objects.—While certain set exercises, in the form of text illustrations, are obviously necessary to serve as guides to one being trained in line drawing, eye measurement, character of lines, etc., yet, when learning to draw three-dimensioned objects, working direct from the object or model itself enables one to draw correctly what is before him instead of merely copying lines from a printed sheet.

One cannot draw correctly until he has first learned to see correctly. Therefore, to draw any object or detail correctly

MODEL DRAWING

one must actually be looking at the object or detail itself, and not at a picture or diagram. All objects in nature have three dimensions, length, breadth, and thickness; whereas, a picture or diagram has only two dimensions, length and breadth. To portray properly such an object one must know its modeling; that is, must understand by actually feeling and handling it that the object has roundness, solidity, thickness, etc. Only after being acquainted with these physical properties of the object, and combining this knowledge with his estimate of how the object appears to him, can he make an accurate portrayal of it.

3. Necessity for Seeing Correctly.—Very few persons use their powers of observation intelligently. The average person will not admit that he has been accustomed to seeing incorrectly; but that he has is easily proved. If asked to draw even so simple an object as a cigar box, he will, in most instances, show the retreating sides parallel instead of converging, simply because he knows that the sides of a cigar box are actually parallel. In like manner, he will draw a circle (when he should draw an ellipse) to show a wheel seen in part profile simply because he knows that a wheel is actually circular. If asked to draw, from memory, a cow, he will most likely place the horns in the wrong relation to the ears. Or, if asked to draw the full length figure of a man, he will make the head too large for the rest of the body; the eyes too large for the face and too near the middle of the cheek; the ears either too low or too high; and, in a profile of the head, a full front view of the eye instead of a side view. These errors are made every day, despite the fact that cigar boxes, cows, men, faces, etc., are constantly being seen. They are not errors in drawing; they are not due to lack of manual dexterity, for even the best professional penman, whose hand and finger muscles are under perfect control, would be liable to such errors; they are due to lack of intelligent observation.

4. The actual appearance of the object itself has a greater influence on the accuracy of the drawing made from that object than is generally supposed. For instance, if one,

MODEL DRAWING

untrained in accurate observation and careful drawing, were asked to draw a cube, it is quite likely he would start by drawing a perfect square and trying to fit other squares on to the sides of the first one. As a matter of fact, there is only one position in which a cube can be placed so that one can see any one of its sides or faces as a perfect square; namely, with the nearest face of the cube exactly parallel to the face of the observer and making right angles with the line of sight from the eye of the observer. In this position, however, it will look like a simple square, not like a cube, because none of the other faces will be visible. Ordinarily, it would be impossible to know the exact form in which to draw any of the faces of a cube unless the drawing were made direct from the cube itself.

5. The distinctive appearance of the actual object, as distinguished from a picture or diagram of the object, is due to a number of causes, but only one of these will be considered in this Section. The three most important of these causes are as follows:

1. The sides of the object appear to retreat and its distant parts appear to become smaller, even though it is known that they do not actually become smaller in the object itself. This is called **foreshortening.**

2. The various faces, sides, or parts, of the object appear brilliant, half-lighted, partly shaded, and in deep shadow, depending on the source and the amount of light. Sometimes these methods of varied lightings appear to change the contours and the shapes and proportions of the parts of the object itself. This is called **light and shade.**

3. Under ordinary conditions of lighting, an object casts a dark image of itself; that is, the object comes between the source of light and some other surface or object in such a way as to interfere with the rays of light, and thus what is known as a **shadow** is cast upon the other surface or object. Sometimes this shadow is of such shape or intensity as to change the apparent form and contour of the object itself.

MODEL DRAWING

MATERIALS AND METHODS OF WORK

MATERIALS REQUIRED

6. Models.—For the purpose of furnishing a practical training in model drawing; that is, in drawing direct from the objects, eight wooden models of convenient size are required. They are the cube, pyramid, hexagonal prism, cylinder, cone, sphere, hemisphere, and vase; and the instruction is arranged to use these to give a progressive training in model drawing. The start is made with the cube, and then the models are taken up in the order mentioned, until the vase with its compound curves is reached and mastered. In this Section the models are drawn in outline only; later they will be studied and sketched from the standpoint of light, shade, and shadow values.

7. Paper.—The most suitable paper for this work is known as "Charcoal paper," and has a surface prepared particularly to receive the strokes made with sticks of charcoal. Charcoal paper can be obtained in various sizes, of which the $19'' \times 25''$ sheet is perhaps the most convenient. Twenty-four sheets (one quire), each $19'' \times 25''$, are required, each of which is to be cut in half through the shorter dimension, thus making forty-eight sheets $12\frac{1}{2}'' \times 19''$. As only four plates of drawing exercises are required in this Section, there will be forty-four $12\frac{1}{2}'' \times 19''$ sheets remaining, some of which may be used for practice work and for any redrawn work that may be required. The remaining sheets may be saved for the drawings to be executed in following subjects.

8. Charcoal.—Charcoal for drawing purposes comes in various sizes and grades. The sticks may be cylindrical or in split form. They may be very hard, thus making a sharp

MODEL DRAWING

brownish line, or very soft making a clear black line or mass with very little pressure. The soft charcoal gives the best results for the work in this Section, so such charcoal is needed.

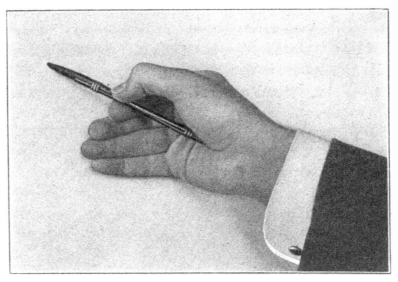

Fig. 1

A dozen sticks will be enough for the present purpose if the charcoal is used with light strokes and unnecessary breaking of sticks is avoided. There should also be enough left for the

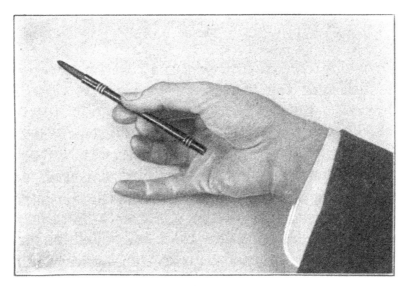

Fig. 2

work on the drawings required for subsequent Sections. Should the supply become exhausted more should be purchased promptly; so as to avoid interruption of the work.

MODEL DRAWING

9. Method of Working With Charcoal.—The method of working with the charcoal stick is as follows: With the palm of the hand turned up, let the charcoal stick (and holder, if required) rest lightly on the ball or side of the first finger, as shown in Figs. 1 and 2, and hold it in place by gently pressing the ball of the thumb down upon it. Steady the hand by letting the other fingers rest lightly upon the paper. If desired, the palm of the hand may be turned down, as shown in

FIG. 3

Fig. 3, in which case two fingers may be on one side of the charcoal stick and the thumb on the other. Care must be taken, however, not to hold the stick rigidly between the thumb and fingers, for freedom and flexibility are necessary if a correct drawing is to be made. When held in either of these positions, the sharpened end of the charcoal stick will point toward the top or the top left-hand corner of the paper.

10. Stomps.—Stomps are made of rolled paper and in various sizes. They are used on a drawing to assist in blending values, making even gradations, softening edges, securing high lights, etc. They are to be used sparingly, as will be explained later, at which time, also, the manner of their use will be described. The stomps will not be needed on the outline charcoal drawings in this Section.

MODEL DRAWING

11. Kneaded Eraser.—Kneaded rubber is a very soft pliable rubber that, as its name indicates, can be worked, or kneaded, into any desired shape, and even drawn to a point. It is very valuable for securing lights after body tones are placed, and for making alterations in a charcoal drawing where an ordinary pencil eraser would not serve the purpose. This eraser will not be needed in this Section, but will be found useful later.

12. Fixatif and Atomizer.—Fixatif is a composition of white shellac varnish and alcohol, light amber in color, and put up in a bottle of convenient form. The atomizer consists of two japanned tin tubes hinged together and, when the smaller tube is placed in the bottle of fixatif and the large end of the other tube is placed in the mouth, is used to spray the fixatif on to the drawing. The purpose of the fixatif is to fix the charcoal on to the paper; that is, to cause the powdered charcoal (for that is all it is when it has been placed on the paper) to adhere to the drawing paper so that it cannot be brushed off.

Fig. 4

13. Spraying a Drawing With Fixatif.—The process of spraying the fixatif on to the drawing is shown in Fig. 4; it is as follows: Lay the drawing horizontally on a table or other surface. Place the end of the smaller tube of the atomizer in the bottle of fixatif, which is held in the left hand, but do not let it touch the bottom; then place the wide end of the other tube between the lips, keeping the two tubes of the atomizer approximately at right angles to each other. Have the bottle and atomizer about 18 or 20 inches above the drawing, inclining them slightly so that the spray will fall gently upon the drawing, then blow easily and steadily through the tube. Do not blow hard, or get the atomizer too near the drawing, for not only will the force of the spray blow away some of the charcoal, but too much fixatif will be spread upon the drawing. The atomizer should be cleaned with clear alcohol each time it is used, to prevent the tubes becoming clogged or gummed.

BLOCKING IN AND PROPORTIONING

14. Placing the Object or Model.—When drawing from a model, one should sit erect in front of a table and hold

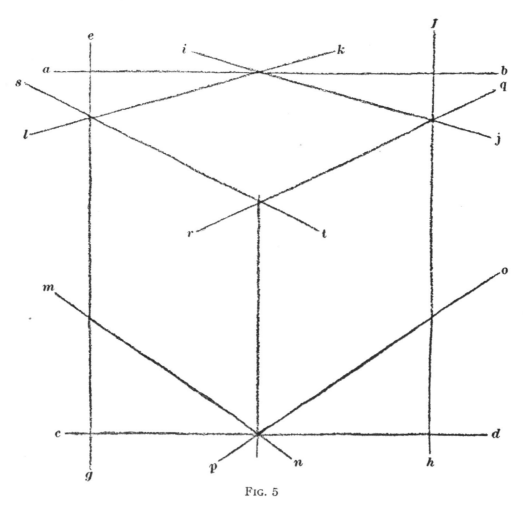

Fig. 5

the drawing board, on which the paper has been fastened, on the knees, but letting the top of the board rest against the edge of the table. If desired, though, one may work at a drawing table, as shown in Figs. 10, 11, and 12. The model should

MODEL DRAWING

be placed about 25 or 30 inches from the eye, with its top about 3 or 4 inches below the level of the eye; to do this, it may be necessary to raise the object several inches above the top of the table by placing it upon books, a box, etc. When the model has been correctly placed, the position should be carefully marked and each of the other models placed there when it is being sketched.

15. Blocking In.—Although later the laws that govern the apparent differences in size and arrangement of parts

Fig. 6

that are actually the same size will be studied, the first effort must be to get the general shape of the entire contour of the model or models properly placed and proportioned on the paper, and their general lines extending in the proper directions. This is called **blocking in.**

The secret of correct blocking-in consists in being able to see the model, or group of models as being included within some regular or irregular geometric figure. The process in the case of a cube seen at an angle, for instance, is first to sketch in lightly the upper and lower limiting horizontal lines

MODEL DRAWING

a b and *c d*, as shown in Fig. 5, then the right and left limiting vertical lines *e g* and *f h*. Then, when the inclined lines *i j*, *k l*, *q r*, *s t*, *m n*, and *o p* are sketched in the approximate contours of a cube seen at an angle, and from above, are indicated. The chief function of blocking-in, however, is to assist in drawing groups. The group must first be seen as a whole, and not as consisting of individual objects; its outside contour

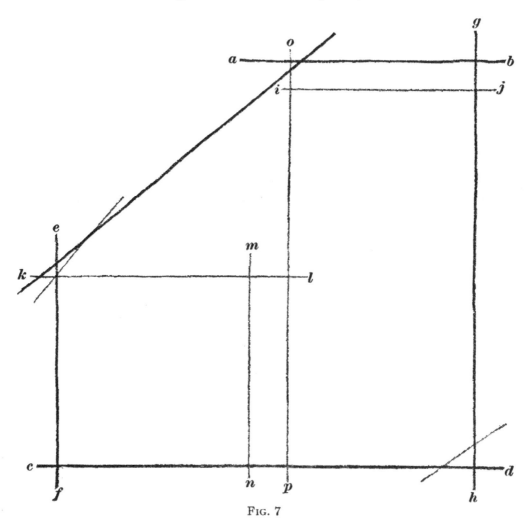

Fig. 7

only must be first considered. This can best be observed by placing the object or the group between one's eye and a bright light, and thus seeing them in silhouette; that is, merely as dark masses with no clear detail within the contours of the masses.

16. Fig. 6 shows a reproduction from a photograph of the cube and the cylinder, and Fig. 7 shows the method of

MODEL DRAWING

blocking-in that must be followed when making a preliminary sketch for the foreshortened outline drawing of these two models. First, the general lines of the outside contour are sketched in lightly, as shown by the bold lines *a b*, *c d*, *e f*, *g h*, and *k o*, and then the subordinate blocking-in lines, *i j*, *k l*, *m n*, and *o p*, are lightly placed. The line *i j* indicates the elliptic top of the cylinder; *k l* locates the rear edge of the top of the cube; *m n* shows the right front edge of the cube; *o p* shows the left contour of the cylinder, etc.

Fig. 8

If the group is a more complete one, as that shown in Fig. 8, where the entire eight wooden models are shown, the principle of working is the same. First, the blocking-in lines, see Fig. 9, for the outside contour or silhouette are placed as shown by the heavier lines *a b*, *c d*, *e f*, *g h*, *i j*, etc., and then the lighter ones are also sketched in as shown. Lines *1*, *2*, and *3* show the vertical center lines of the vase, pyramid, and cone, respectively; *4* and *5* show the tops of the hexagonal prism and cylinder and *6* the top of the cube.

MODEL DRAWING

17. When blocking-in, first the charcoal stick, or soft pencil if desired, held at arm's length, should be passed through the air, as if one were drawing on a vertical plane of glass, following the outside contours of the actual group. Then, lines of similar direction and angles should be drawn on the drawing paper in the manner shown in Figs. 7 and 9; these lines should be lightly sketched in with a soft pencil or with

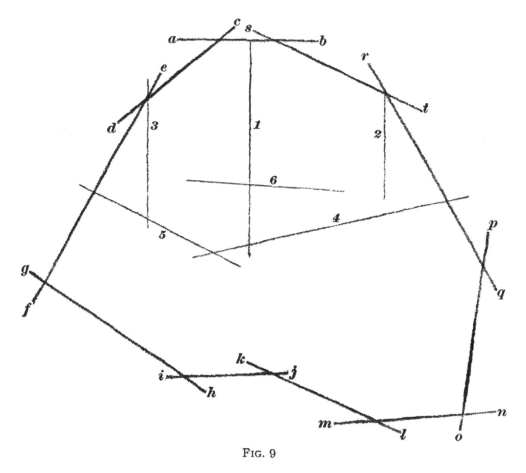

Fig. 9

charcoal. If necessary to correct the placing of a certain blocking-in line, a new one should be drawn but the first one should not be erased. Three or more lines may be found to be necessary before the correct position is secured, which should be properly strengthened so that the masses rendered in charcoal may be properly placed later.

After these general blocking-in lines, to give the outside contour and the approximate positions of the objects, have been placed, the individual objects may be drawn in detail.

MODEL DRAWING

18. Taking Proportions Freehand.—When the contour or mass of the model, or group of models, has been properly blocked in so that it is properly arranged on the paper and

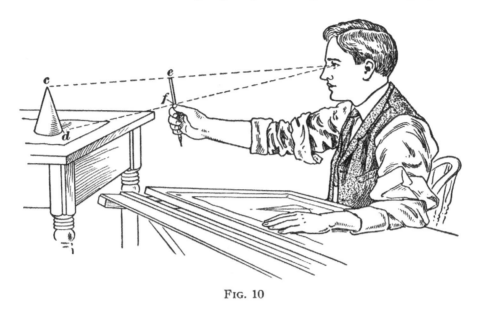

Fig. 10

within the allotted space, the matter of proportioning individual parts is comparatively simplified. These proportions may be easily taken by means of the thumb and pencil or thumb

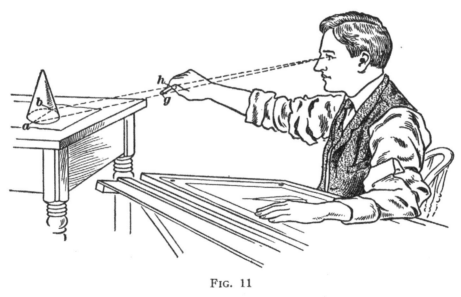

Fig. 11

and charcoal. For example, suppose one were about to make a drawing of a cone. First, he would place the cone in position. Then, holding the pencil at arm's length and at right angles

MODEL DRAWING

to the line of sight; that is, the line of seeing, from his eye to the object, as shown in Fig. 10, closing one eye and looking with the other, he would make the end *e* of the pencil coincide with the apex *c* of the cone, and by sliding his thumb down the pencil until the top of his thumb nail coincides with the bottom of the cone *d* he can locate point *f* on his pencil. The distance *e f* on the pencil then gives the apparent height of the cone *c d*, and this height can be laid off on the lower edge of the drawing paper and the line marked *height*. The width of the cone can then be measured by holding the pencil horizontally, as shown in Fig. 11, keeping the end of the pencil *g* so that it coincides with side *a* of the base of the cone, and marking off the apparent width of the base of the cone *a b*, by placing the thumb nail at *h* on the pencil, *h* coinciding with *b* on the cone. The distance *g h* thus marked off on the pencil will determine the width of the base of the cone; and a line of this length can then be drawn at the bottom of the drawing sheet by the side of the height line and can be marked *width*, this being the standard of width.

19. These lines form standards of measurement from which a cone of any size may be constructed in the same proportions as the original. When making these measurements, one must sit as nearly as possible in the same position in each case and the arm must be extended full length in order that the distance from the eye to the pencil may be uniform; otherwise, inaccurate proportions will be given and a poorly proportioned drawing will be the result. The pencil should also be held at right angles to the line of sight, not slanting perpendicularly or horizontally, as an inclination of the pencil toward the object will invariably render the proportion longer than it should be.

The relative proportions of these two lines will give the relative proportions on which to draw the cone. In this case it will be observed that the width is about one-half of the height and a drawing of any size can be laid off wherein the width of the cone at the base is made one-half of its height. This process is a very simple one when there are but two measurements, but it may be just as readily accomplished

MODEL DRAWING

where there are more measurements, provided sufficient care is taken to gauge them exactly and lay them off proportionate to one another.

20. In Fig. 12 is shown the method of ascertaining, at one operation, the relative proportions of the various sides and edges of a rectilinear solid such as the cube, by using two pencils, held in the hand as shown. In the description of this process reference must be made to the outline proportions shown in Fig. 13, which is the way the outlines of the cube look to the man drawing it in Fig. 12. First, the greatest apparent height of the cube is located, which is distance $a\,g$,

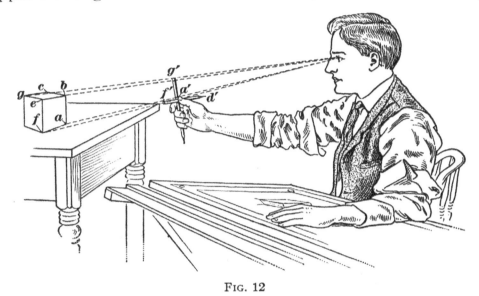

Fig. 12

by marking off with the thumb nail on the vertical pencil the distance $a'\,g'$, and transferring this distance as a line to the lower edge of drawing paper and marking it *extreme height*. Then the extreme width $f\,d$ is marked off on the horizontal pencil as the distance $f'\,d'$ and laid off on the lower edge of the paper as *extreme width*. The apparent height of the nearest edge $a\,b$ of the cube can then be laid off in a similar manner. These three general proportions will give a good foundation upon which to construct the cube.

The sides $e\,f$ and $c\,d$ should then be judged by the pencil and laid out in proper proportion, and the whole figure completed by connecting up the points so located.

MODEL DRAWING

21. The angles formed by the lines *a b*, *a f*, and *a d*, Fig. 13, with the horizontal line *h m*, may be judged approximately by the eye in most cases, but where it is necessary to get them exact they may be carefully measured by means of two pencils held in the hand, as shown in Fig. 12, and so separated that each pencil corresponds with one of the lines meeting to form the angle; that is, the vertical pencil can be held at arm's length so that it coincides with the line *a b*, and the horizontal pencil at the same time coinciding with the line *a f*. In this way the angles may be laid off exactly, and a perfect outline drawing of the cube, as it appears to the eye from a given position, can be made.

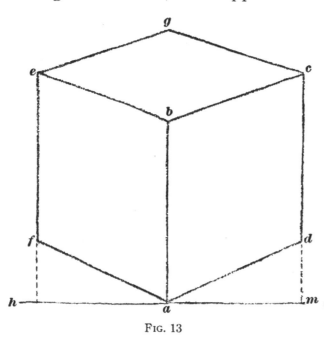

Fig. 13

If the position of the cube is changed so that its nearest side *a b* is not directly in front of the eye but to one side, as shown in Fig. 14, the same method may be used. The entire height from the base line *h m* to the highest corner *g* may be measured; also, the height of line *a b*, and the width from *c* to *e* laid out, while the angles, measured in pencil, may be plotted in their proper places.

Special Note.—When the plates of this Section are laid out the student will be asked to draw the objects *full size;* that is, the cube 2″ tall, the vase 3″ tall, etc., but properly foreshortened. He may wonder how he can lay out the objects full size when they appear to him to be less than full size. His confusion will disappear if he will remember that the "thumb and pencil" system deals only with *proportions,* not actual sizes. The actual sizes of the objects for the plates are specified; namely, the full sizes of the wooden models.

MODEL DRAWING

22. Tests for Accuracy of Drawing.—The secret of learning to draw correctly is first to make the sketch of the object with as few aids as possible, and then to test the accuracy of the drawing, using such aids as may be required. Some of these aids are as follows:

1. *Pencil Measurements.*—The accuracy of a drawing may be tested by making pencil measurements similar to those already described. Care must always be taken, however, to hold the pencil at right angles to the line of seeing. The longer dimension must be taken and then the shorter taken and compared with it. For instance, when measuring the height of an object that is about three times as tall as broad, it is easier to first take the height and then the width, noting that the width is one-third of the height, than to proceed in the reverse manner. These comparisons may be made by swinging the pencil around as if it were on a pivot where the finger and thumb hold it after the height has been obtained and thus getting the width and noting the proportion.

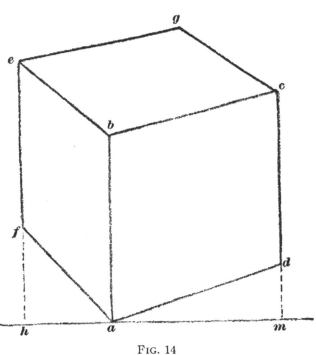

Fig. 14

2. *Cardboard Frame.*—Out of a piece of stiff cardboard about $9\frac{1}{4}''\times12\frac{1}{2}''$ cut a rectangular hole $6\frac{1}{4}''\times9\frac{1}{2}'',$ which gives an opening the size of the rectangle on the drawing plate in which each drawing is to be placed. This frame, which is $1\frac{1}{2}$ inches wide all around, and the method of using it, are shown in Fig. 15. The frame may be set up, vertically or horizontally, in front of the model being drawn and the positions and proportions of the object or model, as related to the inside

MODEL DRAWING

edges of the frame, may be compared with the positions and proportions of the corresponding object or model on the drawing

FIG. 15

plate, as related to the limits of the $6\frac{1}{4}'' \times 9\frac{1}{2}''$ space in which it is placed. In the case of the exercises on the drawing plates the frame would be used horizontally.

3. *Plumb-Line and Horizontal Straightedge.*—Oblique lines may always be compared with the direction of vertical or horizontal lines. The cardboard frame may be used for this purpose to some extent, but for vertical lines a plumb-line consisting simply of a string with a small weight tied to it, should be employed as shown in Fig. 16. For hori-

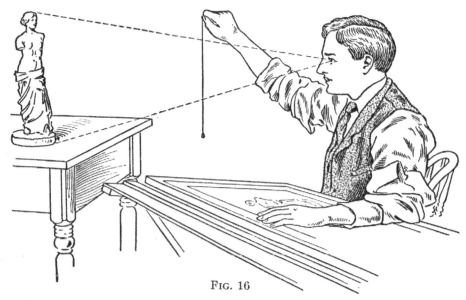

FIG. 16

zontal lines a straightedge, such as the cover of a book, a pasteboard mailing tube, or anything of the kind may be used. If the plumb-line and the horizontal straightedge are moved

MODEL DRAWING

slowly over or up to the oblique line, as seen on the actual model, the direction of the line and the angle it makes with the vertical or horizontal line can be observed readily, and this direction and angle can be duplicated on the drawing and thus accuracy secured.

The purpose of these tests is to enable a person to criticize his own efforts and to detect errors of line and proportion. In this way, similar errors will be avoided in subsequent work. These tests are to be applied to all the work given here, as it is expected that every effort will be made to make correct drawings before sending them in to the Schools for examination.

FORESHORTENING

DEFINITION OF TERM

23. While the true shapes and proportions of the surfaces of objects can be seen only when the nearest surface is directly in front of and parallel with the eye, it is unusual to see objects so precisely placed. Ordinarily, they are looked at obliquely from above so that the top as well as the fronts are seen. Then, the parts of the object farthest from the eye apparently become smaller as the lines extending from the eye, or retreating, appear to converge and the faces are apparently shortened as they extend from the eye. This apparent change in the sizes and proportions of the various parts of an object and of the object itself is called **foreshortening.**

A proper understanding of the principles of foreshortening, and the ability to draw objects in their properly foreshortened positions, must be the foundation of any pictorial work the beginner may hope to do. While learning foreshortening, one is also becoming acquainted with the underlying principles of drawing accurately the objects, landscapes, human figures, etc., such as would be included in a pictorial composition. Training in pictorial composition will be given later. At that time training will be given in the drawing of street scenes and interior views in which proper proportions must be preserved

MODEL DRAWING

between objects in the foreground and those in the middle distance and background.

24. Proper Demonstration of Foreshortening.—Very little can be learned from a series of rules or theories. The only way to know just what foreshortening occurs when objects are viewed in various positions is to view these objects under the conditions named. Therefore, the eight models should be used, at first, to demonstrate the principles of foreshortening. Later, they will be used also to demonstrate light, shade, and shadow, and as models from which rendered drawings are to be made.

FORESHORTENING OF A CUBE

25. Holding Cube Parallel to Body.—The foreshortening of a cube, Fig. 17, when it is held parallel to the body, is shown in Fig. 18. When a cube held upon a table, as shown in (*a*), is seen from directly above, its upper face appears as a square, as shown in (*b*). A cube will also have this appearance if it is held directly in front of the face and parallel to it.

If the cube is raised until it is 2 or 3 inches below the level of the eye and 10 or 12 inches from the face, as in (*c*), the top

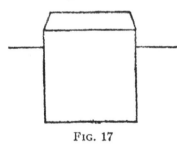

FIG. 17

remaining horizontal, the cube will have the appearance shown in (*d*). The front edge of the irregular rectangle that represents the foreshortened top of the cube now appears to be of the proper length to be the edge of the face of the cube, but the back edge appears to be shorter. Also, the two sides (which are known to be parallel) are not now parallel, but converge in such a way that if continued they would meet in a point. Further, this irregular rectangle is very flat, and not nearly as high as the square that forms the face of a cube.

26. If the cube is raised still farther, keeping its top face horizontal, and all the time the eye of the observer looking at the top face, it is discovered that the height of this irregular

MODEL DRAWING

rectangle diminishes so rapidly that it becomes merely a line, as shown in Fig. 18 (*e*) and (*f*). It is known that the surface observed is in reality a perfect square, and yet what is seen is not a square at all, but more nearly like a line. Further, the front face is apparently larger than any other face of the cube and hides all the others, except the top one when looked down upon, or the bottom one when viewed from beneath. Also, if the cube is viewed from above and in front or from below and in front, with the eye close to it, there will be a tendency for the vertical edges of the front face to converge

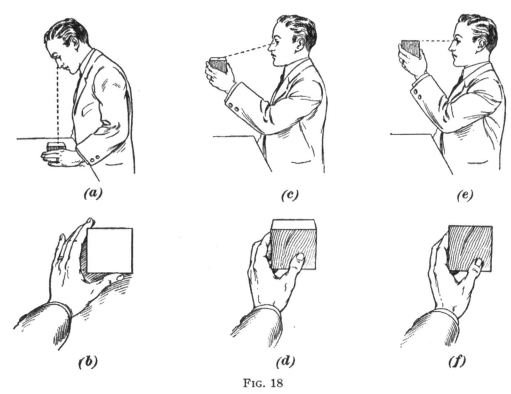

Fig. 18

just as do the horizontal edges of the top face when the cube is held up and its front face is viewed. This tendency, however, is not sufficiently important to be considered in this connection.

27. Tests for Convergence of Lines.—The point where the converging lines would meet, were the retreating sides of a cube extended, may be found as follows: Place the cube upon the middle of a string 4 feet long and wrap both ends of the string around the cube, as near as possible to the front face.

MODEL DRAWING

With the right hand, grasp the two sections of the string so that the string and fingers touch the top face of the cube as close to the front edge as possible without danger of the string slipping off as shown in Fig. 19 (a), the free ends hanging loosely. Supporting the cube with the left hand, lift it until the top edge of the cube and the place where the thumb and fingers of the right hand are pinching together the two sections of string are exactly on a level with the eye. Gradually lower the cube, supported by the left hand, 4 or 5 inches,

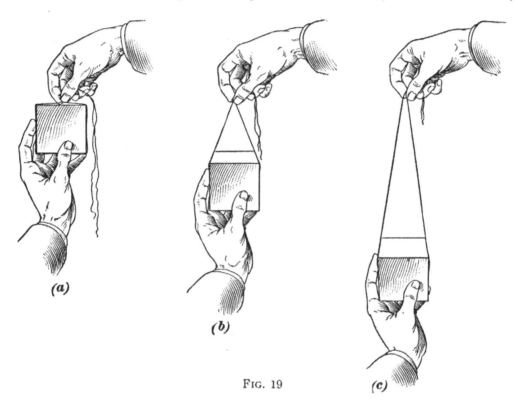

Fig. 19

allowing the two sections of the string to slip through the fingers of the right hand but keeping the two sections of string together and exactly on a level with the eye. In other words, lower the left hand and the cube, but not the right hand. Close one eye and look at the retreating edges of the top face of the cube; it will be found, if the cube has been kept in a perfectly horizontal position, that the retreating edges coincide with the lines made by the string. Thus it is easily understood that the lines of the retreating sides if continued will appear to follow the lines of the string and will thus appear to meet

MODEL DRAWING

at the point where the sections of the string are pinched together by the finger and thumb of the right hand, namely, on a level with the eye, as shown in (b).

28. As a further test, lower the cube still farther below the level of the eye, as in Fig. 19 (c), allowing the sections of the string to glide through the fingers of the right hand, but pinching the two sections of the string lightly together and exactly on a level with the eye and exactly above the middle of the front edge of the top face of the cube. If the cube is now viewed with one eye open it will be observed again that the retreating left edge of the upper face of the cube appears to follow the left-hand portion of the string and the retreating right hand edge appears to follow the right hand portion of the string; which means that were the lines of these edges to be extended they would meet in a point level with the eye, as shown in (c).

29. This principle may be more clearly shown by using a book held horizontally in place of the wooden model, because the larger surface of the book will make sharper retreating angles. In this case the string should be placed under the front cover and close to the back strip of the book, which should be nearest the observer. If while these tests are being made the front cover is slowly raised from a horizontal to a vertical position and then lowered back to a horizontal position, the amount of foreshortening can be clearly demonstrated by noting how the retreating edges correspond with the strings.

30. Results of Convergence Tests.—The tests just made demonstrate that the edges of the horizontal top face of a flat or cubic object always appear to converge toward a point somewhere at a level with the eye. Therefore, when making drawings of similar objects with retreating sides, it is simply necessary first to sketch in the line that is supposed to represent the level of the eye and then, toward a selected point on this line, converge the retreating side lines of the object.

The front side of the cube when seen full face is a perfect square and no other part of the cube can be seen.

MODEL DRAWING

The top face, starting as a perfect square when seen directly from above, appears to become gradually shorter in height as the cube is raised toward the level of the eye, becoming a straight line when the eye level is reached. The rear edge of the top face which is farthest from the observer, appears to be a shorter line than the front edge.

The two side faces and the rear face of the cube held in this position are never visible.

The vertical edges of the front face, when seen slightly above or below the level of the eye appear to converge slightly but in a sketch are usually represented by vertical lines.

These results are not given as rules or theories to be committed to memory, but as points that should be carried in the mind and combined with the beginner's observation of the actual model when making a drawing from the cube seen full face.

31. Holding Cube at 45° Angle.—Objects are most frequently seen at an angle; that is, with one edge, or corner, nearest the observer rather than in the full-face position just described. The simplest angle position is that in which a cube forms an angle of 45° with the body, the position shown in Fig. 20. The foreshortening of a cube held in this position is shown in Fig. 21.

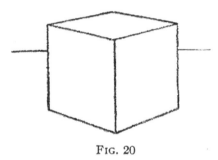

FIG. 20

As before, when looked at from directly above, as shown in (a), the cube appears as a perfect square but its sides make angles of 45° with the body, as shown in (b).

If the cube is raised until it is 2 or 3 inches below the level of the eye and 10 or 12 inches from the face, as in (c), the top face will appear as a diamond shape whose sides, however, are not parallel but converging, as shown in (d).

When the cube is raised to the position shown in (e) the two sides now visible are no longer perfect squares, but, because their distant edges are turned away, these faces are foreshortened and their horizontal edges converge slightly, as shown

MODEL DRAWING

in (*f*). The vertical edges, however, remain unchanged except that those farthest from the eye apparently grow shorter.

32. Tests for Convergence of Lines.—As in the case of the full-face view of the cube, the retreating edges of the sides appear to converge toward common points. But when the cube is in the position shown in Fig. 21 (*d*) there are two points of convergence, instead of one as with the full-face cube. The edges *g*, *f*, and *h* must converge at some point to the right of and above the cube and the edges *e*, *d*, and *i* must converge

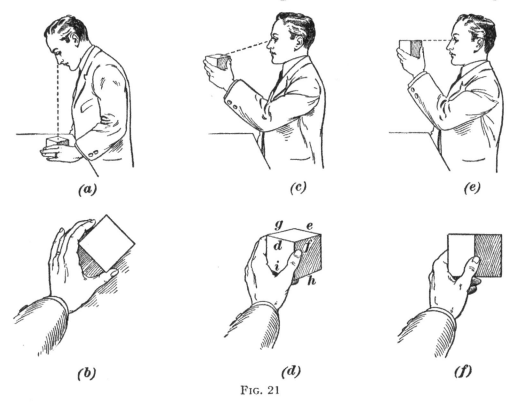

Fig. 21

at some point to the left of and above the cube. To determine these points tests must be made with the actual model, two strings each about 4 or 5 feet long being used. Tie one of the strings tightly around the cube, near one of the faces and knot it tightly at one corner so that it will not slip, as shown at *a*, Fig. 22. This will leave two free ends *c* and *d*, one of which may be cut off if desired. Then tie the other string tightly around the same portion of the cube and knot it tightly at corner *b*, leaving the two free ends *e* and *f*, one of which may be cut off if desired.

MODEL DRAWING

33. Now, holding the cube with the left hand, and in position shown in Fig. 21 (c) and (d), (also Fig. 23), grasp the two sections of the string, one coming from corner a and the other from corner b, in the fingers of the right hand as in previous experiments. These sections of the strings should be at least 2 or 2½ feet long. Now with the left hand hold the cube so that the nearest edge is exactly in front of the eye and about 8 or 10 inches from it. Holding the sections of string in the right hand, and on a level with the eye, move the right hand about 10 inches to the right of the cube and keep moving it until the two strings correspond with the direction taken by edges g and f, Fig. 21, (d), as shown also in Fig. 23, where this experiment is illustrated. If the cube is lowered or

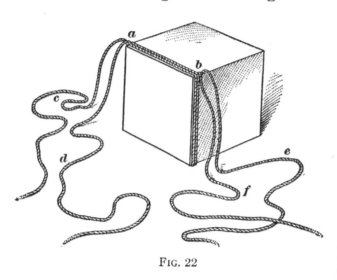

Fig. 22

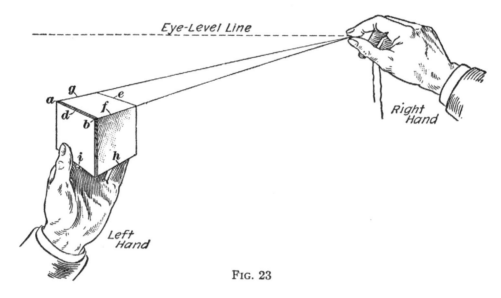

Fig. 23

raised to different positions, but kept always the same distance in front of the eye, the strings will still coincide with the retreating edges g and f. This demonstrates that if the converging

MODEL DRAWING

edges *g* and *f* are continued they will meet in a point that is on a level with the eye.

34. Edge *h* of the base corresponds with edge *f* of the top and if continued will meet in the same point as do edges *g* and *f*. This is evident from the illustration in Fig. 24, which shows how it can be proved by experiment. To save the trouble of retying the strings, the cube should be so turned that knots *a* and *b* of Fig. 23 take the positions of *a* and *b* of Fig. 24. The lettering designating the sides will, however, remain as before. The experiment will reveal that sides *h* and *f* extended will converge at the same point on the eye level, proving also that

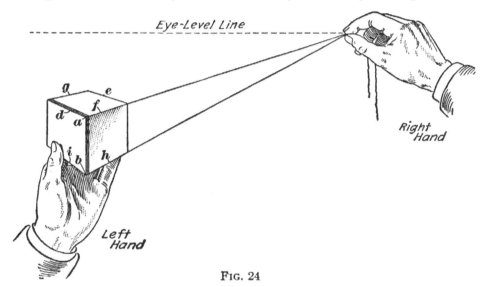

Fig. 24

lines *g*, *f*, and *h* have a common point of convergence. If the edge of the base immediately under *g* could be seen, this experiment would show that this edge extended would also meet the same point as *g*, *f*, and *h*, showing that all parallel lines inclined upwards and to the right have a common point of convergence on the line of eye level. It would also show that this point is the same distance to the right of the line of sight as the nearest edge of the object is from the eye.

35. The other set of converging edges *e*, *d*, and *i*, which extend upwards and to the left will all find their common point of convergence on the line of eye level and a distance to the left of the line of sight, corresponding to the distance of the right-hand converging point from the line of sight.

MODEL DRAWING

This can be proved readily by the experiments illustrated in Figs. 25 and 26, which it is not necessary to describe in detail, further than to say that the strings are held in the left hand

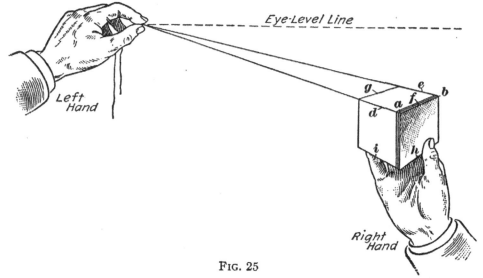

FIG. 25

and the cube supported by the right hand. The corners where the knots come are shifted as shown, the reference letters for edges not being shifted.

36. Results of Convergence Tests.—In addition to

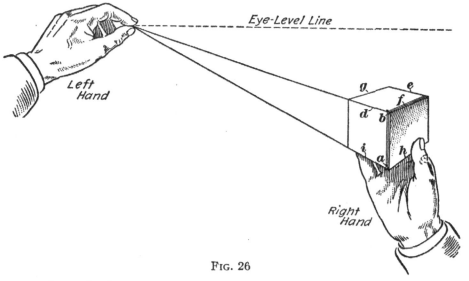

FIG. 26

the results of the convergence tests made with the full-faced cube, the tests just made show the following:

The square top face of a cube seen at an angle appears as a flattened diamond shape with sides not parallel but converging.

MODEL DRAWING

The square faces that are visible appear foreshortened or narrowed, their top and bottom edges converging upwards (to the right or left as the case may be) and their vertical sides remaining vertical.

All horizontal edges extending upwards and to the right converge toward a common point on the level of the eye and at a distance to the right of the line of vision corresponding to the distance of the cube from the eye.

All horizontal edges extending upwards and to the left converge toward a common point on the level of the eye and at the same distance to the left, as the right convergence point is to the right.

When the cube is placed at an angle of 45° with the observer, each visible face appears of the same width, although narrowed.

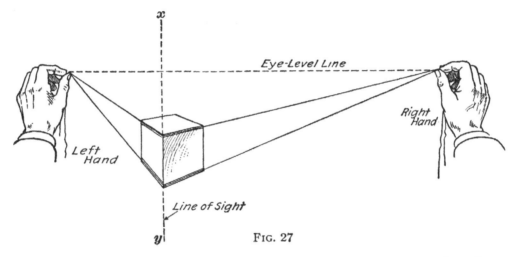

Fig. 27

37. Holding Cube at an Angle Other Than 45°.—Frequently a cube, or cubic object, is seen at an angle other than 45°. For instance, the left visible side of the cube may make an angle of 60° and the right visible side an angle of 30°, as shown in Fig. 27.

The term *making an angle* of a certain number of degrees means that the edges of the base, which is a square, extend backwards at an angle with the imaginary vertical plane that touches the front vertical edge of the cube, this imaginary plane being parallel to the face of the observer. To illustrate this, place a small sheet of glass, such as might be removed from a picture, or a small window pane, vertically against the

MODEL DRAWING

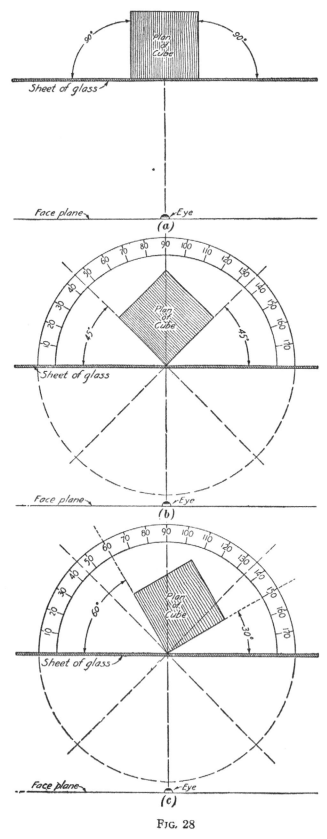

Fig. 28

front edge of the cube, and parallel to the face of the observer; that is, so that the face of the sheet of glass is equidistant from both eyes of the observer when he is in front of it. Now, look directly down on the cube and the glass; the cube will appear as a square and the sheet of glass as a straight line. With a pencil, mark around the base of the cube and along the edge of the glass. Remove both the cube and the glass and look at the pencil marks. It will be found that the sides of the cube make angles with the sheet of glass and therefore with the plane of the face of the observer, as in Fig. 28 (a). It is known that there are 360° in the circumference of a circle, therefore 180° in the semi-circumference and 90° in a quarter circumference. If a circumference is sketched in, as shown in (b), it is

MODEL DRAWING

not a difficult matter to determine roughly what angles are made by the sides of the object. View (a) shows the plan of the cube shown full face making angles of 90°; (b), the plan of the cube seen at a 45° angle; and (c) the plan of the cube with the left side making an angle of 60° and the right side an angle of 30°.

38. When a cube is seen at an angle other than 45°, all converging edges will meet in common points to the right and to the left, just as they do when the object is seen at a 45° angle, as is shown in Fig. 27. Noticeable differences, however, occur in the top and the sides.

39. The foreshortened top face of a cube seen at 60° and 30° begins gradually to lose its diamond shape and to approach again that of the irregular rectangle; as the front point moves to the left the rear point moves to the right.

The greater the angle made by a side the less is seen of that side and the steeper become the converging horizontal edges.

40. Holding Cube Above the Eye Level.—Ordinarily, a cubic object is looked at from above, so that its top face and one or two sides are seen. Sometimes, however, such an object may be above the level of the eye and be seen from below. In such a case, exactly the same principles apply except that in the statement of results, the word upwards must be changed to downwards when referring to converging lines, and the words right (or left) and above must be changed to left (or right) and below when considering points of convergence. Any desired experiment may be made by turning the page bottom side up and looking at Figs. 19, 20, 23, 24, 25, 26, and 27 inverted, and then holding the cube above the level of the eye, when experiments are tried with the strings and the wooden model. It must be borne in mind that, under these circumstances, left and right will become transposed and due corrections must be made. Although objects are rarely drawn in such a position, it is well to know how it is done.

MODEL DRAWING

FORESHORTENING OF A PYRAMID

41. Holding Pyramid Parallel to Body.—The principles of foreshortening that apply to the top face of the full face cube apply also to the full face square pyramid, shown in Fig. 29. The base of the pyramid is a square, the rear edge of which appears smaller than the near edge and the sides of which converge to a point on the eye level. If the pyramid is looked down upon, when in the same position as the cube in Fig. 18 (a), it will have the appearance of a square crossed by two diagonal lines. Lifting it gradually toward the eye level will cause the nearest face to assume its normal shape, that of a tall isosceles triangle (that is, a triangle with two sides of equal length), but will cause the base, if it could be seen, and the two sides to be very much foreshortened.

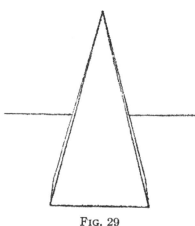

Fig. 29

There are, therefore, only a few new points to be learned from experiments with the pyramid. The first one is to get the apparent height of the pyramid. To do this, the pyramid must be considered as being contained within a prism; that is, a rectangular solid or framework as shown in Fig. 30. The view of the base of the pyramid from above showed a square crossed by diagonals, the apex of the pyramid being apparently at the point of intersection of the diagonals; that is, the center of the square. Therefore, the apex of the pyramid is located somewhere on a vertical line erected above the center of the base o. To determine how far above o is the apex, the pyramid must be placed within a prism. As the wooden model of the pyramid is actually 4 inches high, to construct a containing prism lines ab and cd must be drawn 4 inches high. Line bd is then drawn and the foreshortened square $efdb$ drawn exactly over the base $ghca$, the edges be and df converging as do the edges of the top face of the cube. If diagonals bf and de are now drawn, they will intersect at x, which will be the apex of the pyramid. If lines are

MODEL DRAWING

drawn from *x* to the corners of *g*, *h*, *c*, and *a* of the base, the pyramid will be complete.

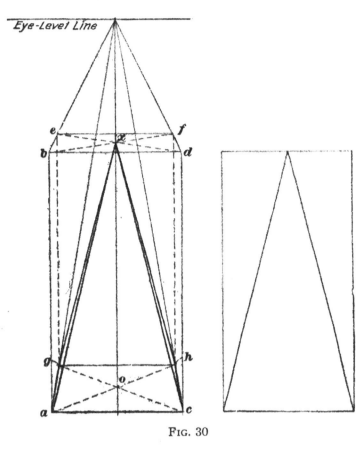

FIG. 30

42. The results obtained by the foregoing are as follows:

In the full-face view of the pyramid, as it is gradually raised to the eye level, the nearest face assumes normal proportions but the two sides become sharply narrowed.

The apex of the pyramid is exactly above the center of the base.

The center of the base, or of any other foreshortened square, is the intersection of the two diagonals.

To get the apparent height of the foreshortened pyramid it must be placed within a prism of the actual height of the pyramid, and a foreshortened view made. The center of the square top, foreshortened, will determine the

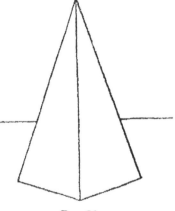

FIG. 31

height of the apex above the base; that is, the height of the pyramid.

43. Holding Pyramid at an Angle.—The square pyramid is usually seen at an angle; that is, with one corner of the base nearest to the observer, as shown in Fig. 31. In such cases the base, if it could be seen, would appear as a flattened diamond with its opposite sides converging, as in the case of the top of the cube seen at an angle. The principles of converging pairs of lines, extending to right and left points

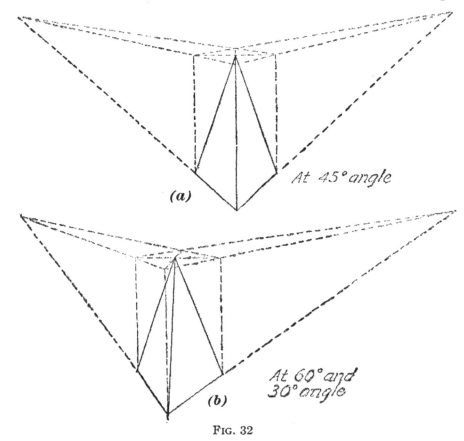

Fig. 32

of convergence on the eye level, apply here as in the case of a cube. Experiments with the wooden model will show that the two foreshortened sides of the pyramid are of exactly the same shape and size and grow taller, but not any wider, as the pyramid is raised to the eye level, if the pyramid is seen at a 45° angle, as in Fig. 32 (a).

If the pyramid is seen at any angle other than 45°, more of one side than of the other will show, as in Fig. 32 (b).

MODEL DRAWING

The method of obtaining the apparent height of the pyramid, foreshortened, when seen at an angle is the same as when the pyramid is seen full face. The enclosing prism is of the angle at which the pyramid is seen. When the center of the top is located the position of the apex is thus found, as is shown in Fig. 32, (a) and (b).

FORESHORTENING OF A HEXAGONAL PRISM

44. Holding Prism Parallel to Body.—The first thing noticeable about the hexagonal prism, shown in Fig. 33, when it is looked down upon from above, is that the top appears as a perfect hexagon; that is, with six edges of exactly the same length, as in Fig. 34. While this hexagon is being considered, it would be well to subdivide it by lines as shown, either on the top of the actual model itself, to be erased later, or on a piece of paper, making the outline full size by placing the end of the hexagon on the paper and drawing a pencil line around it, thus forming the hexagon and then drawing the vertical lines ab and cd, the horizontal line gh, and the diagonals ad and cb.

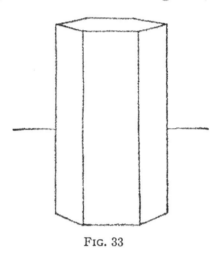

FIG. 33

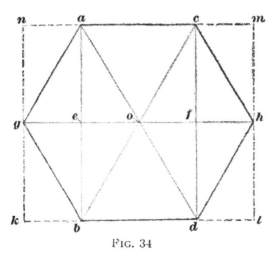

FIG. 34

As the prism is raised nearer to the eye level, and about 7 inches or 8 inches from the eye, the hexagon forming the top, likewise the one forming the bottom, if it could be seen, becomes foreshortened as follows: The rear edge ac appears shorter than the near edge bd, as in the case of the cube, when seen full face, the rectangle $acdb$ instead of being twice as deep as it is wide appears less than one-half as deep as wide.

MODEL DRAWING

Further, the pairs of parallel sides, as ag and hd and ch and gb, appear to converge, just as they do on the top face of the cube seen at an angle. The two sides of the prism, bg and dh, extend backwards at 60° angles, just as does the left side of the cube in Fig. 27 and Fig. 28 (c), each thus being so foreshortened as to appear only one-half as wide as the front face.

In Fig. 34 it is evident that distance ge is only one-half of ef; therefore, when the vertical dotted line gk is projected it is found that kb is only one-half as long as bd, demonstrating that, when foreshortened, the side face of the hexagonal prism appears only about one-half as wide as the front face.

45. Tests for Convergence of Lines.—It is seen from the foregoing that the oblique edges of the hexagonal top of the prism converge under principles that are a combination of those noticed in the cases of the cube seen full face and the cube seen at an angle. When foreshortened, the top of the hexagon as well as its base will show the rectangle $acdb$, Fig. 34, also foreshortened. The sides ba and dc will converge toward a point on the eye-level line immediately above the center of the hexagon. The edges ga, and dh, as well as diagonal bc, will converge to a point on the eye-level line to the right of the center of vision, and the edges bg and hc, and the diagonal da, will converge toward a point on the eye-level line to the left of the center of vision. These facts may be demonstrated by tests with the strings if desired, but it is not necessary to do so, for they were proved by demonstrations with the strings in the case of the cube.

46. Laying Out Foreshortened Full-Face Hexagon. A simple method of laying out a foreshortened hexagon, when sketching the top of the hexagonal prism, for instance, is as follows: Referring to Fig. 35, lay off the front edge bd the actual size of the width of the front edge of the hexagonal top of the prism, obtained by actual eye measurement of the model. Remember that it is the top, the visible hexagonal part, and not the base of the model, that is being considered. Above bd, and parallel to it, lay off a line mn of indefinite extent. The distance of mn above bd depends entirely on

MODEL DRAWING

how much of the top of the model is seen as the observer sits in front of it. This distance can be determined readily by eye measurement.

Converge retreating lines backwards from *b* and *d* toward a point on the eye level exactly above *s*, the middle point of the line *b d*. These converging lines are shown as *b a* and *d c* extended. Where these converging lines cut line *m n*, points *a* and *c* are located, and thus *a c d b* is formed, being the foreshortened view of rectangle *a c d b*, Fig. 34. By means of diagonals *a d* and *c b*, the center *o* of the foreshortened rectangle *a c d b* is located; the position of this point determines the foreshortened position of the line *g h* of Fig. 34, parallel to both *b d* and *m n*, Fig. 35. Through the point *o* draw a horizontal line *x y* of indefinite extent. To locate points *g* and *h*, Fig. 34, in their foreshortened positions for Fig. 35, lay off distances *e g* and *f h* equal to *e o* and *o f*, on the line *x y*. Having located *g* and *h*, it

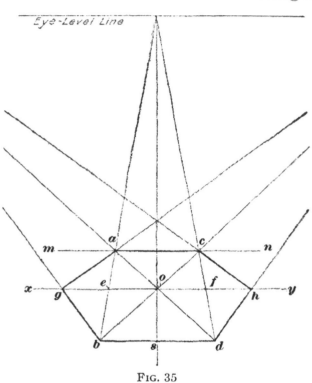

Fig. 35

simply remains to draw lines *b g* and *g a*, and *d h* and *h c*, which will complete the foreshortened view of the hexagon.

47. Constructing Hexagonal Prism.—Theoretically, the hexagonal prism may be drawn by simply constructing two foreshortened hexagons, one for the top and one for the base of the prism, and then connecting the corresponding corners of these hexagons by long vertical lines, strengthening those that are to represent visible edges. This method would be used if the hexagon were to be drawn to scale, and in accordance

MODEL DRAWING

with the rules and measurements of scientific perspective, but cannot be used in this work, because the hexagonal prism seen at close range, is to be drawn *full size*.

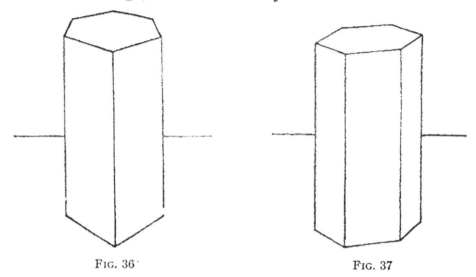

FIG. 36   FIG. 37

As the object is to be drawn full size and as the right and left points of convergence are so close together, it would greatly distort the appearance of the bottom of the hexagonal prism to construct the foreshortened hexagon for the bottom in the same manner used for the top hexagon.

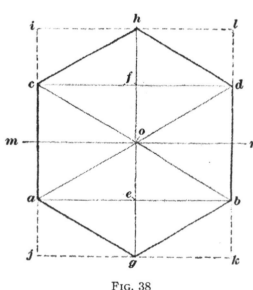

FIG. 38

The method of drawing the hexagonal prism should therefore be as follows: Construct the foreshortened hexagon for the top as described; then, about 4 inches below $b\,d$, lay out the front edge of the base the same length as $b\,d$, calling it $b'\,d'$. When drawing the retreating edges from b' backwards to the left and from d' backwards to the right, simply sketch them in as they appear to the eye; that is, their direction as related to the horizontal base line. Then drop vertical lines from points g, b, d, and h of the top hexagon, and the hexagonal prism will be completed.

MODEL DRAWING

48. Holding Prism at an Angle.—Frequently, the hexagonal prism is seen at an angle instead of full face, either as in Fig. 36 or as in Fig. 37. If seen as in Fig. 36, the two sides visible show an equal amount of foreshortening, but if seen as in Fig. 37 each one of the three visible sides differs from the others in apparent width and in regard to the angles at which the top and bottom edges converge. These matters depend so much on the accurate drawing of the hexagons for the top and the base that these must be considered of first importance.

49. Laying Out Foreshortened Hexagon at Symmetrical Angles.—In Fig. 36 the hexagonal prism is so arranged that a top view of the hexagon appears as in Fig. 38, showing the same lines of subdivision as were used in Fig. 34, with an enclosing rectangle $i l k j$. When making a sketch from the model of the prism, there should first be drawn a horizontal line $j k$, Fig. 39, such as eye measurement shows to represent the extreme

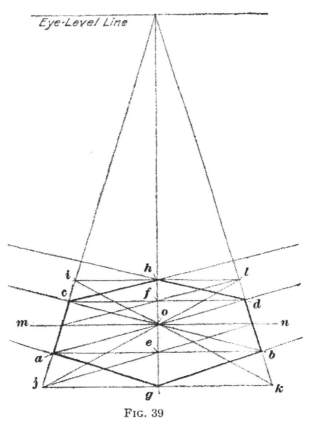

Fig. 39

width of the top of the hexagon. Another horizontal line $i l$ should then be drawn above $j k$ at the distance eye measurement shows to appear between points g and h of the foreshortened hexagon top. Edges $j a c i$ and $k b d l$ are converged until they meet in a point on the eye-level line, thus forming a foreshortened rectangle $i l k j$. By diagonals, the center o is found, through which $m n$ is drawn. Again by diagonals and centers, and then by horizontal lines, points a, b, c, and d are found. This gives all the corners of the hexagon. If lines

MODEL DRAWING

g a, *a c*, *c h*, *h d*, *d b*, and *b g* are drawn, the foreshortened hexagon is complete.

50. Laying Out Foreshortened Hexagon at Irregular Angles.—When a prism placed in the position shown in Fig. 37 is looked at from directly above, its top will appear as in Fig. 40, the lines of subdivision being the same as were used before. In a foreshortened view all the lines will converge, but this view may be drawn according to the plan used in the case of a prism seen full face, with some modifications.

First, the front edge *b d*, Fig. 41, may be laid off by eye measurement the least bit shorter than if it were seen full face and the end *d* slanting slightly away from the observer.

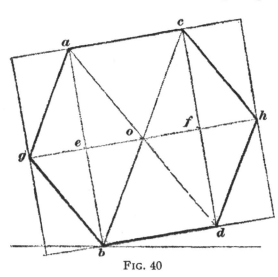

FIG. 40

Lines *b a* and *d c* may be converged upwards toward a point on the eye-level line. This point will not be directly above the center *o* because the line *b d* slants back from the face plane, but will be on a line *p q* perpendicular to the base *b d* at its central point *s*, and passing through *o*. Line *m n* is drawn as before but approximately parallel to *b d*, thus locating the rectangle *a c d b*. By diagonals *a d* and *c b* the center point *o* is located and the line *x y* is drawn approximately parallel to the lines *a c* and *b d*. Lines *a c*, *x y*, and *b d* are not actually parallel, for if extended far enough they would converge to a point on the eye level, but for the present purpose they may be sketched approximately parallel. As the line *x y* extends away from the face plane, distances *g e*, *e o*, *o f*, and *f h* of Fig. 40 are not of exactly equal length on the foreshortened line *x y* of Fig. 41. Distance *o f* is slightly less than *e o*; therefore, *f h* should be made slightly less than *o f* and *g e* made slightly longer than *e o*, because it is nearer the eye. Thus, points *g* and *h* are located and the sides *b g*, *g a*, *a c*, *c h*,

MODEL DRAWING

and *h d* may be drawn, thus completing the foreshortened hexagon. Completing the drawing of the hexagonal prism consists simply of laying out the foreshortened hexagon for the base, four inches below *b d*, and then of drawing vertical lines of the proper length to connect the hexagonal ends, as previously explained.

51. Tests of Accuracy of Foreshortening.—To test the accuracy of the foreshortened lay-outs shown in Figs. 35,

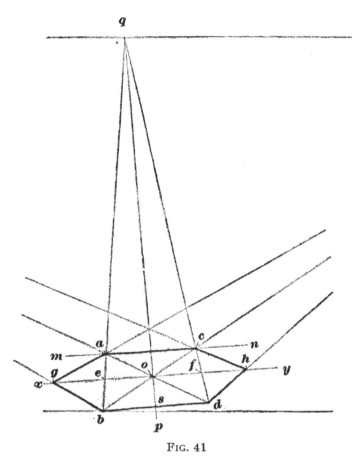

Fig. 41

39, and 41 the pairs of oblique edges, and the corresponding diagonals, should be extended toward their proper points of convergence on the eye.level, to the right and the left, respectively. If they do not so meet, they should be made to meet, and the foreshortened hexagon should be corrected accordingly.

52. Principles Governing Foreshortening of Hexagonal Prism.—The principles of foreshortening underlying the drawing of the hexagonal prism are simply combinations of those observed in the cases of the cube seen full face and the cube seen at an angle. The only new principles are as follows:

In a full-face view of the hexagonal prism, the front face appears full size and in its normal proportions, while each of the two visible side faces appears about one-half as wide as the front face and their top and bottom edges converge to points on the eye level, to the right and left equal distances from the center of vision.

In an edge view of the hexagonal prism, as in Fig. 33, the two visible sides are of equal width; that is, slightly narrower than the full-face view, with top and bottom edges converging as before described.

In the view of the hexagonal prism seen at unequal angles each one of the three visible sides is of different width, to be judged by eye measurement, and all top and bottom edges converge.

To draw properly the appearance of the top and bottom of the hexagonal prism, foreshortened views of the hexagons in their various positions must be drawn, aided by lines of subdivision.

53. Hexagonal Prism Lying on Its Side.—Frequently it is desired to show the hexagonal prism, or some object of which the hexagonal prism is the basis, lying on one side with one end showing, as in Fig. 42. An illustration of this is also shown in the group of models in Fig. 8. If the wooden model is laid on a table, in the position shown in Fig. 42, it will not be difficult to imagine each hexagonal end being enclosed in a rectangle such as n, m, l, k of Fig. 43, and the corresponding corners of these two rectangles connected by straight retreating lines, thus making an imaginary rectilinear box in which the hexagonal prism rests.

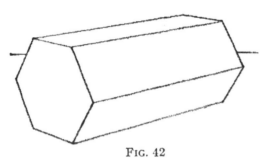

FIG. 42

MODEL DRAWING

54. To draw this prism, first draw the foreshortened box *l k j i p q r s*, using the same principles of converging lines for ends and sides as were used in the case of the 60° and 30° cube. Therefore, first sketch in the vertical edge *k j* of the box at what is thought to be the proper height; that is, the shortest thickness of the rectangle; then back of it place, by eye measurement, the vertical line *l i*. Converge upwards and to the left the top and bottom edges *k l* and *j i* until they meet at a point on the eye-level line. The foreshortened rectangle *l k j i* is then formed. Draw, by eye measurement, the vertical line *q r*,

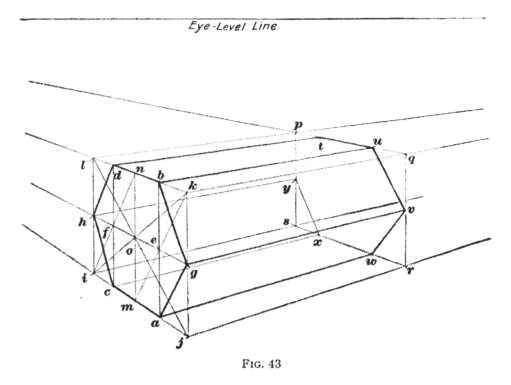

Fig. 43

at the rear end of the box, to the right of the line *k j* and at what appears to be the correct distance between the two ends of the prism, from an inspection of the hexagonal prism lying on the table. Next, draw the converging lines *k q* and *j r* at what appears to be, by eye measurement, the proper slant back, thus determining the length of the line *q r*. The foreshortened rectangle *p q r s* may now be constructed, as previously described. All end and side edges may now be drawn so as to make *l k j i p q r s* appear as a transparent box; that is, so that all edges can be seen.

MODEL DRAWING

55. Within the nearer end *l k j i*, construct a foreshortened hexagon on exactly the same plan as was used in drawing the foreshortened hexagon in Fig. 39. By diagonals, locate the centering and vertical lines, the line *h g*, and points *d, b, g, a, c*, and *h*, which when connected by lines form the desired foreshortened hexagon. Then construct a similar hexagon *t u v w x y* within foreshortened rectangle *p q r s* at the far end of the prism, and after the same method. Then draw retreating lines *d t, b u, g v, a w, c x*, and *h y*, thus completing the drawing of the hexagonal prism. Of course, only edges *d t, b u, g v*, and *a w* are actually visible.

This method is employed whenever one end and the three faces of a prism on its side are shown. The end may show toward the left and the long sides extend toward the right, or the end be shown toward the right, and the long sides extend toward the left.

56. The general principle revealed in the drawing of the prism on its side, in addition to those that have already been learned, is as follows:

To draw properly a foreshortened view of a solid whose upright sides or edges are not vertical, first enclose this solid in an imaginary transparent box, the upright ends, sides, and edges of which are vertical, and the top and bottom of which are horizontal. Then the desired foreshortened view of the object can be plotted in with proper converging lines and thus be drawn accurately.

FORESHORTENING OF A CYLINDER

57. Holding the Cylinder in a Vertical Position. The foreshortening of the cube, the square pyramid, and the hexagonal prism, in various positions, has been described with considerable detail because the principles of foreshortening these three types of solids underlie the foreshortening of all others. The descriptions of the foreshortening of the cylinder, the cone, the sphere, the hemisphere, and the vase, therefore, will be brief. If experiments similar to those made with the cube are made with the cylinder placed as shown in Fig. 44, it

MODEL DRAWING

will be seen that when the cylinder is looked at from directly above, as in Fig. 45 (a), the top view is a circle, as shown in (b). When the top of the cylinder is raised nearly to the eye level, as in (c), the top of the cylinder appears as an ellipse, as in (d). When the top of the cylinder is raised to the level of the eye, as in (e), it appears as a line and the side contours of the cylinder form vertical lines, as in (f).

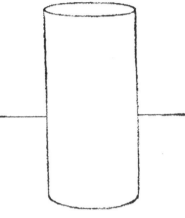

Fig. 44

58. That the bottom of the cylinder also appears as an ellipse can be demonstrated by placing the cylinder on a piece of paper and drawing a pencil line around the bottom of the model. When the cylinder is removed, a person sitting in the regular position for drawing; that is, with the eye about 2 feet away from the pen-

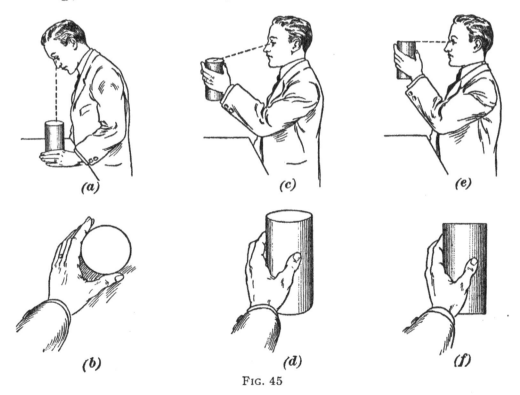

Fig. 45

ciled circle and 10 or 12 inches above it, the circle will appear as an ellipse. The average person is so accustomed to thinking of the base of a cylinder as a circle, because he knows it is actually that form, that he will not allow his eyes to register a correct impression upon his brain as to what he sees when he looks at the circle foreshortened. The result is that he believes he sees a circular shape, when as a matter of fact it is an ellipse that he sees. Demonstration may therefore be needed for one to prove to himself that what he sees is an ellipse and not a circle. He knows that a circle is just as wide as it is high and just as high as wide; in other words, every point on the circumference is equidistant from the center. He also knows that an ellipse is considerably wider than it is high, or considerably higher than it is wide, as the case may be. If, therefore, he will test this penciled circle on the paper, by the system of pencil and extended arm shown in Figs. 10 and 11, first measuring its apparent width, then its apparent height, he will find that it appears considerably wider than high and that therefore it is in appearance an ellipse.

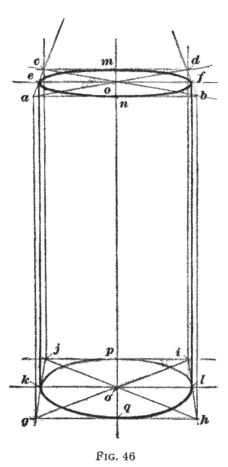

FIG. 46

59. Laying Out Foreshortened Ellipses.—Previous exercises have demonstrated that curved lines and forms are best drawn when dependent on straight lines and forms. Thus, it was learned that a circle can be drawn best by being imagined as being contained within a square, a hexagon, an octagon, etc. But it has been shown that a foreshortened square, the top of the cube, appears as an irregular rectangle with the front and rear edges parallel and the side edges converging. Therefore, the ellipse can best be drawn within such an irregular rectangle. The best method, therefore, of drawing the elliptic top and base, and also the vertical sides

MODEL DRAWING

of the cylinder, is to imagine the cylinder to be placed within a transparent prism, as in the case of the horizontal view of the hexagonal prism; but in this case the square prism will be standing on end. When sketching the cylinder, imagine this enclosing prism and first sketch it in lightly as shown at *a b d c g h i j*, Fig. 46. Care must be taken to get the cylinder its proper size; therefore, first block out, by eye measurement, the apparent greatest width *e f* of the cylinder and then construct the front half of the prism in front of the line *e f* and the rear half back of this line *e f*. When shapes *a b d c* and *g h i j* are drawn, the foreshortened center *o* is located by diagonals and thus points *e* and *f* are found. Points *m*, *n*, *p*, and *q* are already known. The ellipses for the top and the

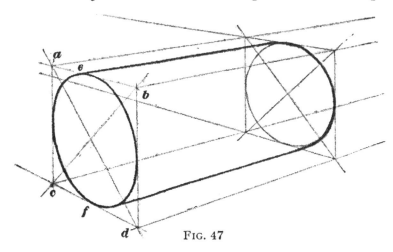

FIG. 47

bottom are then easily drawn in and the vertical lines for the contours put in place. The height of the cylinder is 4 inches, which is the height of the model, and is measured between the centers *o'* and *o*.

60. Holding the Cylinder in a Horizontal Position. A cylinder in a horizontal position is found in the group of models in Fig. 8. As shown in Fig. 47, a foreshortened cylinder lying on one side with one end showing is drawn by the methods used in drawing a hexagonal prism lying on one side.

One important point, however, must be observed. The width or diameter of the cylinder must be made large enough. Therefore, its apparent diameter, as obtained by eye measurement, must be laid off at *e f*, and one-half of the enclosing prism

MODEL DRAWING

must be constructed in front of, and one half back of, this line. Unless this plan is followed the cylinder will appear entirely too thin.

61. Proportion of Cylinder Visible.—The eye cannot see quite half way around a cylinder, particularly if the cylinder is of large diameter and close to the observer. This is shown in Fig. 48, where a cylinder 3 or 4 inches in diameter is seen at a distance of 12 or 15 inches. While a and b are the half way around points, the eye sees only to c and d. Thus the circle is divided into two unequal parts and to be strictly accurate it would be necessary to find line $c\,d$ instead of center line $a\,b$ when placing the ellipse properly within the foreshortened rectangle $a\,b\,d\,c$, Fig. 47. However, on a model of the size

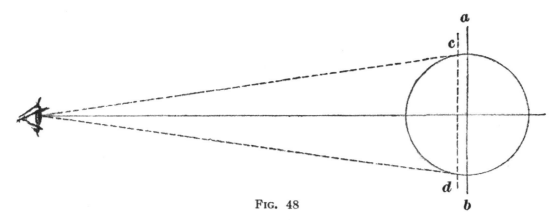

FIG. 48

being used, the end is 2 inches in diameter, and on account of the rather great distance at which it is viewed, the difference may be considered negligible, and to simplify the process the center line may be used, as previously described.

62. The following new points have been revealed by these demonstrations with the cylinder:

The top view of a vertical cylinder is a circle, which becomes foreshortened and appears as an ellipse when nearer the eye level. These principles apply also to the bottom of the cylinder. The side contours are vertical lines.

Foreshortened circles, that is, ellipses, for the ends of the cylinders and the parallel contours of the sides are best drawn in their correct proportions by imagining the cylinder enclosed in a rectilinear transparent prism or box.

MODEL DRAWING

FORESHORTENING OF A CONE

63. Holding the Cone for Demonstration.—The cone will be considered in only one position, standing upright as shown in Fig. 49. As the cone is based on the cylinder, any one who can draw the cylinder will have no difficulty in drawing the cone in its proper measurements and proportions. First, an imaginary, transparent, square prism standing on end should be drawn and a cylinder drawn therein, as in Fig. 46. To draw this cone it is necessary to locate by means of diagonals, the center o in the top and the points k and l in the base. In the case of the cone, Fig. 50, the point o will be the apex of the cone. By connecting the apex o with points k and l the drawing of the cone is completed. This method should always be employed in sketching from the model to ensure correct placing of the apex and the tapering contours.

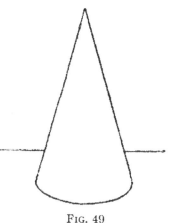

Fig. 49

Or, in other words, a foreshortened cone is drawn by first drawing a cylinder, finding the center of its top, and connecting this by straight lines with the ends of the ellipse showing the foreshortened bottom of the cylinder, which now becomes the base of the cone.

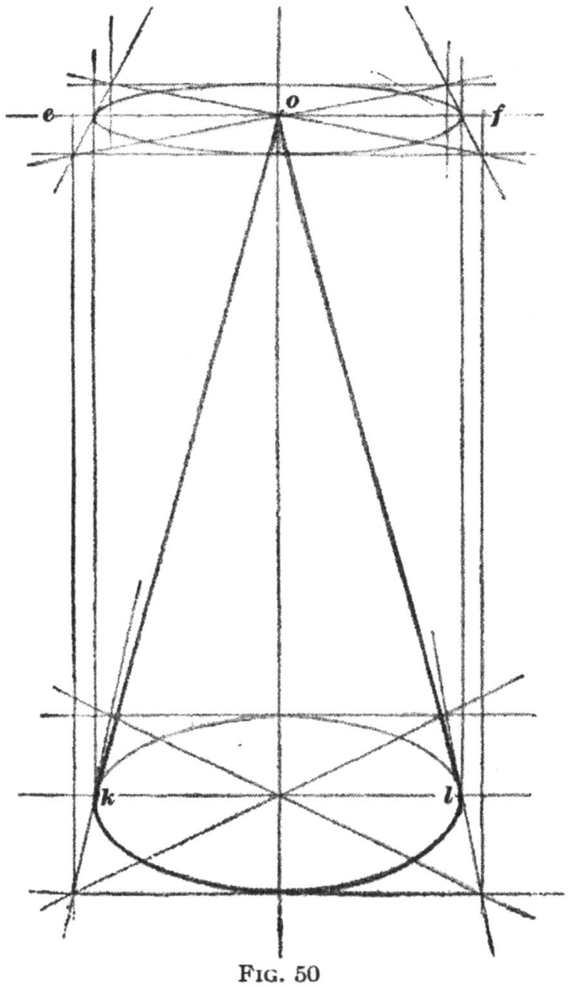

Fig. 50

MODEL DRAWING

64. The cone may also lie upon its side, in which case the foreshortened ellipse for the base will be inclined slightly back from the vertical plane, and the whole cone will be included in a transparent box, as before described, and thus sketched freehand and by eye measurement.

FORESHORTENING OF A SPHERE

65. How Sphere Is Drawn for Plates.—In purely pictorial work, where the sphere is drawn freehand, it cannot be said to be ever foreshortened. No matter what is the angle at which the sphere is viewed, its contour will always appear to be a perfect circle. The sphere may be above, below, to the right of, or to the left, of the eye of the observer, and yet the contour will always be a perfect circle.

In drawing the sphere, where it is required on certain of the drawing plates of this Section, it should therefore simply be contoured as a circle. The size of this circle, however, must always be in the proper proportion to the other objects of similar size. If the sphere is at the front of the group, or is supposed to be drawn "full size," it must be made 2″ in diameter.

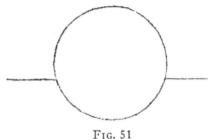

FIG. 51

66. Graphic Foreshortening.—In some kinds of commercial illustrating work, where there are markings or lettering on its surface, the sphere must be graphically laid out; but such a method is not necessary in this subject.

FORESHORTENING OF A HEMISPHERE

67. Holding the Hemisphere for Demonstration. The hemisphere is usually seen with flat portion upwards and horizontal, as in Fig. 52, or with the curved portion upwards and resting on the flat portion, as in Fig. 53. In either case it is simply one-half of a sphere; and any one who can draw a sphere can draw a hemisphere. The important point to remember is that the bisecting of the sphere is done by showing,

MODEL DRAWING

not a straight line, but an ellipse, as in Fig. 52. Beneath (or above, as the case may be) the longer diameter of this ellipse is

FIG. 52   FIG. 53

drawn the semicircle to express the contour, as in Fig. 54, where $a\,c\,b\,d$ is the ellipse, $a\,b$ the long diameter, and $a\,e\,b$ the semicircle.

This method, though, does not portray a hemisphere with absolute accuracy. The strictly accurate method of drawing the foreshortened hemisphere is first to lay out a half cube, and then construct the hemisphere by means of vertical half circles and horizontal circles

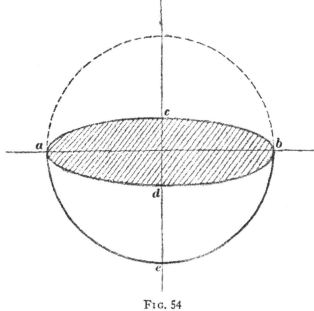

FIG. 54

of decreasing diameters, the ends of the ellipses and semi-ellipses then being connected freehand.

FORESHORTENING OF A VASE

68. Holding the Vase for Demonstration.—By this time it should be a simple matter to recognize the basic form of solid in any object that may be seen. For example, an ordinary cigar humidor will be a cube; a metronome will be a square pyramid; a six-sided waste-paper basket will be a hexagonal prism; a sprinkling can will be a cylinder; an inverted funnel will appear as a cone; a teapot as a sphere; a cup and saucer as a hemisphere on a disk, etc. The beginner will do well to cultivate by observation this faculty of seeing at once the underlying geometric

MODEL DRAWING

solid that is the basis for the contour and modeling of any object.

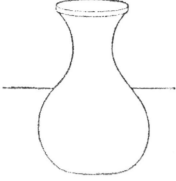

FIG. 55

Applying this principle to the simple vase form, Fig. 55, the model of which should be studied, it will be seen that the vase is a combination of the cylinder and the sphere. To draw the cylinder, it is necessary to lay out the ellipse $e\,f\,g\,h$, Fig. 56, with the diameter $e\,g$ equal to the apparent width of the flat part of the base, which will be slightly greater than the diameter of the flat part of the top. Next, the imaginary transparent cylinder $a\,b\,c\,d\,e\,f\,g\,h$ is constructed by means of the upper and lower ellipses and the vertical lines $a\,e$ and $c\,g$, making its height the same as the apparent height of the vase. The widest part of the vase is a sphere, flattened at the bottom; this may therefore be represented by drawing the contour of the sphere $e\,u\,v\,w\,x\,y\,g$, line $e\,g$ being the flat cut off part.

The curve $e\,f\,g$ is not a part of the contour of the sphere but is the front portion of the ellipse $e\,f\,g\,h$ showing the flat base, and must be so drawn.

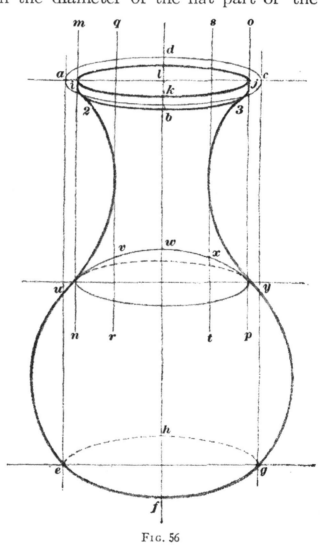

FIG. 56

MODEL DRAWING

69. The neck of the vase and its flat top may be considered as coming within a smaller cylinder, of which *i k j l* is the top. This cylinder is contained within the original cylinder *a b c d e f g h* and its sides are portions of the vertical lines *m n* and *o p*. The narrowest part of the neck is determined by vertical lines *q r* and *s t*. Disk *i k j l* may be drawn for the flat top and the curved lines *2 u* and *3 y* should then be drawn, combining at *u* and *y* with the curves of the spherical contour of the vase. This will complete the outlines of the foreshortened view of the vase.

70. This plan will be found useful, not only when drawing the vase for the regular drawing exercises of this Section, but when drawing any solid with symmetrical curves that one may be required to portray. By employing this plan, an accuracy of proportions of parts can be maintained that could not be secured otherwise.

DRAWING EXERCISES

GENERAL INFORMATION

71. As in the preceding Section, the work required here is in the form of exercises arranged as drawing plates, each plate being $19'' \times 12\frac{1}{2}''$ or one-half of the regular $19'' \times 25''$ sheet of charcoal paper provided. For the first three plates, each $19'' \times 12\frac{1}{2}''$ sheet is to be divided, by vertical and horizontal center lines, into four rectangles $9\frac{1}{2}'' \times 6\frac{1}{4}''$, in each of which one exercise is to be drawn. As each plate is finished it should be sent to the Schools for examination, and while this plate is being examined and returned, work should be done on the plate following.

These exercises are to be drawn in outline only direct from the wooden models and are to be drawn in charcoal lines as described earlier in this Section, and then sprayed with fixatif to protect them. There should be no attempt to shade the drawings nor to indicate the shadows. The rear edge of the table on which the model rests should be indicated by a

MODEL DRAWING

horizontal line back of the model and running entirely across the rectangle. In all cases, the plates are to be drawn according to the methods already given for the different objects and not by any hit-or-miss method. All plates made in a careless manner will be returned without detailed comments or criticisms. Only drawings made from the models according to the rules of foreshortening will be accepted. The blocking-in lines and the construction lines used to secure proper foreshortening should be allowed to remain; drawing plates in which they are lacking will not be accepted. The lines expressing the actual edges of the model itself should be somewhat heavier than the blocking-in lines, or may be accented. In this way, it will be possible to tell whether the student's methods of blocking-in and foreshortening are correct.

72. Fig. 57 will give an idea as to what should be the typical appearance, on a reduced size, of one of these plates. The points of convergence for cube and pyramid will likely be much farther apart on the student's drawing than are those shown in Fig. 57. It is not to be copied from, for all drawings are to be made the full size of the wooden models and direct from them. No other charts for appearance of finished plates are shown in the text, because it is expected that, by this time, the student will know how to arrange the exercises on the plates entirely from the directions given in the text.

PLATE 1

73. Exercise A, Plate 1.—Exercise A is to occupy the upper left-hand $9\frac{1}{2}'' \times 6\frac{1}{4}''$ rectangle. To draw it, make an outline drawing in charcoal or soft pencil, properly blocked in and foreshortened, direct from the wooden model of the cube seen in full front view, the front face being drawn 2 inches square and the other parts in proportion (see "Special Note," bottom of page 16). Allow all blocking-in and retreating lines to remain. Spray the drawing with fixatif and allow to dry.

74. Exercise B, Plate 1.—Exercise B is to occupy the upper right $9\frac{1}{2}'' \times 6\frac{1}{4}''$ rectangle. To draw it, make an outline

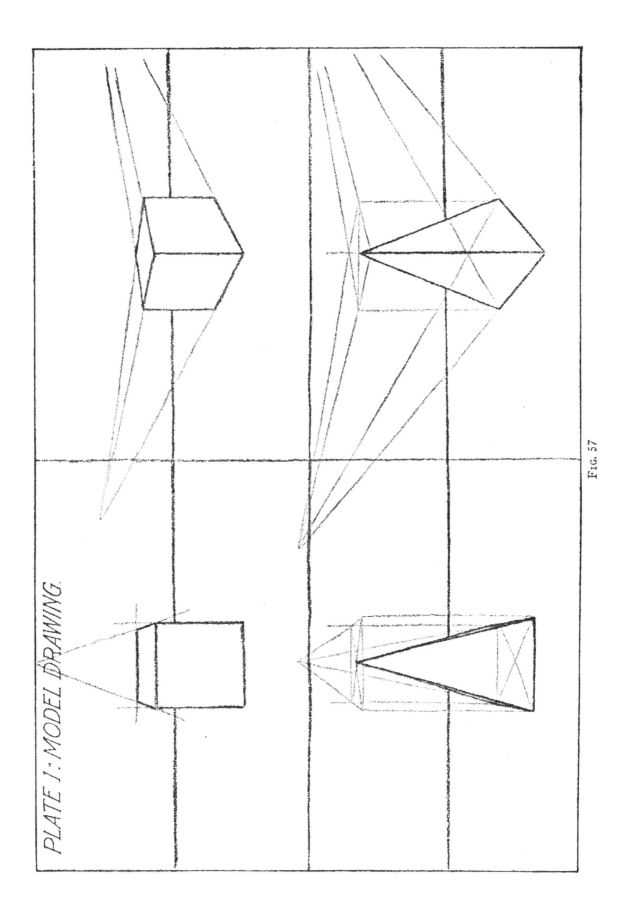

Fig. 57

MODEL DRAWING

drawing in charcoal or soft pencil, properly blocked in and foreshortened, direct from the wooden model of the cube seen at an angle of 45°, the front edge being 2 inches high and other parts in proportion. Allow all blocking-in and retreating lines to remain. Spray with fixatif and allow to dry.

75. Exercise C, Plate 1.—Exercise C is to occupy the lower left $9\frac{1}{2}'' \times 6\frac{1}{4}''$ rectangle. To draw it, make an outline drawing in charcoal or soft pencil, properly blocked in and foreshortened, direct from the wooden model of the pyramid seen in full front view, with the nearest base line 2 inches in length and the other parts in proportion. Allow all blocking-in and retreating lines to remain. Spray with fixatif and allow to dry.

76. Exercise D, Plate 1.—Exercise D is to occupy the lower right $9\frac{1}{2}'' \times 6\frac{1}{4}''$ rectangle. To draw it, make an outline drawing in charcoal or soft pencil, properly blocked in and foreshortened, direct from the wooden model of the pyramid seen at an angle of 45°, same scale as the pyramid in Exercise C, all parts being in their proper proportions. Allow all blocking-in and retreating lines to remain. Spray with fixatif and allow to dry.

77. Final Work on Plate 1.—Letter or write the title, Plate 1: Model Drawing, at the top of the sheet just completed, and on the back, lower left-hand corner, place the class letters and number, name, address, and the date of completing the plate, also letter each exercise, as A, B, etc. Roll the plate, place in the mailing tube, and send to the Schools for examination. Then proceed with Plate 2.

PLATE 2

78. Exercise A, Plate 2.—Exercise A is to occupy the upper left $9\frac{1}{2}'' \times 6\frac{1}{4}''$ rectangle. To draw it, make an outline drawing in charcoal or soft pencil, properly blocked in and foreshortened, direct from the wooden model of the hexagonal prism standing erect and seen full face, the front face being

MODEL DRAWING

4 inches high and other parts in proportion. Allow all blocking-in and retreating lines to remain. Spray with fixatif and allow to dry.

79. Exercise B, Plate 2.—Exercise B is to occupy the upper right $9\frac{1}{2}''\times6\frac{1}{4}''$ rectangle. To draw it, make an outline drawing in charcoal or soft pencil, properly blocked in and foreshortened, direct from the wooden model of the hexagonal prism lying on one side, and extending backwards and toward the right at an angle of 45°. Draw it to the same scale as the hexagonal prism in Exercise A, making all parts in their proper proportions. Allow all blocking-in and retreating lines to remain. Spray with fixatif and allow to dry.

80. Exercise C, Plate 2.—Exercise C is to occupy the lower left $9\frac{1}{2}''\times6\frac{1}{4}''$ rectangle. To draw it, make an outline drawing in charcoal or soft pencil, properly blocked in and foreshortened, direct from the wooden model of the cylinder standing on one end, and 4 inches high, the width being in proportion. Allow all blocking-in and retreating lines to remain. Spray with fixatif and allow to dry.

81. Exercise D, Plate 2.—Exercise D is to occupy the lower right $9\frac{1}{2}''\times6\frac{1}{4}''$ rectangle. To draw it, make an outline drawing in charcoal or soft pencil, properly blocked in and foreshortened, direct from the wooden model of the cylinder lying on one side and extending backwards and toward the right at an angle of 45°. Draw it to the same scale as the cylinder in Exercise C, making all parts in their proper proportions. Allow all blocking-in and retreating lines to remain. Spray with fixatif and allow to dry.

82. Final Work on Plate 2.—Letter or write the title, Part 2: Model Drawing, and the class letters and number, name and address, and date, and the exercise letters (A, B, etc.,) at the proper places on the sheet, mail the plate to the Schools for examination. If Plate 1 has been returned, the criticisms on it should be carefully observed, and if redrawn work has been asked for, it should be done at once and sent to the Schools. Then proceed with Plate 3.

MODEL DRAWING

PLATE 3

83. Exercise A, Plate 3.—Exercise A is to occupy the upper left $9\frac{1}{2}'' \times 6\frac{1}{4}''$ rectangle. To draw it, make an outline drawing in charcoal or soft pencil, properly blocked in and foreshortened, direct from the wooden model of the cone with the longer axis of the ellipse for the base 2 inches in length and other parts in proportion. Allow all blocking-in and retreating lines to remain. Spray with fixatif and allow to dry.

84. Exercise B, Plate 3.—Exercise B is to occupy the upper right $9\frac{1}{2}'' \times 6\frac{1}{4}''$ rectangle. To draw it, make an outline drawing in charcoal or soft pencil, properly blocked in and foreshortened, direct from the wooden model of the sphere, making the diameter 2 inches. Keep the model in a stable position by resting it on a small piece of wax or soap about the size of a pea, so arranged under the model as not to show in the drawing. Allow all blocking-in and retreating lines to remain. Spray with fixatif and allow to dry.

85. Exercise C, Plate 3.—Exercise C is to occupy the lower left $9\frac{1}{2}'' \times 6\frac{1}{4}''$ rectangle. To draw it, make an outline drawing in charcoal or soft pencil, properly blocked in and foreshortened, direct from the wooden model of the hemisphere resting on the curved portion, making the flat portion 2 inches in diameter and perfectly horizontal. The model may be kept in a stable position, as in the case of the sphere, Exercise B, by resting it on a small piece of wax or soap. Allow all blocking-in and retreating lines to remain. Spray with fixatif and allow to dry.

86. Exercise D, Plate 3.—Exercise D is to occupy the lower right $9\frac{1}{2}'' \times 6\frac{1}{4}''$ rectangle. To draw it, make an outline drawing in charcoal or soft pencil, properly blocked in and foreshortened, direct from the wooden model of the vase with its front height 3 inches and its other parts in proportion. Allow all blocking-in and retreating lines to remain. Spray with fixatif and allow to dry.

MODEL DRAWING

87. Final Work on Plate 3.—Letter or write the title, Plate 3: Model Drawing, and the class letters and number, name and address, and date, and the exercise letters, at the proper places on the sheet, and mail the plate to the Schools for examination. If all required redrawn work on previous plates has been finished, proceed with Plate 4.

PLATE 4

88. Exercise for Plate 4.—Arrange the eight wooden models in a group, placing the smaller ones in front and the larger ones in the rear, and make an outline drawing direct from these models, in charcoal or soft pencil, properly blocked in and foreshortened. Group them so as to present an harmonious mass, not scattered units, and have them lighted from the left so that shadows are cast toward the right, but no shadows are to be drawn. Make drawings of the nearest models full size and those in the background in proper proportion to those in the foreground. The arrangement of the eight models must be original, and not like any of the text illustrations. A copy of text Fig. 8 must *not* be made, for such a drawing will not be accepted. Allow all blocking-in and retreating lines to remain. Spray with fixatif and allow to dry.

89. Final Work on Plate 4.—Letter or write the title, Plate 4: Model Drawing, and the class letters and number, name and address and date, and the exercise letters, at the proper places on the sheet, mail the plate to the Schools for examination.

If any redrawn work on any of the plates of this Section has been called for and has not yet been completed, it should be satisfactorily finished at this time. After all required work on the plates of this Section has been completed, the work of the next Section should be taken up at once.

LIGHT AND SHADE

PURPOSE

1. Third Stage in Learning to Draw.—The first stage in learning to draw is limbering up the arm, wrist, hand, and finger muscles and practicing line drawing and eye measurement. The second stage is making drawings in outline direct from objects and models, to familiarize the beginner with form and proportion in three dimensions; length, breadth, and thickness. The third stage, in logical order, is the portrayal of these objects or models pictorially. This means drawing these objects so that the light parts, the shaded parts, and the shadows that are cast, are properly expressed, not only in their forms and contours but also in their correct tone values.

This requires a thorough knowledge of the principles governing light, shade, and the casting of shadows, as well as a training in rendering drawings; that is, in portraying them pictorially. These principles can best be illustrated by placing the wooden models, used when making the outline drawings, in various positions and having the light fall upon them from certain directions, and then studying the light, shade, and shadow effects, and can best be applied by making drawings direct from the wooden models. This plan will be employed in this Section.

These light, shade, and shadow effects, as observed on the simple geometric solids employed, will serve as a foundation knowledge of how to portray lights, shades, and shadows when the objects employed are more complicated, as human figures, etc. For this reason this study of light, shade, and shadow values must not be looked on as being too elementary, but as a necessary foundation for successful pictorial or decorative work.

LIGHT AND SHADE

LIGHT, SHADE, AND SHADOW

SOURCES AND KINDS OF ILLUMINATION

2. Main Sources of Light.—An examination of the wooden models will at once show that there are no absolute outlines in nature. The forms are expressed by various planes of light and shade coming together and the edges of these are seen simply because one plane is of a different tone value, that is, lighter or darker, than its neighbor. The values of these various planes are determined by the kind, the source, and the direction of the illumination that the objects receive.

Broadly considered, there are two general sources of light: *sunlight*, in which the rays of light are parallel, and *artificial light*, in which the rays of light come from a point and diverge.

The sunlight may be direct or indirect. The object may be directly in the path of the sun's rays and thus be brilliantly lighted and cast clear distinct shadows; or it may simply receive light from a window that admits the reflected light from the outside lighted air; that is, the direct rays of the sun do not fall upon the object.

The artificial light may be of many kinds; from an arc or incandescent electric lamp, from a gas flame or burner, or from an oil lamp, a candle, an open-hearth fire, etc.

3. Kinds of Illumination.—Both sources of illumination may light up the objects in many ways. When the light is obtained from a number of directions at once, as from several windows or widely separated lamps, the illumination is known as *diffused lighting*.

When the source of light is in front of an object, so that the nearer parts of the object are lighted and the back is in shade, the illumination is known as *front lighting*.

LIGHT AND SHADE

When the source of light is behind an object, so that the back is lighted and the front is in shade, the illumination is known as *rear lighting*.

When the source of light is overhead, so that the tops of the objects are lighted, the illumination is known as *overhead lighting*.

When the source of light is on one side, so that the side of the object nearest the light is most brilliantly lighted and the

Fig. 1

opposite side is in shade, the illumination is known as *side lighting*.

When the source of light is on the left side of and above the object, the illumination is known as *conventional lighting*.

The different kinds of illumination are here shown by means of photographs of the wooden models, but the actual effects caused by the different sources and directions of the light can best be studied by observing the results produced on the models when placed, singly and in groups, in every possible position.

LIGHT AND SHADE

4. Diffused Lighting.—In Fig. 1 are shown the effects produced by ordinary diffused lighting on the group of models. This is the effect that is produced when the models are placed on a table in a room well lighted by three or four windows; that is, with the light coming from three or four (or more) directions at one time. In this case, the light comes mostly from the front and sides but not from the back and there has been no particular effort made to secure interesting lights and shades. This group is introduced merely to show a typical condition of lighting, but reveals very little that would be clear enough to enable one to formulate principles of light and shade. No gradations of light and shade are shown, neither are there any well-marked shadows. This is due to the fact that the light comes from many sources and kills the greater portion of the shadows. For instance, the typical shadows might be cast toward the right by the light coming from the left, but as light is coming also from the right and from the front these latter rays shine in upon the shadows and, to a great degree, dispel them. Therefore, what little shadow is shown is directly under or very close to the object casting it, and it is very soft or blurred on the edges. The texture, that is the grain, of the wood of the models is beautifully revealed, thus showing that the lighting is clear and adequate.

It will be observed that, as a group, this effect of lighting is flat, monotonous, and far from pleasing, although it is perfectly natural and typical. The importance, therefore, of securing a method of lighting that will bring out properly the light, shade, and shadow effects is quite evident.

5. Front Lighting.—Fig. 2 shows the group of models lighted by direct sunlight coming from back of the observer and shining onto the front of the objects. The effects of surface lighting are interesting when comparison is made, object for object with the same group conventionally lighted, as in Fig. 5. On all the objects, deep shade is absent, because the strong front light dispels it, but a sort of half shade is noticeable on parts of each model. The high lights on all

LIGHT AND SHADE

rounded surfaces tend to approach more nearly the center line instead of the left-hand contour of the object. If the models were of polished metal, the extremely brilliant points and lines of brightest high light would be clearly shown.

The shadows are clear and distinct, but little of them is seen because they are all cast back of the objects. However, should this group of models be looked at from above, the retreating shadows would be plainly seen.

FIG. 2

6. Rear Lighting.—The conditions of lighting for the group shown in Fig. 3 are exactly the reverse of those used for the group shown in Fig. 2, because the objects are lighted from the rear. As the light rays come toward the observer, they illuminate the backs of the models, put into deep shade the fronts of the objects, and cast dark, distinct shadows toward the observer. The most noticeable feature about this group is that, at first glance, it appears composed of black objects, with very little modeling, casting black shadows. Closer examination, however, reveals the modeling of each

LIGHT AND SHADE

object, although largely in shade. With the exception of the top face of the hexagonal prism, which reflects the light rays perfectly, no high lights occur, although a few half lights are shown, as on the tops of the cylinder, the sphere, and the hemisphere. The soft graded lights on each side contour of the vase are beautiful examples of reflected light falling onto an object. The gradation of values from half light to half shade, and then from half shade to deep shade, as shown on

Fig. 3

the hemisphere, is worth careful study. The shadows are, of course, blacker than any of the deep shades, although careful observation is required to detect this at places. All shadows are cast toward the observer.

7. Overhead Lighting.—When the models are lighted from above, as in Fig. 4, the most noticeable features are the bright lights on the tops of the objects and the dark shades at the bottom, the shadows being cast under the objects. In this way, high light, half tone, and shade are expressed,

LIGHT AND SHADE

as in the case of the objects conventionally lighted, but from top to bottom, instead of from upper left to lower right. For instance, the high light on the sphere is exactly at the top and the half tone, if it could be seen, around the lower half, the shade being at the bottom. This is well illustrated by the lower part of the vase, which is practically a sphere. The very bright high light on the flat top of the vase shows very clearly the source of the light.

The shadows naturally have little extent beyond the limits

Fig. 4

of the objects themselves. The peculiar blurred effect of the edges of the shadows is due to the fact that, when the photograph was taken, the group was lighted from an overhead electric chandelier in which there were four or more lamps, each casting a shadow.

8. Conventional Lighting.—In Fig. 5 is shown the effect of having the models lighted from the side and in front, and slightly above, thus casting the rays of light down upon the object at an angle of about 45°; that is, so that the shadow

LIGHT AND SHADE

is about the same length as the height of the object casting it. The system of conventional lighting has been agreed on as a standard that may be used when formulating theories of light, shade, and shadow casting. It will be noted that the shadows are sharper and more readily traced, and the contrasts of light and shade clearer, than under any other condition of lighting.

The cylinder, the hexagonal prism, and the hemisphere are shown in horizontal positions, and the light effects on

Fig. 5

them and the forms of their shadows should be carefully noted. On the lighted surface of the cylinder very little gradation is shown on account of the brilliant illumination and also the reflected light from the other objects. On the prism, however, the hexagonal end shows the high light, the top face shows the half light, the upper inclined right face shows the half shade, and the lower inclined right face shows the shade. The surface lighting of the hemisphere is, in this position, similar to that of the sphere.

LIGHT AND SHADE

The shadow of the cylinder's long straight side would, of course, show parallel edges, if it could be seen unobstructed. The spherical end would cast a long, semielliptic contour on the horizontal supporting surface, but being interrupted by the vertical end of the prism it takes the form shown. The shadows of the prism and the hemisphere follow principles already discussed. The shadow cast by the upper part of the vase onto the lighted face of the pyramid forms an extremely interesting study.

For the present, there will be considered simply the light, shade, and shadow effects seen in Fig. 5. This is to be supplemented, however, by a careful study of the models arranged in the positions shown and conventionally lighted. This study will reveal many interesting shadow effects that are not revealed in a photograph.

LIGHT AND SHADE

DEFINITION OF TERMS

9. In model drawing, the term light, except when considering the source of illumination, refers to the effect on the object illuminated and not to the sun or a lamp. The **light** on an object is, therefore, the lightest or most brilliant part of the object; and, similarly, the **shade** is the darker part of an object; that is, it is the part not in the direct path of the illuminating rays. Care must be taken, however, to distinguish between shade and **shadow,** which is the image cast by an object onto some other body, or by a projecting part of an object onto the object itself.

At present, only the white-and-black values of light and shade will be studied. As every object has color, to portray objects naturally will require the use of colors in the drawing. But before any color work can be done satisfactorily, the contrasts of white-and-black values must be thoroughly understood; that is, the correct portrayal of the object makes it necessary for a person to know whether the part of the object

LIGHT AND SHADE

approaches pure white light or whether it approaches black, which is the absence of light.

10. The treatment of light, shade, and shadow in drawing direct from models and objects differs greatly from their treatment in architectural drawings. The architect is governed by certain geometric rules and principles and makes his so-called shadow tints according to accurately measured projections. As a result, he is able to show, in his elevation drawings, what parts project and what parts recede from the face plane of a building, even before the building is constructed. This kind of shadow projecting is, therefore, a mechanical process of accurately measured points, lines, and angles.

In contouring and portraying lights, shades, and shadows in pictorial and decorative work, there are no hard-and-fast rules for this work, neither are accurately scaled measurements used. The entire process is a freehand portrayal based on accurate laws. Nevertheless, there are certain principles governing the lighting, shade values, and shadow casting, which must be understood before the shadows of objects can be properly contoured.

LIGHTS

11. Direction of the Rays of Light.—As the lights on any object are those portions nearest the source of light and therefore most brilliantly illuminated, their size, luminosity, and general character depend, in large measure, on the direction and the angle of the illuminating rays. Although the illuminating rays diverge as they come from the sun, the sun is such an immense body of light, so many times larger than any object or group of objects on the earth, that, for all practical purposes, these rays may be considered as being parallel when they fall upon the object or objects. This parallel formation or direction is very clearly seen when the direct sunlight is allowed to shine through a small opening, or through several adjacent small openings in the window blind, into a dusty room not otherwise lighted. In Fig. 6, the little arrows x may be considered the beams or rays of light from

LIGHT AND SHADE

the sun falling onto the cube. They are marked "light rays" and are parallel, as shown.

12. Angle of Light Rays in Conventional Lighting. As shown in Fig. 6, in conventional lighting all light rays xa, xb, xc, etc. are not only parallel but also fall upon the object at an angle of 45°. In order to bring out the proper

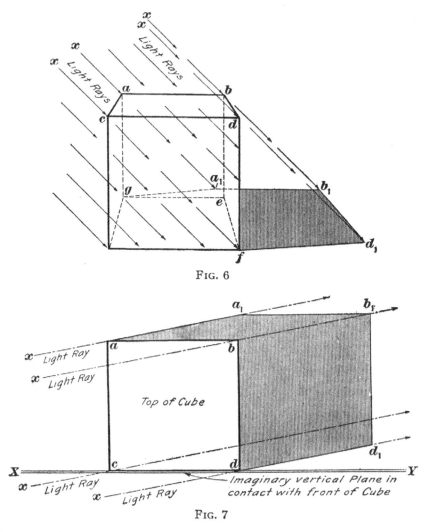

FIG. 6

FIG. 7

lighting and modeling of an object, a human face, a figure with drapery, or a piece of decorative carving, the light is not only assumed to be above and to the left of the object, but slightly in front of the imaginary vertical plane that touches the nearest part of the object. This is shown in Fig. 7, where the light rays xa_1, xb_1, xd_1, which are the rays xa_1, xb_1, xd_1 of Fig. 6 seen from above, come from a source in

LIGHT AND SHADE

front of the vertical plane, of which XY is the base line, and strike against the front of the cube. This may be proved by studying carefully the effects produced by conventional lighting on the wooden models when placed singly and in groups. Only conventional lighting will be used here in the study of lights, shades, and shadows.

13. High Light and Half Light. — The study of the models will show that the lightest part of the object, called

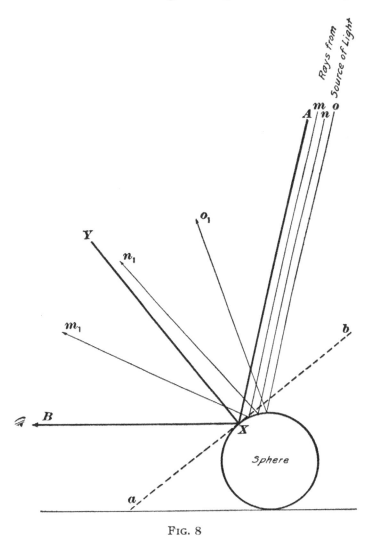

Fig. 8

the **high light**, is not always that part at right angles to the light rays. With the sphere, for example, the lightest part extends from the extreme upper part of the contour, where one would expect to find it, downwards. This apparent

LIGHT AND SHADE

spreading of the high light is due to the fact that the brightest spot is that from which the light rays are reflected from the object to the eye. It is well known that when a ray of light strikes a polished surface, such as a mirror, this ray is cast forwards to another point, say on a wall. The little experiment of catching a ray of light with a small mirror or other polished surface, and by changing the angle of the mirror making the "reflection" dance around over walls and ceiling is a very familiar one. It is also well known that the ray of light reflected from the mirror makes the same angle with the surface of the mirror as is made by the ray of light that falls upon the mirror.

This is shown in Fig. 8, where the light ray A coming from the source of light touches the surface of the sphere at X and is reflected to the eye B of the observer. The direct light ray AX makes the same angle with the curved contour of the sphere as is made by the reflected light ray XB. This is more clearly shown by drawing a dotted line ab, tangent to the sphere at the point X, and a line XY perpendicular to the line ab at the point of tangency X. When the light ray AX comes from the source of light and falls onto the sphere at X it makes a certain angle, say 50°, with the perpendicular line XY. Experiment shows that when this light ray is reflected from the sphere and forms the reflected ray XB, the angle BXY is equal to angle AXY. There are multitudes of other light rays falling upon the sphere, but owing to the angles of reflection only a limited number are reflected direct to the observer's eye, and it is only the part of the sphere from which these are reflected that has the high light. In Fig. 8, light rays m, n, and o strike the sphere and are reflected to m_1, n_1, and o_1; as these reflected rays do not strike the eye, the part of the sphere from which they are reflected has not the high light, but may be considered as being in **half light.**

14. The high light may vary from a minute point of light to a broadly diffused brilliant surface, depending on the nature of the source of light (as the sun, an arc light, an incandescent lamp, a gas flame, etc.) and its brilliancy,

LIGHT AND SHADE

and the texture of the object receiving the light, whether polished, smooth, dull, or rough. In the case of the high light on the sphere, the dull surface caused by the grain of the wood makes a diffused high light. The wooden model of the sphere, brilliantly and conventionally lighted, should be looked at for a demonstration of this diffused high light. However, if this sphere were to be painted white or were to have a polished surface, such as that of a billiard ball, or if the entire surface were a mirror, the exact source of light would be reflected from this portion of the sphere, as, for instance, the shape (curved) of the window and window panes, from which the object is lighted. The high lights on other geometric solids will differ in brightness and form from that on the sphere.

SHADES

15. Half Shade.—A study of the sphere, when conventionally lighted, will show that the parallel light rays are interrupted when half way around the sphere; that is, at the widest part of the sphere. It will also show that, although the upper left-hand part of the sphere, which is facing the light, is quite bright and the lower right-hand part, which is turned from the light, is quite dark, the dividing line between the two is not sharply and distinctly marked. As the surface of the sphere is continually curving, the angles of reflection are continually changing so that the transition from high light to half tone and then to deepest shade is very gradual. Also, the light reflected from other portions of the room or surroundings, and even from the surface on which the object rests, has a great influence on this gradual transition from the light side to the dark side of the sphere. This partially light and partially dark value is known as the **half shade, half tone,** or **semitone.**

16. Deep Shade.—The darkest part of the side of the object turned away from the light is called the **deep shade** and is sometimes quite dark, although not usually as dark as the darkest part of the shadow. If the object is composed of flat planes and sharp edges, such as the cube, the pyramid,

LIGHT AND SHADE

etc., the transition from light to half tone or deep shade may be very abrupt, but if the object is cylindrical or spherical the transition will be very gradual. This can be observed by comparing the lights and shades on the cube, with those on the sphere.

17. Shadow.—Although frequently used interchangeably, the terms shade and shadow have not the same meaning. The shade is that part of an object that receives the least illumination; it is the darkest part of the object. The shadow is the effect produced upon some other surface when the object is between the surface and the source of illumination; in other words, it is the dark image cast upon a neighboring surface.

SHADOWS

18. Formation of Shadows.—In Fig. 6, the light rays $x\,d_1$, $x\,b_1$, $x\,a_1$, etc. emanating from a source above, to the left, and slightly in front of the cube are intercepted by the cube

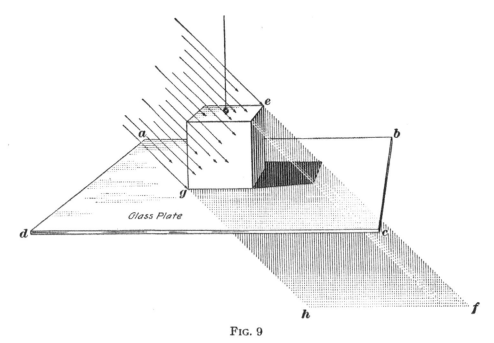

Fig. 9

and therefore cut off. As a result a shadow $f\,d_1\,b_1$ is cast, or thrown, on to that part of the table or other supporting surface on which, if they were not intercepted, these rays would strike.

LIGHT AND SHADE

The reason for this is shown in Fig. 9. When the cube is suspended, the 45° parallel rays of light striking the cube are intercepted and *path of shadow e f h g* is formed. In this path all direct light rays are cut off and the illumination is much reduced; the path is of indefinite length and its sides are always parallel. Ordinarily, however, an object rests upon something; therefore, if a horizontal sheet of glass *a b c d* is held against the bottom of the cube, the path of shadow will go right through the transparent glass. However, if powdered chalk, salt, sand, or some similar substance is sprinkled upon the glass around the bottom of the cube, or if the glass is painted, the glass is made opaque. Then the shadow of the path is interrupted and caused to appear as shown by the very dark value on the glass to the right of the cube. It is of great importance that the art student should know the conformations of the shadows cast by various objects under different conditions.

19. Necessity for Accurate Plotting.—The first thought might be that there is no necessity for plotting shadows accurately when they are already there and need simply be drawn as they appear. That this idea is erroneous can be shown readily if one will attempt to draw cast shadows without knowing how they are actually cast. He will be sure to get the shadows out of place, their limits not definitely defined, and will make them appear simply as a sort of indefinable blur. A test will demonstrate this. Just as one must know, in a general way, the anatomy of the human figure in order to draw properly a man standing, or walking, or in some other posture or action, so he must really know the anatomy of the shadow before he can correctly draw the shadow itself. An inspection of the work of the best artists and illustrators will reveal the evidences of an exact knowledge of shadow casting.

20. Basic Principles of Shadow Casting.—The proper delineation of a shadow depends on two general principles, which—if properly understood and applied—will enable one to draw properly the cast shadow of any object. These are:

LIGHT AND SHADE

The shadow is regular in shape when viewed from above.

This regular shadow must be foreshortened when viewed from in front.

The light rays, coming from the left and above at an angle of 45° (or at some other angle) are parallel when seen from the front, and combine with the plan of these same light rays, when seen from above, as they strike the front of the object at a slight angle, thus forming a regular symmetrical shadow.

This regular shadow, as viewed from above, will appear foreshortened when viewed from the front, and must therefore be drawn according to the principles of foreshortening so as to appear in its proper shape when viewed from the front.

The first principle was clearly demonstrated in Fig. 6, where the rays are seen coming down at 45° and parallel, and also in Fig. 7, where the rays are also parallel but fall upon the face of the object at a slight angle. This is also shown in Fig. 10 (a), where a light ray comes down at 45° and after passing through d, marks off a distance $x\,y$ as the length of the shadow, extending out from right side of the cube. In view (b), this shadow is shown in its true formation at $a\ a_1\ b_1\ d_1\ d\ b$. It must be remembered that as the light comes at an angle against the front face of the cube the rear face $a\ b$ also casts a shadow, as shown, thus giving the peculiar pointed conformation to the whole shadow. In view (c), the lines of views (a) and (b) are combined, thus showing the cube and its shadow foreshortened according to principles that have already been given.

21. A Shadow Cast onto a Horizontal Surface. When drawing from the object it will not be necessary to lay out an elevation and a plan as shown in Fig. 10 (a) and (b). To simplify the process, the general direction of the ray of light foreshortened, that is, the general direction of the front edge of the actual shadow as seen, may first be sketched in at the angle it appears and as a line of indefinite extent, as at $f\,d_1\,x$, Fig. 10 (c). The light rays $e\,b_1\,x$ and $g\,a_1\,x$ are also sketched in, following the same general direction as $f\,d_1\,x$ but with a slight convergence, so that, if continued, they will eventually

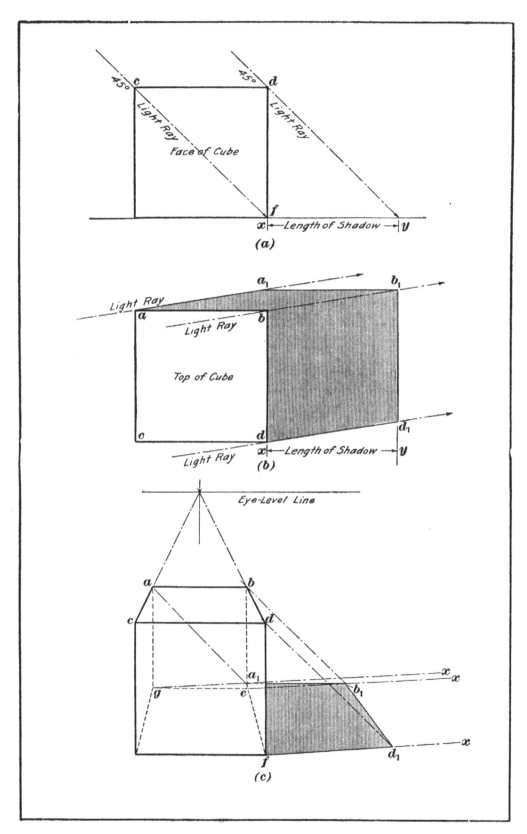

Fig. 10

LIGHT AND SHADE

meet at a point on the eye-level line, thus foreshortening these rays. It simply remains, therefore, to draw lines downwards at 45° through the corners a, b, d that cast shadows and where these 45° lines cut the converging rays $f\,d_1\,x$, $e\,b_1\,x$, and $g\,a_1\,x$, will determine the limits of the shadow.

Note that when the 45° line is drawn through a certain point it must stop at the horizontal converging ray that goes through the point directly under the corner through which the 45° light ray passes. Thus the 45° line through corner d must stop on light ray $f\,d_1\,x$ (at d_1); the 45° line through corner b must stop on light ray $e\,b_1\,x$ (at b_1); and the 45° line through corner a must stop on light ray $g\,a_1\,x$ (at a_1).

Of course, the shadow will start at the nearest edge f that casts a shadow, and will end at the farthest edge g that casts a shadow. This will make the contour of the shadow $f\,d_1\,b_1\,a_1\,g\,e$; only that part to the right of edge $d\,f$ will be seen from the front, however.

22. While by this time lines may be drawn, by eye measurement, at any desired angle with a reasonable degree of accuracy, in some cases absolute accuracy is required. An accurate 45° angle may be obtained by drawing upon a square piece of cardboard, a diagonal from the upper left-hand to the lower right-hand corner, and cutting the cardboard on this diagonal. Either of these pieces will then serve as a convenient means of drawing 45° lines. The lower edge should be moved along the base line until the oblique edge touches the point through which it is desired to draw the 45° line, and this line is then drawn until it is stopped by the light-ray line extending outwards and slightly backwards to the right, as previously described.

23. A Shadow Cast Also Onto a Vertical Plane. Frequently, an object is so placed that its shadow falls not only on the horizontal supporting plane but also upon a neighboring vertical plane or other object. In casting the shadow upon such a neighboring plane or object, the same principles are followed as in the case of the horizontal plane, except that the horizontal light rays, as soon as they touch the vertical plane,

LIGHT AND SHADE

are diverged from their path and go up along the face of the vertical plane, and thus become vertical lines. This is shown in Fig. 11, where the shadow of the cube is cast partly onto the horizontal supporting surface and partly onto the vertical plane $m\,n\,o\,p$.

To plot this shadow, the cube $a\,b\,d\,c\,g\,e\,f$, and the vertical plane $m\,n\,o\,p$ are drawn in their proper foreshortened positions, the vertical plane being parallel to the right-hand face of the cube; that is, edges $p\,o$ and $m\,n$ of the vertical plane will converge at the same point in the eye-level line as the edges $b\,d$ and $e\,f$ of the cube. Next, the horizontal light rays $f\,d_1\,x$, $e\,b_1\,x$, and $g\,a_1\,x$ are drawn, slightly converging, as before. As these rays are interrupted at d_1, b_1, and a_2, by the bottom edge $m\,n$ of the vertical plane, they must be deflected upwards and follow the surface of the vertical plane; they therefore no longer converge but become vertical lines $d_1\,x_3$, $b_1\,x_2$, and x_1. It simply remains to draw 45° lines through points a, b, and d until they cut light rays $g\,a_1\,x_1$, $e\,b_1\,x_2$, and $f\,d_1\,x_3$ and

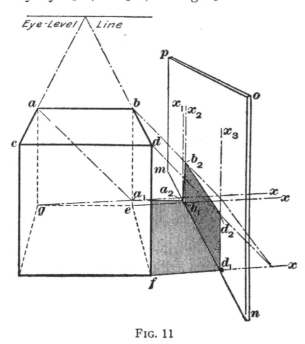

FIG. 11

thus locate point a_1 on the horizontal plane, points b_2 and d_2, as the limits of the vertical shadow. Point a_2 is found by drawing a line from b_2 to the point where the horizontal part of the original shadow touches the base $m\,n$ of the vertical plane $m\,n\,o\,p$. The contour of the shadow, partly on the horizontal plane and partly on the vertical plane, is thus completed, as shown at $f\,d_1\,d_2\,b_2\,a_2\,a_1\,g\,e$, in Fig. 11.

24. A Shadow Cast onto Neighboring Planes or Objects Not Vertical.—The neighboring plane may not

LIGHT AND SHADE

always be vertical, but may slant toward or away from the cube, as in the case of a pyramid or a hexagonal prism lying on its side. In such cases the same principles are followed as before, the horizontal light rays being deflected upwards to follow the face (foreshortened) of the plane receiving the shadow; but the shadow lines of the vertical edges of the cube will not follow, and be parallel with, the ends of the inclined plane. Experiments should be made of placing a cube so that it casts a shadow on a vertical plane (as a piece of cardboard or an envelope held vertically) as in Fig. 11.

Fig. 12

Keeping the bottom of the plane $m\,n$ in contact with the horizontal supporting surface and not shifting it at all, the top edge $p\,o$ should be swung downwards and away from the cube, so that front edge $n\,o$ makes an angle of 60° or 45°. It will then be noticed that the shadow edge $d_1\,d_2$ does not remain parallel to edge $n\,o$ but inclines backwards and away from it and the upper edge of the shadow $b_2\,d_2$ remains parallel (foreshortened) with the lower edge of the plane $m\,n$, as before.

LIGHT AND SHADE

If the vertical plane is inclined toward the cube instead of away from it, the upper corner d_2 of the shadow comes forwards toward the edge $n\,o$, instead of retreating from it.

An application of these principles of shadows cast onto inclined planes will be made on the regular plates in this Section. It will not be necessary to plot out such shadows according to definite measurements, if the principles learned so far are applied when doing the freehand sketching of the shadows that are actually seen.

25. A Shadow Cast onto a Curved Surface.—When the shadow is cast onto a curved surface, the first noticeable effect is that the shadow contour consists of curved lines. The

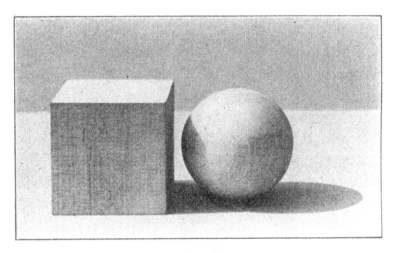

FIG. 13

plotting of this shadow is governed by the general principles of shadow casting, so that a careful study of the various forms of shadows cast by objects of different contours upon curved surfaces will enable any one, knowing these principles, to draw such shadows accurately.

In Fig. 12 is shown the contour of a shadow cast, by a cube, upon a cylinder, where only the horizontal edges of the cube cast a curved shadow. The vertical edges cast a vertical shadow because the cylinder is not curved in a vertical direction; only in a horizontal direction.

However, in the case of the shadow cast by the cube upon the sphere, Fig. 13, the lines forming the contour of the shadow

LIGHT AND SHADE

are all curved because the receiving surface, that is, the surface of the sphere, is itself curved in all directions.

26. The Shadow of an Object Having Curved Contours.—When the object that casts the shadow is cylindrical or spherical in form, the contours of the shadows of the curved portions must be curved, whether the receiving surface is flat or curved. The graphic plotting of these shadows will be described in connection with the description of the cylinder, sphere, hemisphere, and vase, and therefore need not be given here.

DEMONSTRATIONS WITH THE WOODEN MODELS

INTRODUCTION

27. To understand clearly the effects of light, shade, and shadows, the wooden models should be carefully studied when conventionally lighted. But to secure the best results from this study one of the following plans should be adopted:

1. If the demonstrations with the models are made during the spring or summer, place the model upon a table that has been put outdoors where the sun's rays can strike it, as in an open yard, upon a flat roof, on a veranda, etc. Then, between 9:30 and 11:30 A. M. and between 1:30 and 3 P. M. the shadows cast by the sun will be sufficiently satisfactory to give conventional lighting even though the rays may not be at an angle of exactly 45°.

2. If the work is done in some other season, or if conditions are such that these demonstrations cannot be made out of doors, the models may be placed on a table, with a window to the left of it through which the direct rays of the sun shine in upon the model at a 45° angle. The demonstrations must be made, as before, between 9:30 and 11:30 A. M. (preferably at 10 o'clock) and 1:30 and 3 P. M. (preferably at 2 o'clock). Depending on the season or the geographical location, these hours may have to be altered. In all cases good judgment must be used in selecting the proper times for these demonstrations.

I L T 159B—12

LIGHT AND SHADE

3. If direct sunlight is not available, a good north light coming from a window at the left of the table upon which the object is placed will give fairly sharp shadows.

4. If it is necessary to work by artificial light, the model can be illuminated in such a manner by an electric bulb, an inverted gas light, an ordinary portable gas reading lamp, or even an oil lamp, as to give sharp shadows. Of course the light rays from such artificial light will not be perfectly parallel, as in the case of sunlight rays, but the shadows will be sufficiently sharp to study.

The models should be studied under at least one of these conditions so that the effects produced may be fully understood. In all cases, though, an effort should be made to secure a brilliant concentrated light as the source of illumination. The models should be placed about 2 feet from the eye and from 10 to 12 inches below it. A piece of light gray cardboard should be set up vertically, back of the models, but not so as to obstruct the light, and also beneath them. This is the manner in which the models were arranged when they were photographed for Figs. 1 to 5, and 12 to 32.

THE CUBE

28. Demonstration With the Cube Full Face.—The cube should now be placed in such a position that the model and its shadow will appear about as in Fig. 14. This illustration is given simply as an aid in arranging the cube properly and the lighting should be so arranged that the lights, shades, and shadows of the wooden model are about as shown in the illustration.

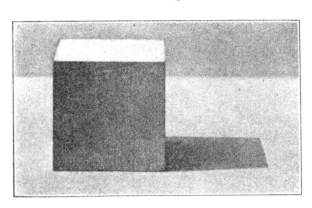

Fig. 14

After that, no further reference should be made to the illustration, but all demonstrations should be made with the wooden model itself, and all observations made from it.

LIGHT AND SHADE

Only the front and the top of the cube are visible and neither of these are very brilliantly lighted because the direct rays of light are reflected beyond the eye to the right. The top appears brightest because it is at the proper angle in relation to the light rays and to the line of sight; that is, it is parallel with the supporting surface. The end grain of the wood also increases its brightness. The top, therefore, may thus be considered the high light. The front face is slightly duller than the top, although not directly in shade, because it receives an oblique light. In fact, no distinct dark shade is evident in this full-face view of the cube; one would have to move toward the right and look at its right side to discover the shade.

29. The shadow of the cube full face, in conventional lighting, is a simple one, and the method of plotting was given when the graphic diagrams of the plotting of this shadow, given in Fig. 10, were described. The shadow cast by the model should be carefully studied to see how nearly it conforms to the principles of plotting the location, the direction, and the extent, that have already been given. If the light rays do not make an angle of exactly 45°, the shadow may be longer or shorter but the principles of plotting the shadow will remain the same.

30. Demonstration With the Cube at an Angle. The cube should now be placed with one vertical edge toward the observer, that is, cornerwise, as shown in Fig. 15, the conventional lighting being arranged as previously described.

In this position, three faces of the cube are visible, and the three gradations of lighting, high light, half shade, and deep shade, are now

Fig. 15

evident. The top of the cube is most brilliantly lighted, and is the high light, not only because it is nearest to the direct rays,

LIGHT AND SHADE

but because the angle at which the light rays strike it is such as to throw them direct to the eye. The left side is not quite so brilliant, because it is sharply inclined away from the eye, thus shedding the reflecting rays, and is the half shade. The character of the grain of the wood has some influence on these relative lights.

The right side receives no direct rays at all, because it is turned away from the source of light and is the darkest part of the object, and is therefore called the shade. The only reason the shade side of the object is not totally dark is because it receives reflected light from other objects or surfaces in the room. The shadow appears as dark as it does because it is in such a position (horizontal) that it does not receive much of this reflected light, although in this instance it receives some. It will be noticed that the shade side of the cube varies in its degree of shade, being darkest near the bottom, that is, nearer the shadow.

31. It will be seen at once that the shadow cast by the cornerwise cube is of quite a different shape from that cast by the full-face cube. The method of plotting this shadow, however, is exactly the same as that used in the case of the full-face cube. In Fig. 16 (a) is shown a front elevation of the cube, both the left and the right sides showing, with the light rays coming down through d and b at a 45° angle and marking off at d_1 and b_1 the limits of the length of the shadow. In (b) is shown the true formation of this shadow when viewed from above, and which must be foreshortened just as the cube that casts it is foreshortened. In (c) is shown the foreshortened cube and its shadow.

The practical method of getting this shadow is, as before, first to sketch in the horizontal light rays $g\, a_1\, x$, $e\, b_1\, x$, and $f\, d_1\, x$, directly under points a, b, and d, respectively. The 45° light rays are then drawn through a, b, and d. Where the one through a cuts ray $g\, a_1\, x$ marks a_1; where the one through b cuts ray $e\, b_1\, x$ marks b_1; and where the one through d cuts $f\, d_1\, x$ marks d_1. By connecting g, a_1, b_1, d_1, f, e, and g, the contour of the shadow is defined. Section $g\, e$ remains hidden.

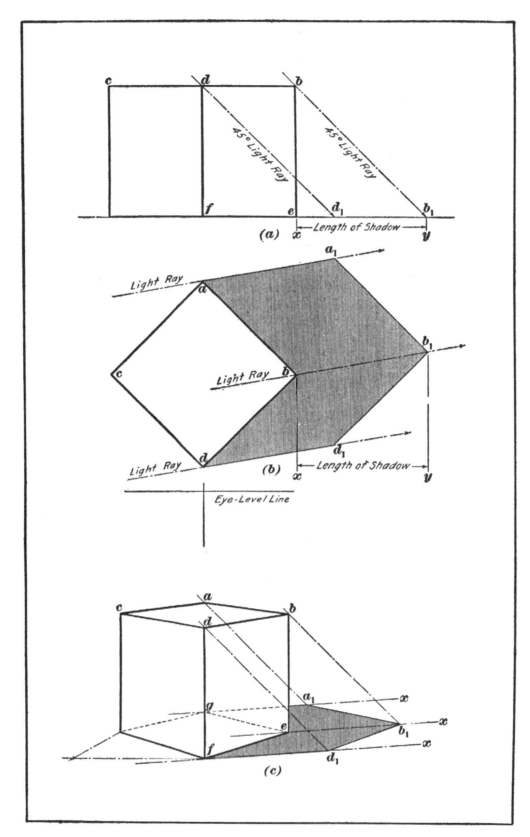

Fig. 16

LIGHT AND SHADE

THE PYRAMID

32. Demonstration With the Pyramid Full Face. Place the square pyramid in conventional lighting, with one face toward the observer, as shown in Fig. 17. For these various demonstrations with the models the same arrangement of lighting must be maintained, the models must always be placed at the same position or spot on the table (it would

Fig. 17

be well to mark it with pencil or chalk), and the observer should always sit at the same relative position in front of the model.

The front face of the pyramid will be bright, although the small portion of the left side, if visible, may be equally bright, depending on the angle of light. The right side is in shade, being turned entirely away from the source of light. The tone value of this shade and of the shadow and their variations follow the same principles as were described for the cube seen full face.

33. Shadow of Pyramid Cast onto a Horizontal Plane.—It will be observed at once that a pyramid casts a shadow with two long sides meeting in a point. The method of plotting it, however, is the same as was used in the case of

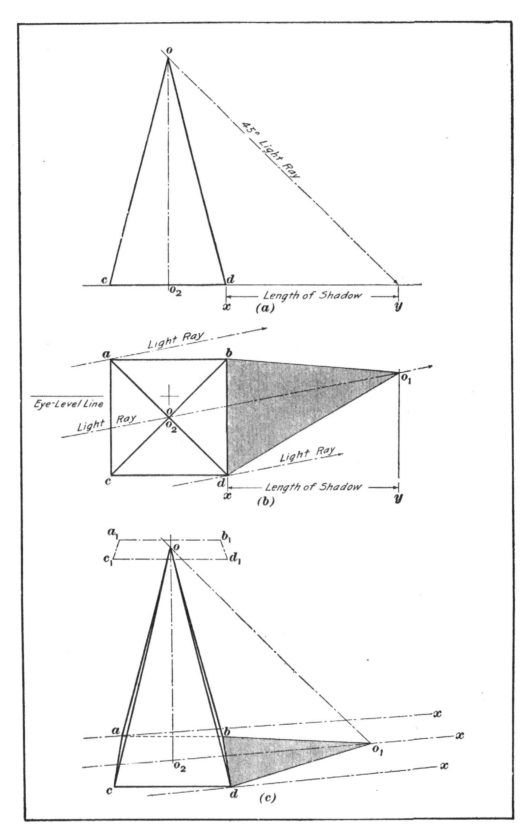

Fig. 18

LIGHT AND SHADE

the cube; this is shown in Fig. 18, where (a) is a front elevation of the pyramid full face, which is a triangle. The 45° light ray marks off $x\,y$ as the complete limit of the length of the shadow. The true formation of the shadow is shown in (b). It must be remembered that the shadow is cast by the edges running up to the apex o, which apex is exactly above the center of the base, as is shown in (c) by apex o at the center of foreshortened rectangle $a_1\,b_1\,d_1\,c_1$ directly above base $a\,b\,d\,c$.

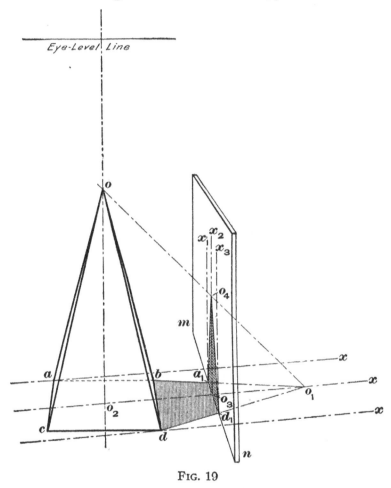

FIG. 19

Therefore, the horizontal light rays must be drawn through base corners a and d, and through center o. In (c) is shown how the 45° light ray cuts the horizontal light ray $o_2\,x$ at o_1, this point then being connected with b and d, thus completing the shadow $b\,o_1\,d$.

34. Shadow of Pyramid Cast onto a Vertical Plane. The method of plotting the shadow that falls partly onto a

LIGHT AND SHADE

horizontal and partly onto a vertical plane has been described in connection with the shadow cast by a cube. Fig. 19 shows that the same principle of plotting applies to the shadow of the pyramid. When the horizontal shadow lines meet the bottom of the vertical plane $m\,n$, that is, at a_1 and d_1, they are deflected upwards. The shadow of the apex will fall upon a vertical line drawn upwards from o_3, and at a point on this line where the 45° ray cuts it, namely point o_4. This point o_4 is connected with points a_1 and d_1, thus forming the contour of the part of the shadow that falls on the vertical plane.

Fig. 20

The same general principles apply when the shadow falls onto inclined planes, curved surfaces, etc., of neighboring objects. It is therefore not necessary to give directions and diagrams for plotting such shadows. Knowing the principles of casting the shadow of the pyramid onto the horizontal and the vertical planes, one can draw, with sufficient accuracy, shadows on inclined and curved surfaces, as they appear to him.

35. Demonstration With the Pyramid at an Angle. Using the same lighting as before and keeping the same position from which to view the model, turn the pyramid around so that one corner of the base is nearest the observer, as in Fig. 20. Now two faces are visible. The left one is in full light and

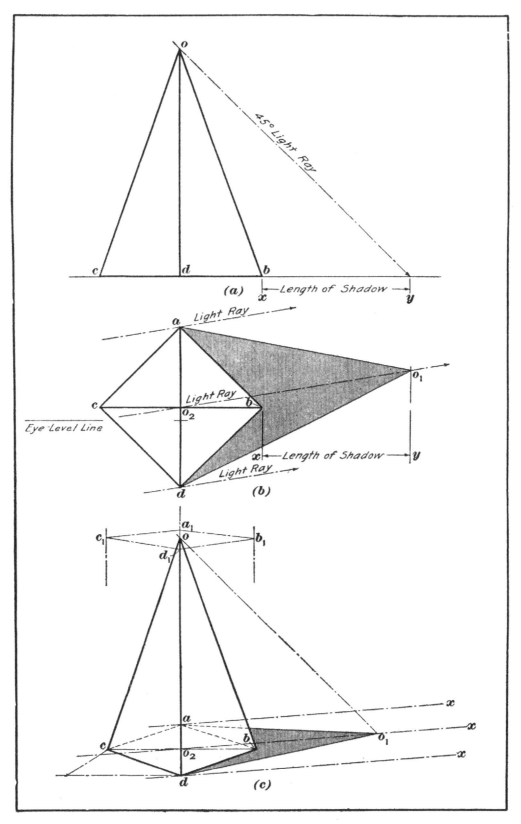

Fig. 21

LIGHT AND SHADE

quite bright because it reflects the light rays directly to the eye, and the right is one in shade because it is turned away from the source of light. There is thus high light and shade only; there is no half shade. The shade side and the shadow vary in depth of tone, as before explained. It should be observed that the shade sides of objects are deepest in tone value at the near edge, thus contrasting with the light side, and gradually appear less dark as they recede from the eye.

36. The plotting of the shadow for the pyramid seen at an angle contains no new principle, the same method being employed as was used in the case of previous models. The diagram showing this method is given in Fig. 21 (*a*), (*b*), and (*c*), and needs no description. Care must always be taken to run the horizontal light ray, upon which the shadow of the apex is to be located, through the central point *o* of the base, found by means of diagonals, for the apex is always directly above this central point of the base. The shadow of the cornerwise pyramid can be plotted also on vertical and inclined planes, and on curved surfaces, as previously explained.

THE HEXAGONAL PRISM

37. Demonstration With the Prism Vertical.—The hexagonal prism standing on end, should now be viewed with one flat face toward the observer, as shown in Fig. 22. Three sides and the top are visible. This is an excellent example of high light, half shade, and shade, all on the same object. The top, that is, the upper end, is the high light because it is turned toward the source of light and reflects the light rays to the eye. The left visible side is well lighted but not so brilliant as the top, and may be considered as half light. The front face is obliquely lighted and is the half shade. The right visible side is turned away from the source of light, and is in shade; this shade and the shadow vary in evenness of tone value, as before described.

These graded values, distinctly marked by the edges of the prism faces and showing high light, half light, half shade

LIGHT AND SHADE

and shade, will serve as an introduction to the more subtle gradations of high light, half light, half shade, and shade to be observed later on the curved surfaces of the cylinder, cone, sphere, hemisphere, and vase.

38. Just as the foreshortening of the hexagonal prism is done on the principles used in the foreshortening of the cube full face and the cube at an angle, so the shadow of the hexagonal prism is plotted by using a combination of the methods used for the plotting of shadows cast by the full-face

Fig. 22

cube and those cast by the cube at an angle. Fig. 23 (a) shows the 45° light rays locating the extent of the length of the shadow; view (b) shows the actual shape, $a\,a_1\,b_1\,c_1\,d_1\,d\,c\,b$, of the shadow when seen from above, in which it is observed that horizontal edges cast shadow edges parallel to themselves; as $a_1\,b_1$ parallel to $a\,b$; $b_1\,c_1$ parallel to $b\,c$; and $c_1\,d_1$ parallel to $c\,d$. View (c) shows the practical method of foreshortening the shadow directly, without plan and elevation drawings.

The method of plotting the shadow of the prism on a vertical plane and also on inclined planes and curved surfaces is the same as has been described for the plotting of shadows of the cube and the pyramid on similar surfaces.

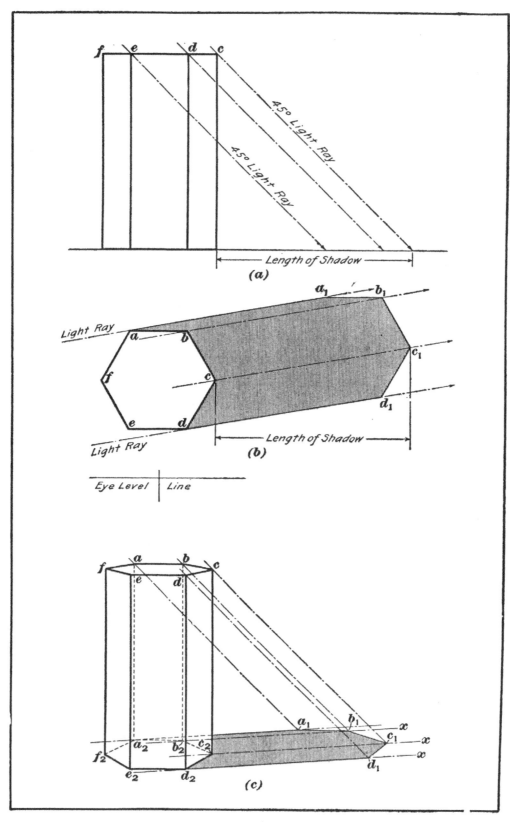

Fig. 23

LIGHT AND SHADE

39. Demonstration With the Prism on Its Side. The light-and-shade effects of the prism lying on one side can be observed by placing the model in such a position, so that one end, foreshortened, and three long faces, very much foreshortened, are seen. The long face at the top and the one on the left adjacent to it, although not seen by the observer, will receive the brightest light; the right upper and the left lower faces will be in half shade and the right lower face will be in shade. This is shown in the case of the horizontal prism in Fig. 5.

The shadow will be simple in shape; therefore, no diagram for plotting need be given. It will appear similar in shape to the shadow of the cube at an angle, with the lower right-hand corner of the shadow cut off. A demonstration with the prism in this position should be made.

THE CYLINDER

40. When the cylinder is standing on end, as shown in Fig. 24, the circular top is lighted about the same as the tops of

Fig. 24

the cube and hexagonal prism. But the lighting on the rest of the surface of the cylinder is quite different from any heretofore observed. So far only flat planes of light have been shown,

LIGHT AND SHADE

each with a definite extent and sharp limiting edges. The curving surface of the cylinder, however, shows light and shade values blending into each other.

The high light is a vertical band of light a short distance in from the left-hand contour of the cylinder. The position of the high light is determined by the angle at which the rays of light strike the cylinder and are reflected to the eye; only a few planes of rays are thus reflected. This was fully shown in Fig. 8, and explained in the accompanying text, to which the student should again refer. This high light would be extremely brilliant if the surface of the cylinder were made of some polished metal, or even if this wooden cylinder were painted white and varnished, or were enameled with white enamel paint. This can be demonstrated by using any cylindrical tin, nickel, or silver object, such as a tin can, some cylindrical kitchen utensil, or the nickel-plated container in which sticks of shaving soap are put up.

41. The high light on the wooden cylinder shows a gentle gradation into a half light or half shade at the left contour of the cylinder, and a similar gentle gradation toward the right. As the high light diminishes as it goes toward the right, the half light comes about opposite the eye of the observer, that is, on the nearest part of the cylinder, the half shade is a little to the right of that, and between the half shade and the extreme right-hand contour of the cylinder is the shade. On a polished cylinder, however, the shade does not extend up to the extreme right-hand edge, for along this edge there is a narrow band of light. This is caused by reflected light rays and other causes it is not necessary to specify here. This band of half light bordering on the shade at the extreme edge of the cylinder may not be so observable in Fig. 24, but on a polished cylinder it is always visible, and must be looked for and portrayed when a polished cylindrical object is being delineated.

The shadow, as before, is darker in tone value than the shade on the object, unless strongly affected by reflected light and it is darkest near the base of the cylinder.

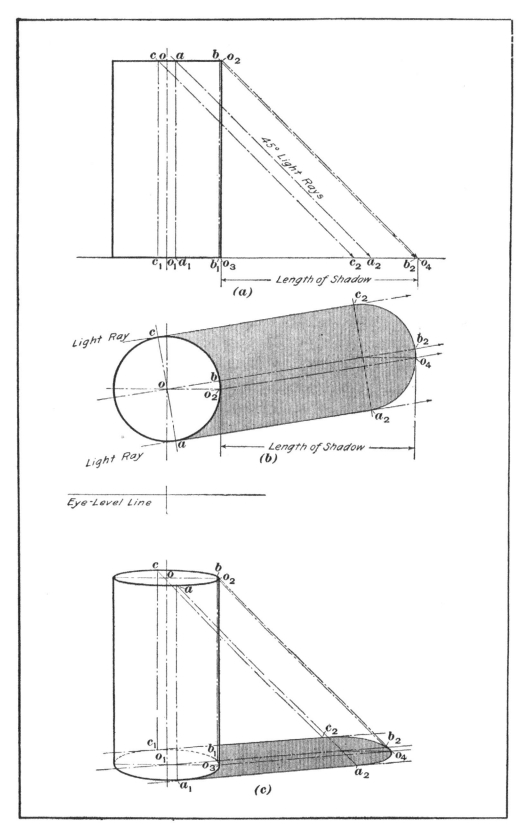

Fig. 25

LIGHT AND SHADE

42. As seen in Fig. 25 (a), (b), and (c), the principles of plotting the shadow of the cylinder are the same as used for plotting the shadows of the other models, but care must be taken to pass the 45° light rays through the proper points and the horizontal light rays through the corresponding points directly underneath them. View (b) shows that the slight angle at which the horizontal light rays strike the cylinder makes them tangent thereto, that is, makes them touch the cylinder, at points a and c; the lines showing the light rays must be drawn through those points.

Point o_2 in all views is the greatest extension of the right side contour of the cylinder, and in (c) point b_1 is the point where the horizontal light ray through center o_1 cuts the circumference. Lines for the horizontal light rays must be drawn through these points. In view (a), these points c, a, b, and o_2 are shown at their relative positions when viewed from the front and the 45° light rays are then drawn through these points to cut the corresponding horizontal light rays, thus locating points c_2, a_2, b_2, and o_4. When these points, in views (b) and (c) are connected by curves, and the straight lines $c_2 c_1$ and $a_2 a_1$ are drawn, the contour of the shadow is completed as shown. Part of the shadow will of course be hidden by the body of the cylinder, as shown in (c).

Frequently the cylinder is shown lying on its side, making an angle with the eye of the observer. The principles under which such a foreshortened view of the horizontal cylinder is drawn have already been presented in an earlier Section. The shadow projected by the cylinder in this position is plotted in the usual way, by passing 45° light rays through established points on each end of the cylinder so as to cut the horizontal light rays at the proper points, these points then being connected so as to make the contour of the shadow. This shadow contour, as well as the light and shade values, in one position, is shown in the case of the horizontal cylinder in the group in Fig. 5. Experiments and demonstrations with the wooden model of the cylinder will reveal other shadow formations, not only on a horizontal surface, but also on vertical surfaces, inclined surfaces, curved surfaces, etc.

I L T 159B—13

LIGHT AND SHADE

THE CONE

43. The study of the cone, Fig. 26, will show that the same effects of high light, half light, half shade, and shade will appear on the cone as were observed on the cylinder. As the surface of the cone is not vertical, but converges upwards toward the apex, the high light, half shade, shade, etc., will appear not as parallel bands, but as very pointed triangles. There will also be a tendency for the cone to be somewhat

FIG. 26

brighter toward the apex than at the base, depending, of course, on the exact angles of the rays of light.

The plotting of the shadow of the cone is a simple matter, as can be seen from Fig. 27 (*a*), (*b*), and (*c*). The apex casts its shadow at 45° onto the horizontal ray $o_2\, x$, view (*c*), running through the center of the base, thus establishing point o_1. Through point o_1 are then drawn lines tangent to the foreshortened base of the cone at *a* and *b*, thus forming the shadow $a\, o_1\, b$, part of which is hidden by the body of the cone.

The shadow of the cone on vertical and inclined planes and on curved surfaces is plotted as was the shadow of the pyramid on similar surfaces.

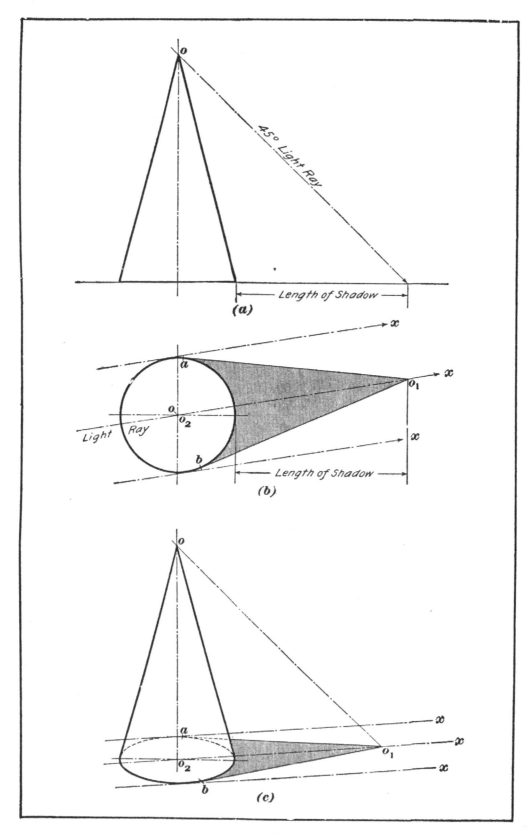

Fig. 27

LIGHT AND SHADE

THE SPHERE

44. Demonstration With the Sphere.—Any one who has carefully made all the demonstrations with the various models so far described, and has observed the effects of light, shade, and shadow that occur in the case of objects that have flat sides and sides curved in one direction, will have no difficulty in the study of the sphere. The appearance of this model conventionally lighted is shown in Fig. 28. A small piece of wax or soap placed beneath the sphere will keep it steady while it is being studied.

Fig. 28

The lights, shades, and shadow of the sphere in conventional lighting should be studied long and carefully, for this spherical shape is the underlying base of many objects that will be drawn later.

45. As the surface of the sphere is continually curving convexly in all directions, there are no planes and therefore no abrupt divisions of light and shade because the rays of light falling on this curved surface are reflected at all possible angles from this surface. As previously described, only a few light rays strike the curved surface of the sphere in such a way as to make a really bright spot of high light on the upper left-hand section of the visible surface of the sphere. From this spot of high light the values gradually deepen to half light, then to half shade, and finally to shade on the lower right-hand section of the sphere. The sphere rests, theoretically, on a point and therefore the half shade and the shade are observed not only on the right side of the sphere but also partly on the under side. The shadow cast by the sphere falls not only to the right, but actually under the sphere.

LIGHT AND SHADE

46. It has already been shown that, to draw the sphere, one need make no attempt to foreshorten it but should simply draw a circle, depending on the rendering later to portray the effect of roundness and solidity. Likewise, in drawing the shadow of the sphere one need not plot the shadow according to definite principles, but need simply draw it as he sees it when cast by the actual model, and as illustrated in Fig. 28.

47. When necessary, however, the shadow cast by a sphere may be plotted graphically in the same manner as shown in the constructive diagrams, Fig. 29. The sphere may be considered as a large transparent ball upon which a series of opaque black rings may be painted. These rings may be represented in the elevation (a) as straight lines $a\,b$, $c\,d$, $e\,f$, $g\,h$, and $i\,j$; and in the foreshortened view (c) as ellipses. The 45° light ray that passes through the point b, in view (a), strikes the horizontal supporting surface at b_1; another 45° light ray passes through point a and strikes the horizontal supporting surface at a_1, thus forming the extent, or length, of the shadow of the painted ring $a\,b$ in view (a). This is clearly shown in view (c), where the projected shadow of ring $a\,b$ is shown by ellipse $a_1\,b_1$. The shadow is of course centered on the central horizontal light ray $x\,x_4$. In a similar manner the shadows of the other painted rings are projected; ring $c\,d$, view (c), gives shadow $c_1\,d_1$; ring $e\,f$ gives shadow $e_1\,f_1$; ring $g\,h$ gives shadow $g_1\,h_1$; and ring $i\,j$ gives shadow $i_1\,j_1$. The actual shapes and positions of these shadows when seen in plan, are shown in view (b), where the five overlapping circles are shown, but to prevent confusion are not lettered.

48. It is understood, of course, that the depth of these shadows, the lengths of which have already been obtained, are influenced by the positions of their appropriate horizontal light rays. View (b) shows that the depth of the largest ring $e\,f$, view (a), is determined by the parallel light rays passing through e_2 and f_2, namely light rays $x\,x_1$ and $x\,x_7$, thus giving the actual depth of the shadow in plan as $e_3\,f_3$, view (b); and its actual depth foreshortened as $e_3\,f_3$ in view (c). In a

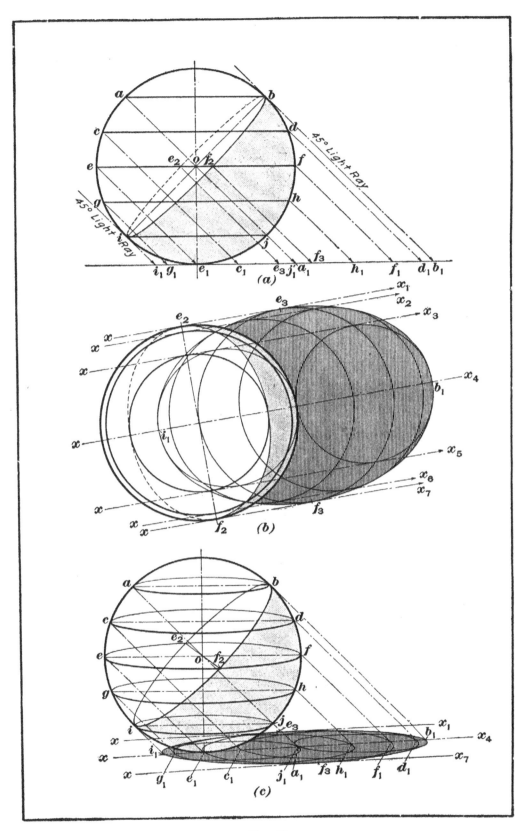

Fig. 29

LIGHT AND SHADE

similar way the depths of the shadows of the other rings are obtained.

There are now formed five circular shadows placed as shown in (b) of Fig. 29, and five elliptic shadows as shown at (c) of Fig. 29. As shown, these shadows will overlap, and it therefore simply remains to enclose them all in one large elliptic shape [foreshortened in (c) of Fig. 29], i_1, e_3, b_1, f_3, and to shade it in as shown, which will represent the shadow of the sphere. As before, a portion of this shadow will be hidden by the body of the sphere itself.

49. Simple Method of Plotting Shadow of a Sphere. While the principles of plotting the shadow of a sphere should be understood, the following working plan may be used: As the light rays fall parallel and at 45°, the points of tangency made by them on the sphere form what may be termed the *great circle*, which is shown as the oblique ellipse $i\,e_2\,b\,f_2$, view (c). This circle is inclined at a 45° angle with the ground because it is at right angles to the 45° light rays falling on the sphere. The upper end b of the great circle casts shadow point b_1 and the lower end i casts shadow point i_1, thus determining the length of the shadow. The depth of the shadow is determined, as before, by the limits of the parallel horizontal light rays. The large ellipse to portray the shadow may then be sketched in freehand without further difficulty.

When sketching direct from the sphere, these diagrams need not be employed literally, but they should be kept in mind while working. The working plan should be to draw two 45° tangent lines, the right-hand one touching the upper right-hand curve of the sphere's contour, and the left-hand one touching the lower left-hand curve of the sphere's contour, thus locating on the horizontal supporting surface the extreme right end and the extreme left end, respectively, of the shadow. The depth of the shadow may be judged by eye measurement and then the shadow be drawn freehand as an ellipse.

50. When the shadow of the sphere falls upon a vertical plane, the horizontal light rays used as guides for the depth of the shadow cast horizontally are deflected upwards along

LIGHT AND SHADE

the vertical surface and thus become vertical lines. These vertical lines are then cut by the 45° light rays passing through certain selected points on the inclined great circle, thus determining points to contour the foreshortened curve of the shadow. The same principle is used for the casting of the sphere's shadow upon inclined planes and curved surfaces, but in these cases the directions of the ascending lines of light rays must be plotted as they appear.

Fig. 30

THE HEMISPHERE

51. The model of the hemisphere should be so arranged that the flat portion is up, and is perfectly horizontal. This can be accomplished by sticking a small piece of wax, or soap, onto the rounded portion of the hemisphere upon which it rests, and then pressing the hemisphere down until it touches the table or other object upon which it rests, keeping the flat part absolutely level and horizontal, as is shown in Fig. 30.

The circular flat portion of the hemisphere will be lighted exactly as was the circular top of the cylinder; and the curved surface of the hemisphere will be lighted about like the lower half of the sphere.

The plotting of the shadow is also a simple matter for one who has plotted

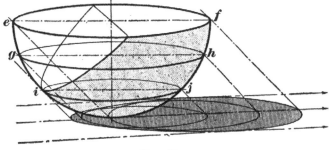

Fig. 31

the shadow of the sphere. As shown in Fig. 31, it is only necessary to cast, on the supporting surface, the overlapping shadows of ellipses ef, gh, and ij. These elliptic shadows are then extended and rounded off so as to make one large ovate

LIGHT AND SHADE

ellipse, or oval, which is the shadow of the hemisphere. In other respects the casting of the shadow of the hemisphere onto horizontal, vertical, and inclined surfaces, and onto curved surfaces, is done as in the case of the shadow of the sphere.

THE VASE

52. Although the vase is apparently very simple in its curves and contours, yet a study of it when placed in conventional lighting, as in Fig. 32, will reveal combinations of effects seen singly on the cylinder and the sphere, as well as many other points about light, shade, and shadow that will be of great interest.

The top of the vase is in a sort of very bright half shade, just as were the tops of the cylinder and the hemisphere.

Fig. 32

The brightest part, the high light, is about midway between the top and bottom of the vase and near the left contour. The widest part of the vase is in reality spherical and the high light falls as it does onto the sphere. Blending with this high light is the one on the neck, which is similar to the high light on a cylinder. The half lights, half shades, lines of reflected light at the right contour, etc. are located as has been described already for the sphere and the cylinder. A

LIGHT AND SHADE

careful study of the model will reveal many other details, to which it is not necessary to call attention at this time.

53. As in the case of the sphere, it will not usually be necessary to plot accurately the shadow cast by the vase. An accurate plot, however, may be made when required by casting the shadows of circles, or disks, centered on the central horizontal light ray, and then combining and overlapping these shadows so as to make a complete shadow, as shown

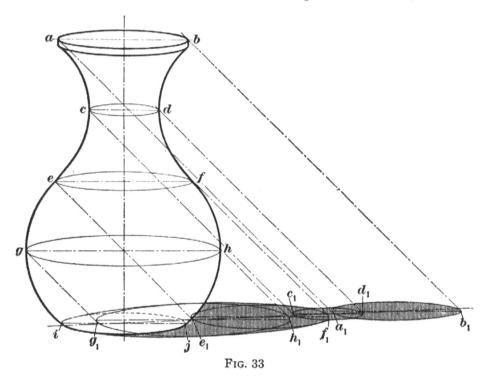

Fig. 33

in Fig. 33. First the shadow of the top $a\,b$ should be cast upon its appropriate horizontal light rays, when it will appear as the elliptic shadow $a_1\,b_1$. Next, the shadow of the narrowest part of the neck $c\,d$ should be cast; this will appear as the small elliptic shadow $c_1\,d_1$. The casting of the shadows of circles representing the spherical portion of the vase $e\,f$, $g\,h$, and $i\,j$ is simply a duplication of what has been done in the case of the sphere; these make shadow $i\,f_1$. These separate elliptic shadows are then combined by softening off and joining the curves, thus making the complete shadow as shown.

The principles of plotting shadows of cylindrical and spherical objects onto various planes have already been explained.

LIGHT AND SHADE

MATERIALS AND METHODS OF WORK

PRELIMINARY PRACTICE

54. Portraying Tone Values.—In the portraying of tone values, broad tints and tones are placed upon the paper by means of charcoal, which is used because with it the effects of even and graded tone values are secured with the least amount of trouble. Better tone values may sometimes be obtained by means of pigment and a brush, but skill in their use is more difficult to acquire. In all cases, however, an outline drawing of the model must be prepared in order that the parts of the object that are to be represented in light, shade, and shadow will be properly contoured. In this way, the matter of portraying these values is greatly simplified.

There should be remaining, from the work on the preceding Section, a supply of materials sufficient not only for the work of this Section, but for some of the work in subsequent Sections. However, should the supply of any necessary material run short at any time, a new supply should be purchased at once.

55. Practice Strokes.—Fasten a $19'' \times 12\frac{1}{2}''$ sheet of charcoal paper to the drawing board, placing under it several sheets of newspaper, a large blotter, or even a piece of heavy cloth, so that a softer and more resilient surface will be secured. With a stick of charcoal, that has not been sharpened to a point but is in its natural form, practice making strokes in the same manner the stroke practice work was done in the preceding Section. With a full-arm movement, holding the charcoal between the thumb and the first two fingers with palm of hand turned sidewise or downwards, as previously described, draw oblique and curved strokes from the upper right-hand corner to lower left-hand. Draw these strokes lightly at first and then gradually increase the pressure so

LIGHT AND SHADE

that heavier and heavier lines result, until finally broad black lines are drawn. At first, white spaces may be left between the lines but, as the pressure on the lines is increased, the broad black lines may be brought close together and, as their edges blend into each other, a flat tone will be formed.

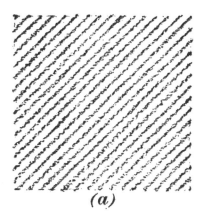
(a)

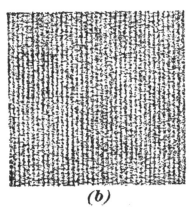
(b)

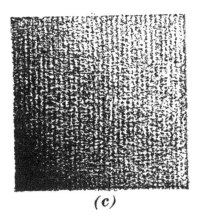
(c)

FIG. 34

56. Practice in Flat and Graded Tones.—For practice, draw a square about 2 inches on each side, and render the surface, by means of parallel oblique lines, in even monotone, as shown in Fig. 34 (a). Being able to secure a uniform shade in this manner, attempt spacing the lines more closely so as to produce an even tint without apparent lines except those formed by the tooth of the paper, as shown in (b). By using more pressure and a greater number of lines on one side, the tint can be graded until an effect similar to that shown in (c) is obtained. When doing this, the whole square is shaded over in the lightest tone first, and then the darkest tone is applied in the lower left-hand corner. The dark tone is then extended, gradually lessening the pressure with which it is executed, until it blends softly into the lighter tone without any line of demarcation. Generally speaking, but three degrees of shading are made use of in the drawing—the deepest shade, half shade, and white. These are then blended one into the other where necessary, in order to produce intermediate gradations.

LIGHT AND SHADE

57. Oftentimes shadows stand out very prominently and in sharp contrast with a very light surface. Other times they will blend into a dark shade so that their edges can hardly be discerned. Owing to the influences of reflected light, shadows sometimes start in a very dark tone and gradually become paler until they softly blend into the lightest tone of the drawing. It is necessary to be prepared to portray any of these conditions; therefore, such practice as the blending of dark into light, as shown in (*c*), is of the greatest importance.

RENDERING FROM THE MODEL

58. Preliminary Observation of Models.—When making a charcoal drawing of an object, for instance the cube seen at an angle, the first thing to do is to view the object through half-closed eyes in order to eliminate details and to see, in their proper proportions and values, the masses of light and dark values. By viewing it in this manner, the object will appear as in a hazy or blurred photograph. The most prominent value observable in the present case will be the dark value or mass composing the shaded side of the cube and shadow, which blend together without any sharp line of distinction. Next, will be seen the half shade of the left visible side of the cube; and, third, the light value of the top of the cube. This demonstration must be made as this text is read so that the proper method of observation may be practiced.

59. Stages of Rendering.—The rendering of the contours, and light, shade, and shadow values of the object, is done in four steps, or stages. In the first stage, shown in Fig. 35, the outlines of the object and the table line are lightly blocked in, to govern the placing of the tone values.

The second stage, shown in Fig. 36, is the placing, roughly, of the three main values, as seen with half-closed eyes. In this case, by means of bold broad strokes, quite a dark value should be filled in, to represent the shaded side of the cube and the shadow of the cube; next a lighter value should be

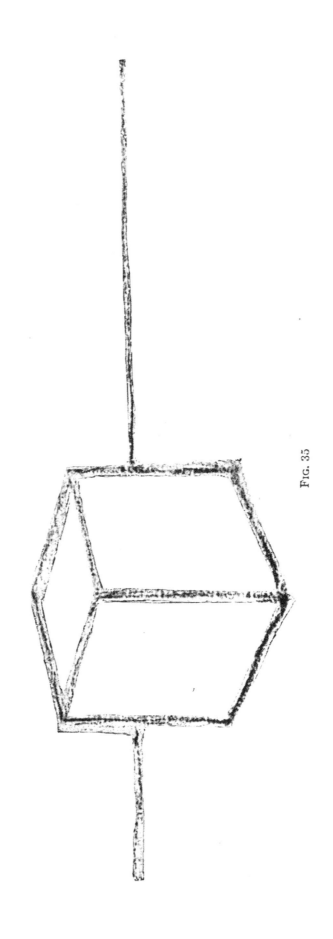

Fig. 35

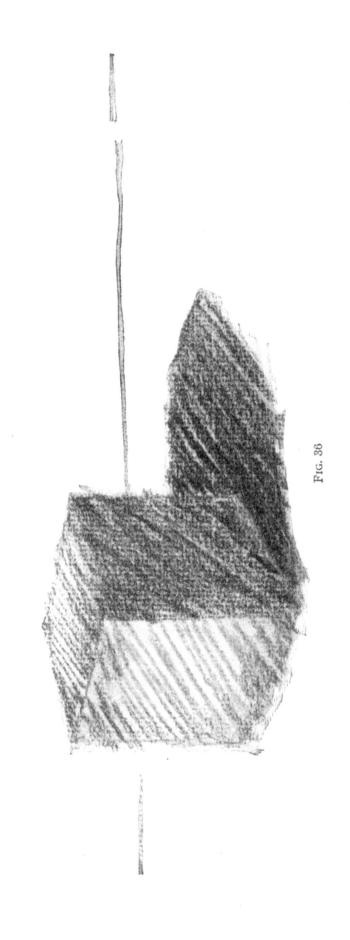

Fig. 36

FIG. 37

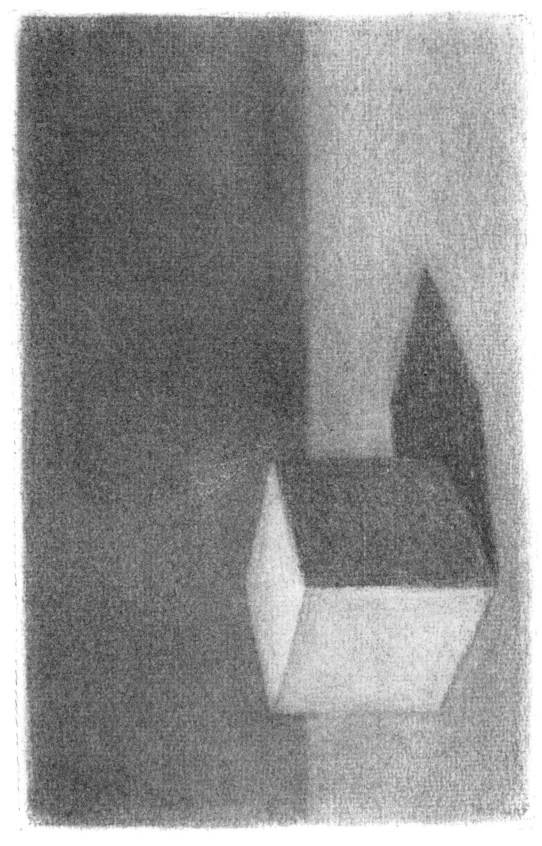

Fig. 38

LIGHT AND SHADE

placed for the left visible side of the cube; and, third, a still lighter value should be laid for the top of the cube. No attempt should be made to show sharp dividing edges; the strokes forming one value will overlap those forming another value, and should be left so. No attempt should be made to put in background or foreground. The only work should be that done with the strokes of the charcoal, and should not be touched by the fingers or anything else. The whole operation should take only a few minutes, but should be done with great care.

60. For the third stage the foreground and background values should be put in by strokes only, and the various values and their limits should then be worked up more clearly, as shown in Fig. 37, all work being done by strokes and hatchings drawn directly with the charcoal, untouched and unrubbed by finger or other means.

For the fourth and last stage, as shown in Fig. 38, the evidence of individual strokes or hatchings should be eliminated by lightly rubbing the charcoal with the tip of the finger or with one of the paper stomps. Great care is needed that the rubbing is not too hard or vigorous. The finger or stomp should be passed lightly over the charcoal in a circular motion, which will spread the particles over the paper, touching only the raised lines or dots in the paper; as the sunken spots between the dots remain white, because untouched by the charcoal, they give transparency to the tone. If the charcoal is rubbed hard, it will fill up the sunken portions, thus making a muddy black smudge. After this general softening off has been done, some of the darker values may be given more definite limits, lines of shadow may be put in (such as the dark lines showing where the cube rests upon the table); and other finishing touches may be added with a stick of charcoal sharpened to a chisel edge. Further, there will very likely be planes of light values that have been overlapped by the strokes forming the darker values, which can be evened up by means of the kneaded rubber worked to a chisel edge or to a point. The kneaded rubber can lift off the charcoal, not only for

FIG. 39

LIGHT AND SHADE

this purpose but also to take out the dark values to form high lights where needed. A little practice with the kneaded rubber will enable any one to regulate the half lights and high lights by softening off or actually removing the charcoal where desired.

61. Specimen Rendering in Charcoal.—The general description just given for handling the medium will cover its use in the case of any kind of charcoal drawing. In Fig. 39 is shown a charcoal drawing of the group of models, conventionally lighted, in order to illustrate the methods employed in the case of curved surfaces, blending of shaded values, various kinds of high lights and half lights, etc. When making this drawing, the outside contour of the group of objects was first blocked in, then the individual models were lightly drawn at their proper places. The darkest values (shades and shadows), the half shades, and the lights, were then observed through half-closed eyes as before, and placed upon the paper in their proper positions with quick broad strokes of the unsharpened charcoal stick. The four stages of making a charcoal drawing were then passed through.

In the touching-up work it was necessary to use the kneaded rubber to get the proper gradations of light to dark on the cone, the vase, the sphere, the cylinder, and the hemisphere. These differences in tone values were partly secured by the stroke work, but the smooth blending was accomplished by lightly rubbing with the fingers and then lifting off charcoal, where desired, with the kneaded rubber. On the top of the vase, the upper left-hand contour of the cone, the upper left-hand part of the vase, the pyramid, the cylinder, the sphere, and the hemisphere, the brilliant lights were secured by lifting off practically all the charcoal with the kneaded rubber. The reproduction in Fig. 39 is considerably smaller than the original drawing, as can be seen by the reduced scale of the texture of the charcoal paper.

LIGHT AND SHADE

DRAWING EXERCISES

GENERAL INFORMATION

62. In this Section the drawing plates, as before, will consist of drawings made direct from the wooden models themselves, *not* from any text illustrations. These drawing plates are to be prepared so that each plate is first made as an *outline* charcoal drawing of the objects specified, the model itself to be shown properly blocked in and foreshortened, and the contour of the shadow also laid out according to the definite rules of shadow plotting. Then the blocking in, foreshortening, and shadow projection lines will be lightly erased, and the objects and their shadows *rendered* in tone values by means of charcoal, and sprayed with fixatif to prevent the charcoal from brushing off.

The finished rendering must look like a pictorial photographic portrayal of the model (in black, gray, and white, of course), and therefore a foreground and a background should also be included in the rendering. Suggestions for arranging these backgrounds may be had by looking at the backgrounds of Figs. 14, 15, 17, 20, 22, etc. The horizontal surface of the table on which the model rests may be the lighter portion of the background, and the vertical background, the upper part of the study, may be the darker portion, although this arrangement may be varied to suit conditions of light and shade on the model.

63. Each subordinate rectangle on the plates, except in the case of Plate 7–8, is $9\frac{1}{2}$ inches wide by $6\frac{1}{4}$ inches high. To portray the background properly, it should extend to about $\frac{1}{2}$ inch from the edge of the rectangle, thus making the space in each rectangle covered by the background about $8\frac{1}{2}$ inches wide, by $5\frac{1}{4}$ inches high. In this way there will be a generous

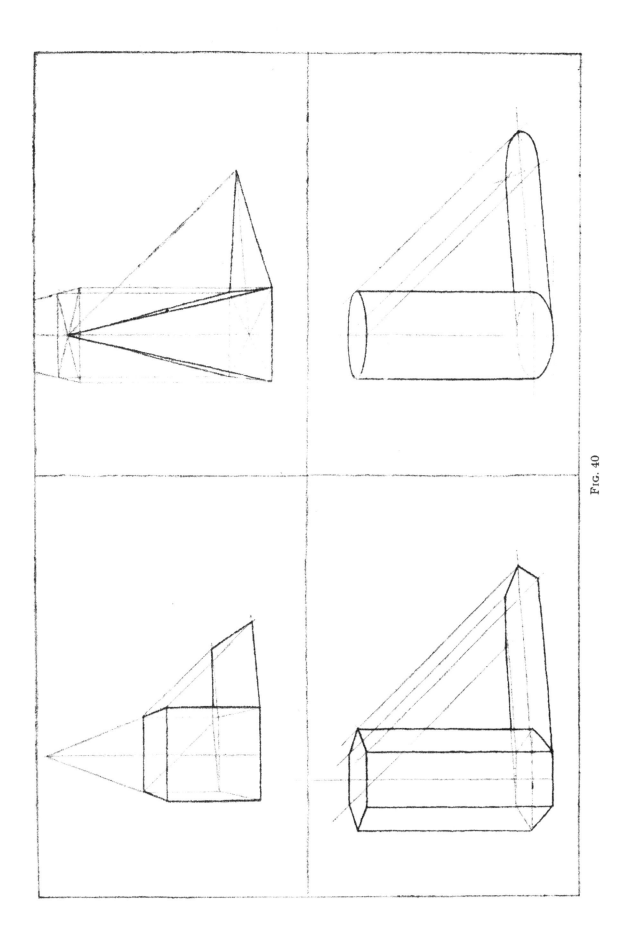

Fig. 40

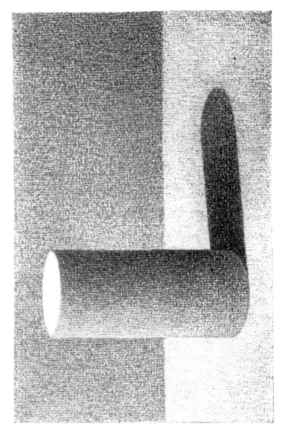
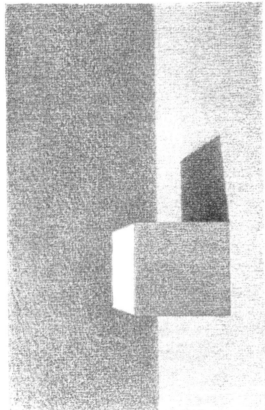

Fig. 41

LIGHT AND SHADE

white margin all around each rendering, separating it from its neighbor. Fig. 40 illustrates, on a much reduced scale, how the first sketch for Plate 1-2 is to be laid out in outline, with the shadow contours accurately plotted. Fig. 41 illustrates, also on reduced scale, how the rendering done over the outline work will appear, being composed of fully rendered studies of the same models that were first blocked in in outline. The other plates are to be prepared according to the same plan; different models, however, are to be used.

Each exercise of the four on each plate should be completed in every respect, sprayed with fixatif, and allowed to dry, before the next exercise on that plate is begun. When working on any exercise, the other three rectangles on the plate should be covered with a sheet of paper. These plates should be sent in to the Schools for examination one at a time as were the plates drawn heretofore.

Starting with the Section on *Light and Shade* the plates will bear double numbers instead of single numbers as in the two preceding Sections. Instead of being known as Plate 1, Plate 2, Plate 3, etc., as heretofore, the plates from now on will be marked Plate 1-2, Plate 3-4, Plate 5-6, etc. This change is made to designate that each plate is practically two stages or processes—an outline drawing and a rendered drawing. The student need simply letter the title of the plate, in each case, exactly as designated in the directions given below.

PLATE 1-2

64. Exercise A, Plate 1-2.—Exercise A is to occupy the upper left-hand $9\frac{1}{2}'' \times 6\frac{1}{4} \times$ rectangle. To do this exercise, make an outline drawing direct from the wooden model of the full-face cube, making the front face 2 inches square, properly blocked in and foreshortened. Place it slightly to left of center line so that the shadow can be properly accommodated within the rectangle, plot in the contour of the cast shadow accurately, in outline only, according to rules for such plotting given in this Section. Then the exercise should be rendered fully in charcoal, the proper margin of

LIGHT AND SHADE

white paper being left around the rendered exercise, and the rendering sprayed with fixatif. The method of working shown in Figs. 35 to 38 should be employed, the finished Exercise being as in Fig. 41. No outlines should appear around the objects when the renderings are completed. Only charcoal *tone values* should portray the modeling.

65. Exercise B, Plate 1-2.—Exercise B is to occupy the upper right-hand $9\frac{1}{2}'' \times 6\frac{1}{4}''$ rectangle. To do this exercise, make an outline drawing direct from the wooden model of the full-face pyramid, making the nearest base line 2 inches in length and the other parts in proportion. Place it in the rectangle so as to accommodate the shadow, and properly plot in the cast shadow. Render the study in charcoal tones, as described for Exercise A, and shown in Fig. 41.

66. Exercise C, Plate 1-2.—Exercise C is to occupy the lower left-hand $9\frac{1}{2}'' \times 6\frac{1}{4}''$ rectangle. To do this exercise, make an outline drawing direct from the wooden model of the full-face hexagonal prism standing erect, making the front face 4 inches high and the other parts in proportion. Place it in the rectangle far enough to the left to properly accommodate the shadow cast toward the right. Plot in the shadow accurately. Render the study in charcoal tones, as described for Exercise A, and shown in Fig. 41.

67. Exercise D, Plate 1-2.—Exercise D is to occupy the lower right-hand $9\frac{1}{2}'' \times 6\frac{1}{4}''$ rectangle. To do this exercise, make an outline drawing direct from the wooden model of the cylinder standing erect, making the front height 4 inches and other parts in proportion. Place it in the rectangle far enough to the left to properly accommodate the shadow cast toward the right. Plot in the shadow accurately. Render the study in charcoal tones, as described for Exercise A, and shown in Fig. 41.

68. Final Work on Plate 1-2.—When all renderings are completed and are sprayed with fixatif and allowed to dry, the title, Plate 1-2: Light and Shade, should be lettered or written at the top of the sheet, and the name, class letters

LIGHT AND SHADE

and number, address and date placed on the back of the sheet. The plate, protected on its face by a thin sheet of tissue paper, should then be placed in a mailing tube and sent to the Schools for examination.

PLATE 3-4

69. Exercise A, Plate 3-4.—Exercise A is to occupy the upper left-hand $9\frac{1}{2}'' \times 6\frac{1}{4}''$ rectangle. To do this exercise, make an outline drawing direct from the wooden model of the cone, with longer axis of ellipse for the base 2 inches and other parts in proportion. Place it in the rectangle so as to accommodate the shadow. Properly plot in the shadow. Then the exercise should be rendered fully in charcoal, the proper margin of white paper being left around the exercise, and the rendering sprayed with fixatif. The method of working shown in Figs. 35 to 38 should be employed. No outlines should appear around the objects when the renderings are completed. Only charcoal tone values should portray the modeling.

70. Exercise B, Plate 3-4.—Exercise B is to occupy the upper right-hand $9\frac{1}{2}'' \times 6\frac{1}{4}''$ rectangle. To do this exercise, make an outline drawing direct from the wooden model of the sphere, making the diameter 2 inches. Keep the model in a stable position by a small piece of wax or soap as previously described. Place it in the rectangle so as to accommodate the shadow, and plot this shadow accurately. Render the study in charcoal tones, as described for Exercise A.

71. Exercise C, Plate 3-4. Exercise C is to occupy the lower left-hand $9\frac{1}{2}'' \times 6\frac{1}{4}''$ rectangle. To do this exercise, make an outline drawing direct from the wooden model of the hemisphere, resting on the curved portion with the flat portion upwards. Make the flat portion 2 inches in diameter and perfectly horizontal. Place the drawing in the rectangle so as to accommodate the shadow, and plot this shadow accurately. Render the study in charcoal tones as described for Exercise A.

LIGHT AND SHADE

72. Exercise D, Plate 3-4.—Exercise D is to occupy the lower right-hand $9\frac{1}{2}'' \times 6\frac{1}{4}''$ rectangle. To do this exercise, make an outline drawing direct from the wooden model of the vase, with its front height 3 inches and other parts in proportion. Place it in the rectangle so as to accommodate shadow, and plot this shadow accurately. Render the study in charcoal tones as described for Exercise A.

73. Final Work on Plate 3-4.—When all renderings are completed and the drawings sprayed with fixatif and allowed to dry, the title, Plate 3-4: Light and Shade, should be lettered or written at the top of the sheet, and the name, class letters and number, address and date placed on the back of the sheet. The plate, protected by a thin sheet of tissue paper or thin waxed paper, should then be rolled and should be placed in a mailing tube, and sent to the Schools for examination. If all required redrawn and rerendered work on previous plates has been completed, work on Plate 5-6 may be begun.

PLATE 5-6

74. Arrangement of Vertical Plane for Plate 5-6. Each model on Plate 5-6 is to be represented as standing to the left of a vertical plane somewhat higher than the object, say about $4\frac{1}{2}$ inches or 5 inches high and about 5 inches or 6 inches long, as shown in Figs. 11 and 19. The intention is first to show the contour of the shadow, and later to show the model's shadow rendered in tone values, as cast upon this vertical plane in conventional lighting. The vertical plane should be arranged so that its lower edge extends backwards at a 45° angle with the plane of sight, and so that it is about $\frac{1}{2}$ inch from the nearest portion of the wooden model.

This vertical plane may be a flat brick wrapped tightly in white paper and standing on one long edge; or it may be the lid of a pasteboard box, the cover of a book, or any convenient light-colored object held in a vertical position by a weight. This vertical plane should be so arranged as to have its lower edge extending backwards toward the left at

LIGHT AND SHADE

about 45°, so that the shadow of the wooden model conventionally lighted will be cast partly onto the table and partly onto the vertical plane, and can be plainly seen while drawing.

75. Exercise A, Plate 5-6.—Exercise A is to occupy the upper left-hand $9\frac{1}{2}'' \times 6\frac{1}{4}''$ rectangle. To do this exercise, make an outline drawing, direct from the wooden model of the cube, seen at 45°, and the vertical plane. Make the drawing full size, as before, the cube having one corner edge toward the observer and being 2 inches high. Place the vertical plane to the right of the model, parallel to the rear right retreating face of the cube, and $\frac{1}{2}$ inch from it. Plot carefully, in outline, the contour of the shadow of the cube cast partly onto the table and partly onto the vertical plane. Then the exercise should be rendered fully in charcoal, the proper margin of white paper being left around the exercise, and the rendering sprayed with fixatif. The method of working shown in Figs. 35 and 38 should be employed. No outlines should appear around the objects when the renderings are completed. Only charcoal tone values should portray the modeling.

76. Exercise B, Plate 5-6.—Exercise B is to occupy the upper right-hand $9\frac{1}{2}'' \times 6\frac{1}{4}''$ rectangle. To do this exercise, make an outline drawing, direct from the wooden model of the pyramid, and the vertical plane, with a corner of the base toward the observer, and seen at 45°. Make the greatest diagonal of the base about $2\frac{3}{4}$ inches and the other parts in proportion. Place the vertical plane, as before, to the right of the model, parallel to the rear right retreating edge of the base of the pyramid, and $\frac{1}{2}$ inch from it. Plot carefully, in outline, the contour of the shadow of the pyramid cast partly onto the table and partly onto the vertical plane. Render the study in charcoal tones, as described for Exercise A.

77. Exercise C, Plate 5-6.—Exercise C is to occupy the lower left-hand $9\frac{1}{2}'' \times 6\frac{1}{4}''$ rectangle. To do this exercise, make an outline drawing, direct from the wooden model of the sphere, and the vertical plane, making the sphere 2 inches in diameter. Place the vertical plane, as before, to the right of the model

LIGHT AND SHADE

and about ½ inch from it. Plot carefully, in outline, the contour of the shadow of the sphere cast partly onto the table and partly onto the vertical plane. Render the study in charcoal tones, as described for Exercise A.

78. Exercise D, Plate 5–6.—Exercise D is to occupy the lower right hand $9\frac{1}{2}'' \times 6\frac{1}{4}''$ rectangle. To do this exercise, make an outline drawing, direct from the wooden model of the vase, and the vertical plane, making the vase 3 inches high and the other parts in proportion. Place the vertical plane, as before, to the right of the model and about ½ inch from it. Plot carefully, in outline, the contour of the shadow of the vase cast partly onto the table and partly onto the vertical plane. Render the study in charcoal tones, as described for Exercise A.

79. Final Work on Plate 5–6.—When all renderings are completed and the work sprayed with fixatif and allowed to dry, the title, Plate 5–6: Light and Shade, should be lettered or written at the top of the sheet, and the name, class letters and number, address and date placed on the back of the sheet. The plate, protected by a thin sheet of tissue paper, should then be rolled and should be placed in a mailing tube, and sent to the Schools for examination. If all required redrawn and rerendered work on previous plates has been completed, Plate 7–8 may be begun.

PLATE 7–8

80. Blocking in and Rendering for Plate 7–8.—Plate 7–8 contains but one exercise, which occupies the entire plate. To draw this exercise, arrange the eight wooden models in a group, placing the smaller ones in front and the larger ones in the rear, and have them conventionally lighted so that shadows will be cast toward the right and will be inclined slightly backwards, onto the table and onto neighboring models. The grouping of these models must be an original arrangement, and not a copy of any illustration in the text. The nearest models are to be drawn full size and those in the background in pro-

LIGHT AND SHADE

portion. Plot carefully, in outline, the contours of all shadows that are cast. Then the whole study should be rendered completely in charcoal to show all light, shade, and shadow effects. Proper generous margins of white paper should be allowed to remain. The rendering should then be sprayed with fixatif. The method of working shown in Figs. 35 to 38 should be employed. No outlines should appear around the objects when the renderings are completed. Only charcoal tone values should portray the modeling. There should be a white margin.

81. Final Work on Plate 7-8.—The title, Plate 7-8: Light and Shade, should be lettered or written at the top of the sheet, and the name, class letters and number, address and date placed on the back of the sheet. The plate, protected by a thin sheet of tissue paper, should then be rolled and placed in a mailing tube, and sent to the Schools for examination. If all required redrawn and rerendered work on previous plates has been completed, Plate 9-10 may be begun.

PLATE 9-10

82. Character of Exercises, Plate 9-10.—The exercises on Plate 9-10 are to consist of rendered drawings, properly foreshortened, of common household objects whose shapes are based on the cube, the cone, the sphere, and the hemisphere. Suitable objects would be a cigar box, a funnel, a spherical teapot, and a cup and saucer. These should be blocked in and foreshortened as were the wooden models for the preceding plates, and the contours of the shadows accurately plotted as before; after which they should be rendered.

The objects should be drawn about the same size and scale as the wooden models on whose shapes the forms of the objects are based, and should be arranged in their respective rectangles so that all shadows will fall within the limits of the rectangles.

83. Exercise A, Plate 9-10.—Exercise A is to occupy the upper left-hand $9\frac{1}{2}'' \times 6\frac{1}{4}''$ rectangle. To do this exercise, make an outline drawing, direct from the object itself, of a

LIGHT AND SHADE

cigar box or other box with the lid standing open, seen at a 45° angle, properly blocked in and foreshortened. Place it slightly to the left of the center line of the rectangle to accommodate the shadow. Plot in the contour of the shadow. Then the exercise should be rendered fully in charcoal, the proper margin of white paper being left around the rendered exercise, and the rendering sprayed with fixatif. The method of working shown in Figs. 35 to 38 should be employed. No outlines should appear around the objects when the renderings are completed. Only charcoal tone values should portray the modeling.

84. Exercise B, Plate 9–10.—Exercise B is to occupy the upper right-hand $9\frac{1}{2}'' \times 6\frac{1}{4}''$ rectangle. To do this exercise, make an outline drawing, direct from the object itself, of a funnel resting on its circular rim, spout pointed upwards, or of some other conical object, properly blocked in and foreshortened. Place it properly in the rectangle to accommodate the shadow. Plot in the contour of the shadow. Render the study in charcoal tones, as described for Exercise A.

85. Exercise C, Plate 9–10.—Exercise C is to occupy the lower left-hand $9\frac{1}{2}'' \times 6\frac{1}{4}''$ rectangle. To do this exercise, make an outline drawing, direct from the object itself, or of a small spherical teapot, properly blocked in and foreshortened. Place it properly in the rectangle to accommodate the shadow. Plot in the contour of the shadow. Render the study in charcoal tones, as described for Exercise A.

86. Exercise D, Plate 9–10.—Exercise D is to occupy the lower right-hand $9\frac{1}{2}'' \times 6\frac{1}{4}''$ rectangle. To do this exercise, make an outline drawing, direct from the object itself, of an ordinary hemispherical teacup resting in a saucer, properly blocked in and foreshortened. Place them properly in the rectangle so as to accommodate the shadows. Plot in the contours of the shadows. Render the study in charcoal tones, as described for Exercise A.

87. Final Work on Plate 9–10.—When all the renderings are completed and the drawings sprayed with fixatif

LIGHT AND SHADE

and allowed to dry, the title, Plate 9-10: Light and Shade, should be lettered or written at the top of the sheet, and the name, class letters and number, address and date placed on the back of the sheet. The plate, protected by a thin sheet of tissue paper, should then be rolled, placed in a mailing tube, and sent to the Schools for examination.

If any redrawn or rerendered work on any of the plates of this Section has been called for and has not yet been completed, it should be satisfactorily finished at this time. After all required work on the plates of this Section has been completed the work of the next Section should be taken up at once.

THE HUMAN FIGURE

PURPOSE

1. Fourth Stage in Learning to Draw.—The use of the human figure usually occupies a prominent part in the composition and drawing of pictorial and decorative work. But the human figure is extremely difficult to draw, being composed of so many subtle curves and contours, and such delicate gradations of light and shade in its modeling, that, before these can be drawn and rendered properly, training must be had in drawing more simple forms. For that reason training has been given in line drawing and eye measurement, in model drawing in outline, and in drawing from inanimate models to portray light, shade, and shadow, this preliminary training serving as a series of graded steps leading up to the drawing of the human figure. The next natural and logical step is to draw the human figure, which may be considered the fourth stage in learning to draw.

2. Proper Foundation for Figure Drawing.—Before one can draw the human figure he must be thoroughly familiar with the proportions, measurements, and contours of the human figure as a whole, and of each of its individual parts. To give such a familiarity is the purpose of this Section, which may be considered as a sort of reference book. The information given here must be thoroughly understood, and practice secured in actually sketching such proportions, before the practical work of drawing human figures in various postures and actions can be taken up. In the following Sections the training in figure drawing is extended to include drawing the figure in repose and in action.

THE HUMAN FIGURE

Owing to the demand, by a certain class of art students, for a short-cut method of drawing the human figure, unprincipled persons posing as instructors have denied the necessity of a well-laid foundation for drawing the human figure. Their so-called short cuts for teaching the drawing of this, the most complicated of all subjects, however, do not train one to do original work in actually drawing from the living model. They teach only facility in copying the work of others, an accomplishment that is of no practical value to the prospective illustrator.

3. Foundation for Caricaturing and Cartooning.—A careful systematic study of the human figure is absolutely necessary for any one who desires to draw caricatures and cartoons. Many persons, because of the attraction of the pictures in the comic sections of newspapers and in humorous weekly and monthly magazines, acquire a strong desire to do work of this kind. They, therefore, often study the work of their favorite cartoonists thinking that when able to copy this work satisfactorily their training is done. These persons confuse the ability to copy with the ability to originate.

It is impossible to compose and draw cartoons, caricatures, or original pictures of any kind, unless one has had a thorough graded training in drawing, and no one can draw the human figure without a full knowledge of the rules governing its proportions, etc. Caricatures are but drawings of a face or figure with its features exaggerated and cannot be drawn, except from a copy, until the ability to draw the face or figure in its normal proportions has been obtained. This ability is acquired only by a systematic study of figure drawing, facial expression, etc., such as will be given in this and following Sections.

The student is strongly advised against the practice of copying caricatures and cartoons made by professional artists, or making comic drawings in imitation of some cartoonist's individual style. Such a practice will be of absolutely no value in training him to draw the human figure, or in acquiring an individual style

THE HUMAN FIGURE

PROPORTIONS OF HUMAN FIGURE

FRAMEWORK OF FIGURE

4. Application of Principle of Structural Forms. The transition from drawing inanimate models in outline and light and shade to drawing the human figure is not, in reality, an abrupt one. As the curved line is based on the straight line and can be drawn more easily and accurately if straight construction lines are drawn, and as solids with curved sides and edges are based on solids with straight sides and edges, so may the human figure and its individual parts be based on rectilinear shapes of given proportions. This is well shown in Figs. 1 and 2, which give the full-front and side views of the same figure. In each case, (*a*) shows the fully modeled figures; (*b*) shows the figure and all its parts enclosed within their proper frameworks; (*c*) shows the frameworks alone.

5. From these two illustrations it is evident that certain principles govern the drawing of the human figure. These principles must be clearly understood and kept in mind at all times; they are as follows:

1. The human figure is a solid, for it has length, width, and thickness; it is not, however, a hard, rigid, unbending solid like a piece of wood or marble.

2. Each individual part, such as the head, the trunk, the arm, etc., is also a solid.

3. The head may be enclosed within an imaginary block form slightly longer than a cube; the neck within a half cube; the trunk, from the neck to where the legs join the body, within a solid about twice as high as wide but not quite as thick, or deep, as it is wide; the legs and arms within hinged pairs of solids, each section of the pair (corresponding to upper arm or upper leg and lower arm or lower leg) being about twice as long as wide; and the feet within wedge-shaped blocks as shown.

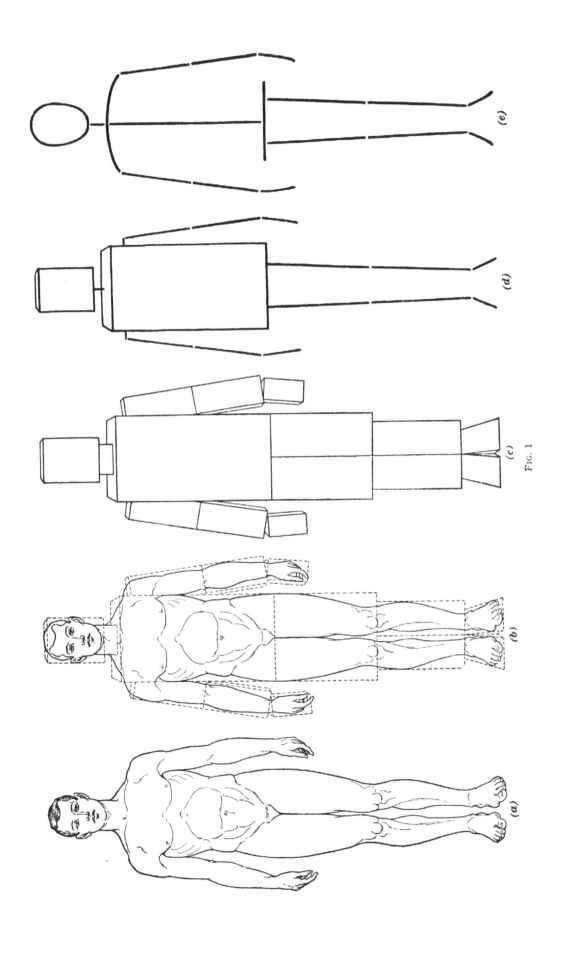

Fig. 1

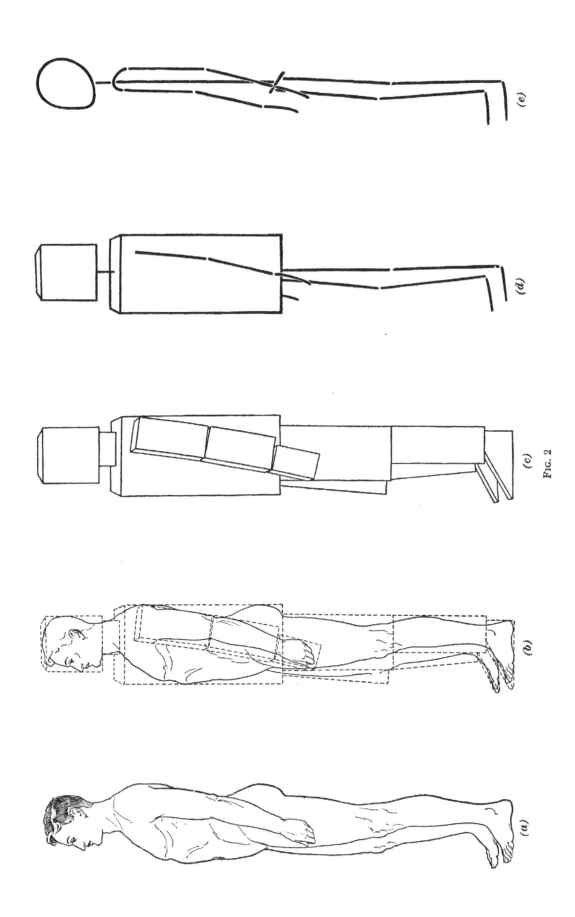

Fig. 2

THE HUMAN FIGURE

4. These blocks or solids are not fastened rigidly together at their points of joining, but may be considered as being hinged so as to be able to move in various directions.

If these few general blocking-in shapes are fixed well in mind it will always be possible to think of the figure, no matter how placed or in what complicated postures, as being made up of flexible solids, properly joined, and of the proportions given. The purpose, therefore, of these illustrations is not to furnish a quick method of drawing the figure, but to show the basic framework of the figure and its parts, considered from the exterior.

6. **Foreshortening of Human Figure.**—As people do not always stand erect, soldier like, but assume postures in which one part of the body is much closer to the observer than other parts, the principles of foreshortening must often be applied to drawings of the human figure. The application of these principles, however, is not difficult when the body is thought of as being enclosed within flexible rectilinear solids. Whenever it is desired to show the figure in any foreshortened position, it is simply necessary to draw the proper enclosing rectilinear solid in foreshortened position and then sketch in the enclosed curved lines of the figure.

Suppose, for example, that one were looking at a man stretched out upon the ground, as if he had fallen after being wounded, the feet of the man being nearest the observer. The proper procedure is to sketch a foreshortened square prism, like a 6-foot piece of squared timber, then on this to mark off the proper lengths for the head, trunk, and legs. The rectilinear solids enclosing the individual members may then be drawn in their proper foreshortened positions within the large main solid. It simply remains, therefore, to draw in the contours of the head, neck, trunk, legs, and feet, in their proper enclosing rectangles to complete the foreshortened view of the figure.

7. This procedure must be followed whenever a figure is to be drawn in a foreshortened position, and there is no conceivable position of the figure in which some part of it is not foreshortened. This idea of foreshortening must be kept in

THE HUMAN FIGURE

mind all the time as the proportions and characteristic appearances of human figures are studied and when actually drawing human figures in repose and in action. It will then not be necessary to refer to the foreshortening in detail whenever a certain position or action of the figure is being studied; the beginner must observe this foreshortening and must be careful to portray it properly in the drawings he prepares.

8. Study of Skeleton.—In the present study of the framework of the body, the study of the bones and muscles is purposely avoided. That the support and action of the human figure are dependent on the positions of the bones of the skeleton, and that they are held together and moved about by the muscles, is admitted. But the study of these parts is for the student of anatomy and physiology, rather than for the illustrating student. He desires only to familiarize himself with the human figure for use in his pictures. All he needs to know at this time is the result of this bony and muscular posture and action, as it shows typical postures and actions of the figure, as standing, sitting, walking, running, gesturing with arms and hands, etc. The methods of showing such action will be discussed later.

9. Simplified Structural Forms.—The blocked-in forms in Figs. 1 (c) and 2 (c) are too awkward and cumbersome in their parts to be carried in the mind or to be used when sketching human figures. They may, therefore, be reduced to simpler forms by representing the neck, arms, and legs by heavy lines, very much as a heavy bent-iron framework is used as the foundation of large plaster-of-Paris statuary models. The result of this simplification is shown in (d), where only the head and trunk are rectilinear solids, and the neck, arms, and legs are heavy lines. The breaks in these heavy lines indicate the joints at the shoulders, elbows, wrists, thighs, knees, and ankles.

To reduce the block forms to still simpler shapes, the corners of the rectilinear solid for the head may be rounded off to give more the appearance of the actual head and the body indicated by one of the heavy lines or pipes, as shown in (e).

THE HUMAN FIGURE

If care is observed to keep the proportions of these simplified figures correct; that is, to see that the arms and legs are not made too long or too short for the body, and that the joints come at the proper places; these simplified forms will be of great practical use when it is required to make drawings from the figure, in repose or in action.

METHODS OF PROPORTIONING ENTIRE FIGURE

10. Figure Based on Center Lines.—Vertical and horizontal center lines are a great aid in the correct proportioning of the human figure, in the same manner as these lines aid in line drawing and when working from wooden models. The following method of procedure will, therefore, be found helpful when proportioning any object or figure as a whole when sketching it.

First, observe and mark off the greatest dimension of the object or figure, whether it is height or width, and then the shortest dimension. Next, locate the middle of the object or figure by vertical and horizontal center lines and note some prominent feature that most nearly corresponds with that middle point. Subordinate details may then be sketched in readily.

The human figure is evenly balanced on each side of a vertical center line that passes down midway between the eyes, over the tip of the nose, the middle of the mouth, chin, and neck, midway between the nipples, down over the navel, corresponds to the inside line of the legs, and ends where the insides of the two heels touch. In an erect front view figure this is a perfectly straight vertical line.

If a horizontal line is drawn for the crown of the figure's head, another for the bottom of the feet, and a third exactly halfway between the first and second, there will be located the bottom of the trunk of the figure; this is the place where the inside lines of the legs join the body. The use of these lines of proportion is clearly shown in Fig. 3, where ab is the vertical center line upon which the figure is equally balanced, cd is the horizontal line for the crown of the head, and ef the horizontal line for the soles

THE HUMAN FIGURE

of the feet. Line *g h*—exactly midway between *c d* and *e f*—locates the bottom of the trunk where the inside lines of the legs join the body. This shows how simple and easily remem-

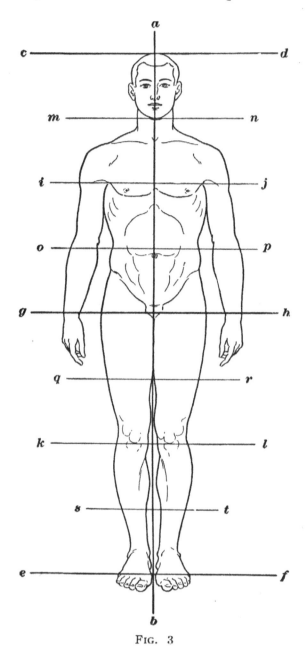

Fig. 3

bered is the first and most important step in locating the proportions of the human figure.

11. Locating Parts of Figure.—When the figure is divided into two equal parts, the head and trunk and the legs,

THE HUMAN FIGURE

the natural inclination is to subdivide these parts in order to locate others. By dividing the upper half, Fig. 3, into two

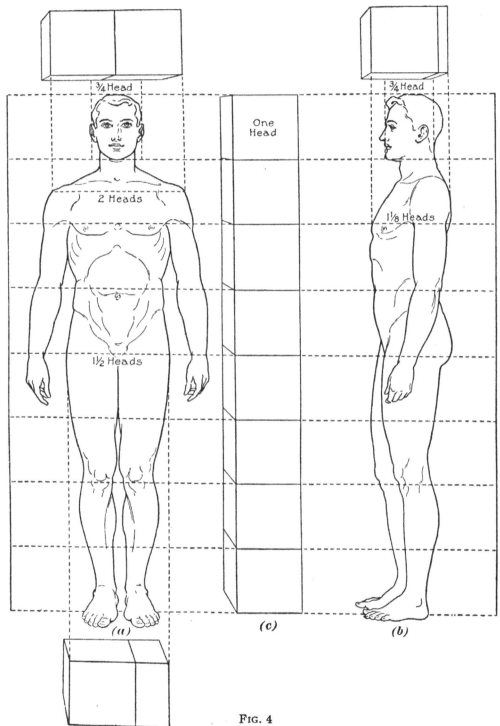

Fig. 4

equal parts, by the line $i\,j$, the armpits are located; that is, the points where the inside lines of the arms join the body. When

THE HUMAN FIGURE

the lower half of the body is bisected by the line $k\,l$, the knees are located.

The figure is now divided into four equal parts horizontally. If the uppermost one of these is bisected by horizontal line $m\,n$, it locates the bottom of the chin; a similar bisecting of the three remaining horizontal fourths locates other points or features of the figure, as at lines $o\,p$, $q\,r$, and $s\,t$. This divides the figure horizontally into eighths, which is also the distance from the crown of the head to the bottom of the chin. Therefore, the average human male figure is eight heads high. Some authorities have reduced this to seven and one-half heads, for the male figure, but this proportion makes the figure too stunted.

12. Proportioning Figure According to Heads.—To be able to proportion the various parts of the figure in terms of heads is a great convenience, as the head is one-eighth the height of the entire figure. But the system of heads must not be used for the first blocking-in of the figure. The preliminary blocking-in must be done by first getting top and bottom lines and then a bisecting horizontal line to locate the middle of the figure. If one were to try to lay out the figure by starting with the head and then plotting out the rest of the figure, he would get the figure either too long or too short.

13. Fig. 4 illustrates how the system of heads can be used for proportioning parts. In (a) is shown the front view and in (b) the side view of the figure. In (c) are shown, graphically, eight solids, each of which would contain a head and may therefore be termed *heads*. It will be observed that when eight of these heads are piled one on top of the other they correspond to the height of the male figure; the other proportions are as follows:

Height of Figure
From top of head to bottom of chin	1 head
From top of head to armpits	2 heads
From top of head to bottom of trunk	4 heads
From top of head to knees	6 heads

Width of Figure
Width of head at temples	¾ head
Width across shoulders	2 heads
Width at bottom of trunk (hips)	1½ heads

THE HUMAN FIGURE

THICKNESS OF FIGURE
Thickness from front of face to back of neck.......... $\frac{3}{4}$ head
Thickness from front of breast to back of shoulder.... $1\frac{1}{8}$ heads
Thickness through waist.......................... $\frac{3}{4}$ head

Many other points and proportions can be established with the head as a unit of measurement, such as lengths of arms,

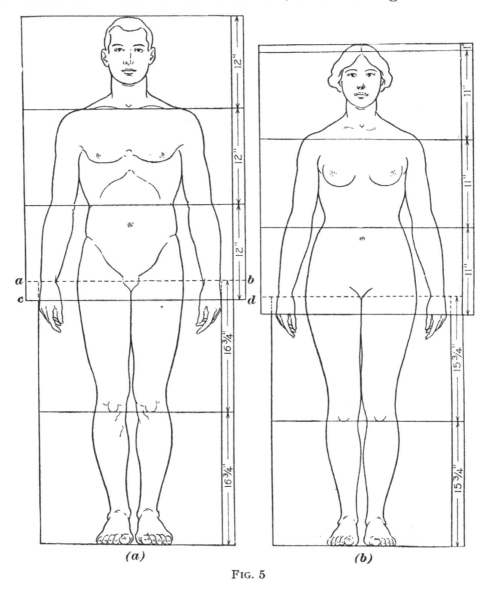

FIG. 5

hands, and feet, thickness of thigh and calf, etc. But for the present it will only be necessary to familiarize oneself with the proportions given, for with these proportions well in mind the actual drawing of the figure will not be difficult when later such sketching from the human figure is required.

THE HUMAN FIGURE

14. Proportioning Figure by Actual Measurements. Based on averages, it may be said that the average male figure is 67 or 68 inches (5 feet 7 or 8 inches) tall, and the female figure 63 or 65 inches (5 feet 3 or 5 inches) tall. These average actual measurements, however reliable and exact, cannot in themselves be very useful to the illustrator, for the simple reason that he must always foreshorten parts of the figure. He must, therefore, depend on relative proportions; for he can foreshorten these. However, a knowledge of actual measurements reveals a system of proportions that not only locates points in the body not previously obtained, but establishes a system of workable proportions that is always used in practical work. Further, these show clearly the difference between the proportions of the male and the female figures. These accurate measurements reveal that the line of the shoulders and the line of the waist fall about at thirds between the crown of the head and a little below the extreme lower end of the trunk. These measurements are shown in Fig. 5 (*a*) and (*b*).

15. A careful study of Fig. 5 (*a*) and (*b*) will reveal the relative heights and proportions of parts of the average male and female figures. If the horizontal line *a b*, view (*a*), that bisects the male figure is dropped a little, say 2 or 3 inches, as shown by the line *c d*, the distance from the top of the head to the extreme bottom of the trunk is found to be 36 inches. By dividing this distance in three parts of 12 inches each, the shoulders and waist will be located.

In the female figure, shown in (*b*), the corresponding distance is 34 inches. By allowing the 1 inch in excess in the top section and dividing the rest of this distance into three parts of 11 inches each, the shoulders and waist will be located. The lower half of either the male or female figure need only be bisected horizontally as before to locate the knees.

Fig. 6 shows the application of this principle to the rear view of a figure.

16. Practical Application of These Proportions. When actually drawing the figure, whether from life or from memory, it is the proportions and not the measurements that

THE HUMAN FIGURE

are applied. First, the horizontal lines for the top of head and soles of feet are sketched in, the horizontal center line that locates the bottom of the trunk is placed in, and then the lower end of the trunk is slightly dropped, and the space from this line to top of head is divided, by horizontal lines, into even thirds to locate the shoulders and the waist. If the main

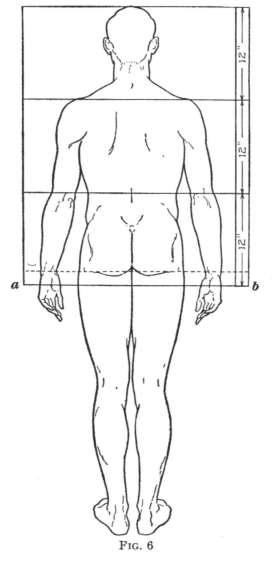

FIG. 6

points of the figure have already been blocked in, the process of locating the shoulders and the waist is the same, but simplified.

Figs. 7, 8, and 9 show, graphically, how this system is applied. Fig. 7 shows a rear view of the female figure. The lines establishing the top of the head, shoulders, and waist are slightly inclined away from the horizontal because the head, shoulders,

THE HUMAN FIGURE

and waist of the figure are tipped toward the right. The line for the bottom of the trunk is horizontal, because this part of the figure is in its normal position The line for the knees is sharply tipped because the left knee is lower than the right one (in the drawing) because of the position of the legs.

In Fig. 8, which is a front view of the female figure, the principle is again applied. The division lines to mark positions

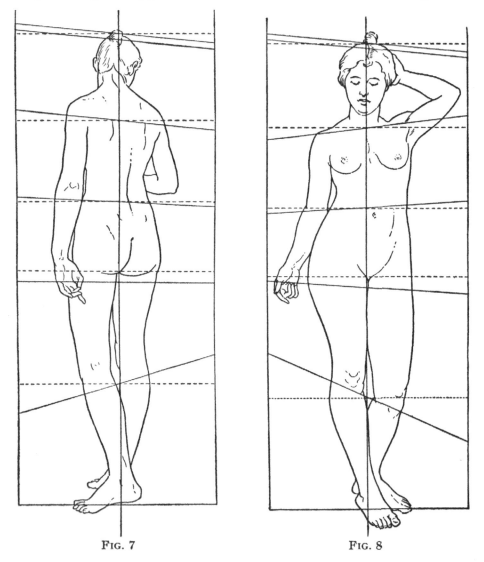

Fig. 7   Fig. 8

of parts are again tipped because these particular parts of the figure are tipped, as shown.

In Fig. 9, the principle is applied to the seated female figure. In such a case, the distance to be divided into thirds is from the crown of the head to the seat. When so divided, the shoulders

THE HUMAN FIGURE

and waist are located as before. It will be noted that the knees, even in the seated figure, are midway from the bottom of the trunk to the soles of the feet.

17. Comparative Proportions of Child and Adult Figures.—The proportions of the human figure that have been given are those of the adult figure, and of course are those that are most needed by the illustrator, as adult figures are most common in illustrations. However, as occasions for the use of

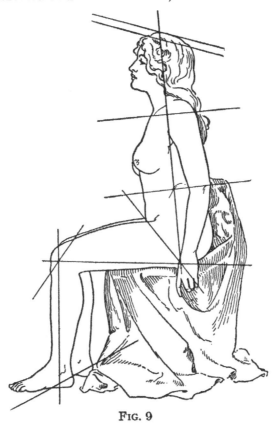

Fig. 9

figures of infants and children frequently arise, the illustrator should know the relative proportions of parts in the infant and the child body. It is common to see drawings of children in which the head is disproportioned to the rest of the body, or the legs are too long; and the young illustrator must be prepared to avoid such errors.

Fig. 10 (*a*) to (*d*) shows the figures at various ages. View (*a*) is an infant of 6 months; (*b*) a child of 5 years; (*c*) a youth of 9 years; and (*d*) an adult. It will be noted that as the age increases, the relative proportion of head to body, expressed

THE HUMAN FIGURE

in number of "heads" increases. At 6 months, view (*a*), the child is only $3\frac{3}{4}$ heads high; at 5 years, view (*b*), about $5\frac{1}{2}$ heads high; at 9 years, view (*c*), about 6 heads high; and in the adult, view (*d*), 8 heads, as previously discussed. Expressed conversely, this means that the infant's head is quite large for the body, the 5-year-old child's head (while actually larger than the infant's head) is relatively smaller as compared to its body;

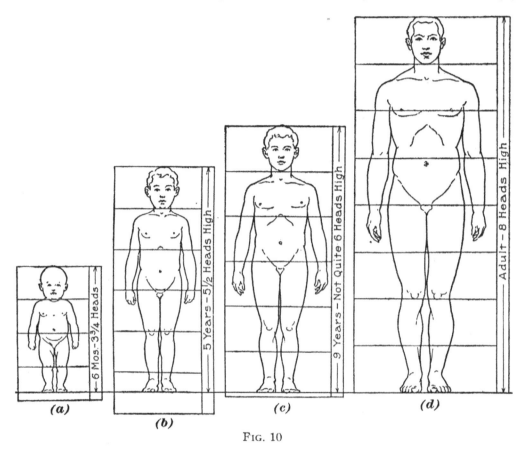

FIG. 10

the 9-year-old youth's head is still relatively smaller; and the adult's head is smallest of all, as compared to the size of the body.

It must be remembered, also, that in extreme old age, the body diminishes somewhat in height; not only on account of the stooped posture that often comes with old age, but because of the sagging of muscles and tissues. However, one who becomes familiar with the proportions of the normal adult figure in the prime of life can readily make the alterations in proportions, as well as in drawing of individual parts, so as to portray old age properly.

I L T 159B—16

THE HUMAN FIGURE

METHODS OF PROPORTIONING PARTS OF FIGURE

IMPORTANCE OF INDIVIDUAL PARTS OF FIGURE

18. The framework of the human figure as a whole, and the placing and proportioning of its various parts in relation to the entire figure and to one another, have been discussed so far. However, before one could expect to make an accurate drawing of the figure either from life or from memory, he must have a

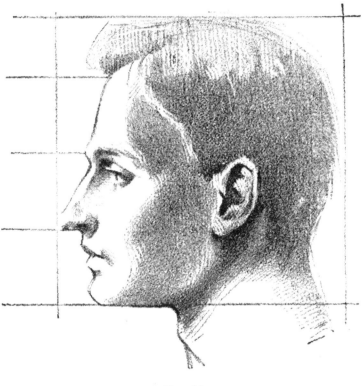

Fig. 11

more detailed knowledge of just what is the construction and appearance of each individual part or feature of the human body. Having familiarized himself with all these details he is then ready to combine them; to draw the head, the neck and shoulders, the breast and abdomen, the arms and hands, the thighs, the legs, and the feet, each one of proper size and properly rendered, and in harmonious relation to the entire figure and to every other individual part.

THE HUMAN FIGURE

THE HEAD

19. Profile View.—Viewed in profile, the head may be enclosed in a perfect square; and, in either profile or in full-face view, the face divided into thirds from the roots of the hair to the chin, as shown in Fig. 11. These thirds may be marked: *1*, from the roots of the hair to the brows; *2*, from the brows to

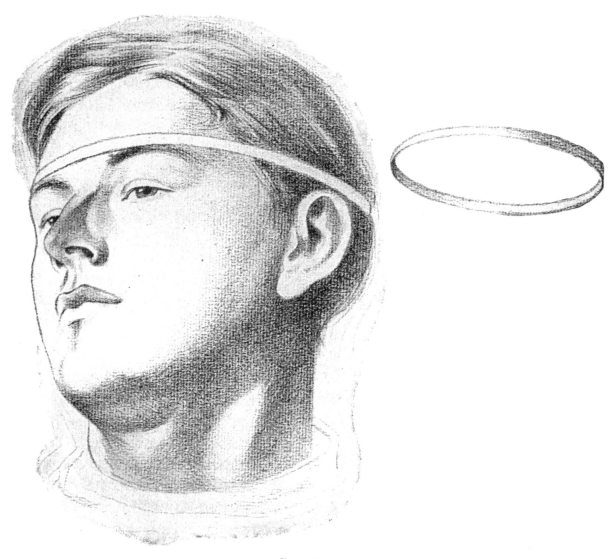

Fig. 12

the base of the nose; and *3*, from the base of the nose to the bottom of the chin. The distance from the crown of the head to the roots of the hair is one-fifth the height of the head. These measurements vary with each individual and cannot be taken

THE HUMAN FIGURE

absolutely, but for general drawing may be considered as a basis for construction

20. Full-Face View.—In the front, or full-face, view, the head may be considered as five eyes in width, the space between the eyes and on each side occupying a distance equal to the length of the eye itself. If a cross-section of the head were made at the height of the eyebrows, it would be nearly oval in shape with the fulness in the back; the ordinary band of a hat illustrates this. If a piece of tape is tied around the head at the line of the brows so that it touches the tip of the ears it will describe an oval and form a means of locating certain features of the face when the head is thrown backwards or for-

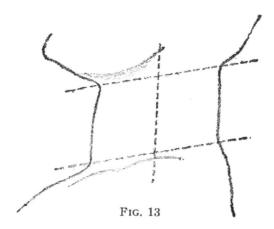

FIG. 13

wards so as to change the relative position of the features, as shown in Fig. 12. Thus, in drawing the head from any standpoint, whether the eye is far beneath, looking up to the model, or above, looking down on him, the brows and tips of the ears will always follow this oval strip, or tape, and can always be accurately located. However, the human head is so varied in proportion that it must be drawn as seen, irrespective of any set rules, for adherence to them is likely to be productive of a stock face or figure that soon becomes devoid of interest and novelty.

NECK AND SHOULDERS

21. After placing of head, the neck and shoulders must be considered; a line from the point of one shoulder to the point of the other gives the general direction. Where the

THE HUMAN FIGURE

neck joins the back of the head it rises much higher than at its junction with the fleshy part of the face under the jaw, but the junction of the neck with the back at the line of the shoulders is correspondingly higher than its junction at the pit of the throat. Thus, the column of the neck has a downward, oblique direction from its points of junction in the back to its points of junction in the front part of the body, as shown in Fig. 13.

The shoulders, which in the common acceptance of the

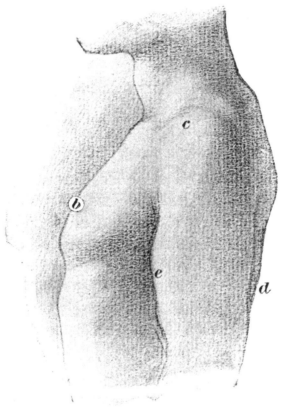

FIG. 14

word, include all the space from the neck to the muscle that caps the end of the bone of the upper arm, rise above the collar bones, and form a sort of muscular defense for them.

BREAST AND ABDOMEN

22. Muscles of Breast.—The two rather massive prominences on the breast of the male figure, shown at b, Fig. 14, are the breast muscles. They are separated by a slight indentation or hollow extending from the pit of the throat downwards.

THE HUMAN FIGURE

In repose, their surface is unbroken by any muscular markings, but under strong action they are well defined. Their contour is indicated by the shape of the shadows that fall on them. The various forms on the chest are very readily located by the relative positions of the nipples, which in the standard male figure are one head below the chin.

23. Muscles of the Abdomen.—Beneath the massive breast muscles, on each side of a perpendicular line, are the muscles of the abdomen. These also are somewhat indistinct when in repose, and are frequently obliterated entirely by an excess of fat. In the thin or muscular figure they are sharply defined when in action and appear as three separate masses on each side of a median line from the base of the breast muscles to the bottom of the trunk.

24. The Female Breasts.—In drawing the breasts of a female figure, the forms and shadows are very subtle. In the front view, where there are no contouring outlines, the expression of these details depends entirely on the careful rendering of the marginal shadows and the correct estimate of their proper tones. The position of the nipples and their relative position to the navel should be accurately determined, as these three points are of primary importance in the construction of the torso, or trunk, of the figure.

SHOULDER, ARM, AND HAND

25. Bones of Arm and Hand.—In the upper part of the arm there is a single large bone called the humerus. At its upper extremity it joins the shoulder, and at its lower extremity it unites with two smaller bones, called the ulna and the radius, and forms the elbow. The ulna and the radius unite at the wrist with several smaller bones that extend to the joints of the fingers. In the construction of the forearm, as the lower portion of the arm is called, the radius is on the side of the arm that connects with the thumb, while the ulna is on the side that connects with the little finger.

THE HUMAN FIGURE

26. Muscles of Shoulder and Arm.—Over the shoulder joint where the humerus connects with the clavicle is stretched the deltoid muscle, which caps the shoulder like an epaulet, as shown at *c*, Fig. 14. The biceps muscle *e*, which is that one made prominent in the front of the upper arm, is forwards of the humerus, and the triceps muscle *d*, corresponding with it on the back of the arm, is on the opposite side. Thus, the upper arm is deeper than it is wide owing to the fact that these two muscles lie on opposite sides of the bone, and its greatest dimension is seen when viewed from the side.

27. Pronation and Supination.—When the arm is in the act of *pronation*, that is, in the position shown in Fig. 15, the muscles of the forearm assume a widely different appearance from that seen when the arm is in the act of *supination*, as shown in Fig. 16. During pronation the position of the bone of the forearm is distinctly seen by the shadow that runs to the point of the elbow. During supination the bone is not seen, and the shadow shown is under the muscle. The contours on the upper and lower lines are changed completely, especially about the wrist. Familiarity with these forms is only reached through long practice in drawing from the figure and close observation. Therefore, the details of the arm in both these attitudes should be carefully studied, so that the memory will be stamped with the difference in the contours of the muscles. In pronation, the forearm has reached what is practically its extreme limit of range in one direction, and in supination it has reached the extreme limit in another direction. There are varieties of action between these two extremes that change the position of the muscles to such an extent that one must be thoroughly familiar with them in order to have the arm in good drawing, no matter in what position it may be.

28. Arms in Various Positions.—In Fig. 17 is shown the male arm as seen from a low point of view, in consequence of which it is considerably foreshortened. The shoulder cap, or deltoid muscle, here becomes clearly defined, and the muscles of the forearm are shown rigid and full near the elbow, owing to the fist being clenched. The shadow on the inside of the

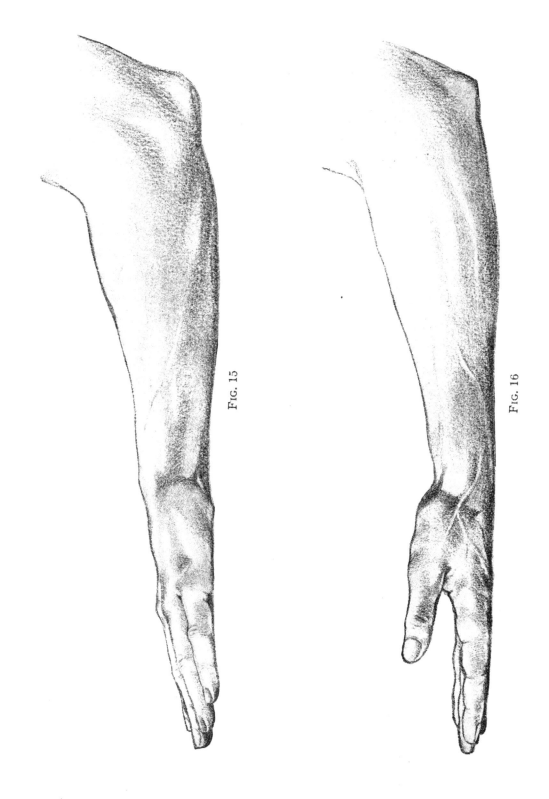

Fig. 15

Fig. 16

arm indicates the intersections of the planes that give the contour in this position.

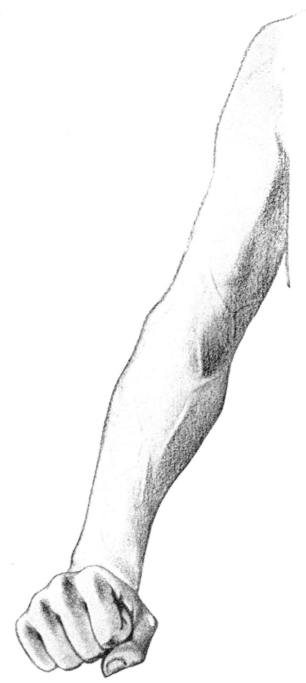

Fig. 17

In Fig. 18 the female arm is shown with a clenched fist. By being drawn up tight against the upper arm, the forearm is given a fulness near the elbow that is seen in no other position.

THE HUMAN FIGURE

The characteristic smoothness of the female arm is also shown. Even in this position the muscles are not knotty and hard as in the male arm, but the curves round off gracefully, one into the

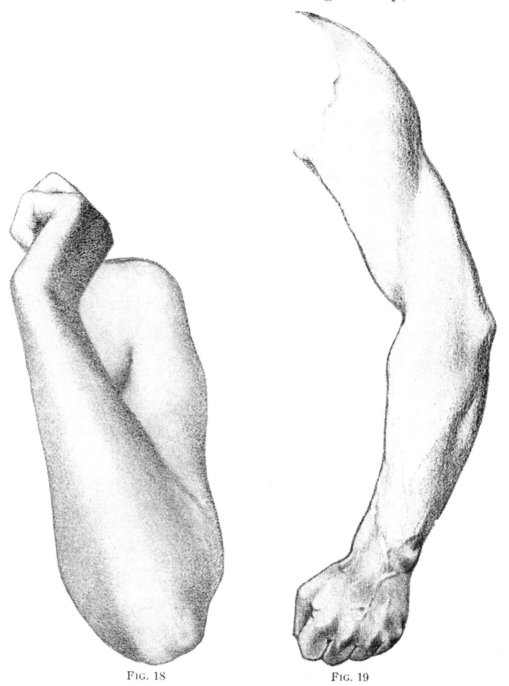

Fig. 18   Fig. 19

other, forming gentle undulations rather than sharp, emphatic curves. This is a characteristic that distinguishes all the contours in the female figure from similar contours in the male figure.

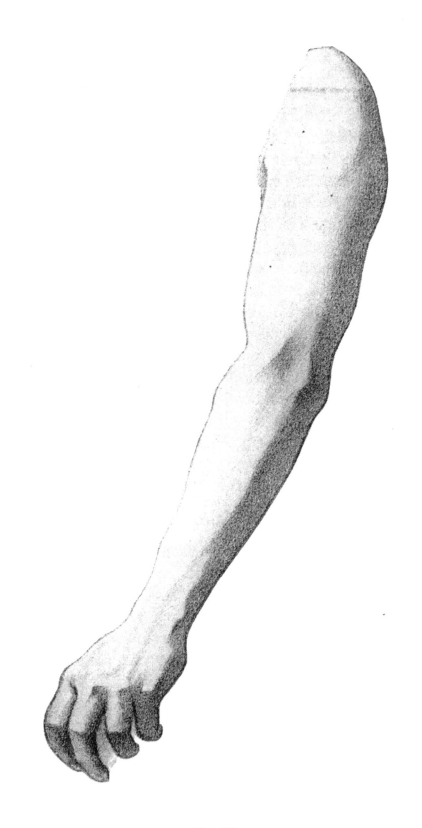

Fig. 20

THE HUMAN FIGURE

29. Fig. 19 shows a muscular arm of the male figure, the development of which is clearly shown. The deltoid muscle of the shoulder can be seen reaching like an epaulet from the top of the shoulder to the side of the arm and entering it in a blunt point between the biceps muscle and the triceps. The triceps bulges slightly at the back of the arm, but its fullest part is nearer the shoulder than the nearest part of the biceps. The muscles of the forearm are emphasized, as in Fig. 19, by the clenching of the fist, but if the hand were gradually opened the muscles on each side of the forearm would gradually flatten out and the fulness of the forearm spread somewhat toward the wrist.

Fig. 20 shows the male arm in a relaxed state, but the muscular development is sufficient for one to observe the power contained therein. Down the full length of the arm the plane of shadow indicates the shape of the muscular forms beneath the skin and follows each concavity or convexity of surface on the side away from the light. The position of the elbow becomes marked by a sharp angle in the shadow, while on the back of the hand each knuckle and joint is expressed by a modeling of small planes of light and shade. This illustration will bear careful study; the prominent bone on the outside of the wrist and each of the joints of the fingers are expressed by a little plane of light located in just the right place.

30. Fig. 21 shows the construction of the arms and location of the planes of light and shade, when these members are seen from behind. The muscular development is slight and the position one of complete inaction and listlessness. The feeling of inaction is expressed by the flatness of the muscles and the evenness of the curves from one plane to another. Note the creases and folds in the skin that give character to the elbows and also to the expression of the ligaments in the wrist as they run from the muscles of the forearms to the fingers. Though none of the muscles are contracted, the plane of shadow on the inside of the left arm shows all the gradations of bone structure and muscle, and in many cases will even indicate the form, branching, and general distribution

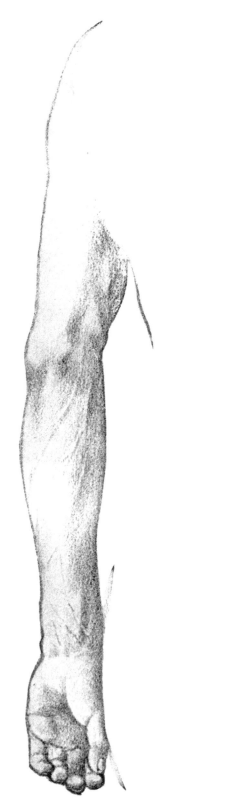
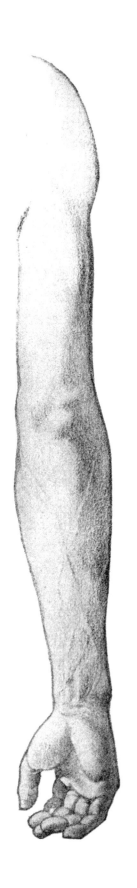

Fig. 21

THE HUMAN FIGURE

of the veins. In the right arm note particularly the thin appearance of the upper part; this is due to the fact that the biceps and triceps are set one before the other with the bone between them, so that the smallest dimension of this portion of the arm is shown. But the position of the forearm is such that the bones and accompanying muscles are seen from their widest standpoint. The relative widths and positions of the various proportions of the arms as they are turned in different positions should be carefully studied.

In Fig. 22 is shown a profile view of the female right arm, The upper arm appears rather short for the forearm, owing to the fact that when making this drawing the model was placed far above the eye. This foreshortening gives the effect of elevation to the figure. The left arm resting upon the small of the back shows the smooth, graceful curves of the outside line of the female arm in this position, contrasted with the sturdy and abruptly changing planes of the male arm. In both the left and right arms, the unbroken smoothness of line characteristic of the female figure is strongly illustrated.

31. In Fig. 23, the thin, undeveloped arms of a young girl are shown. Here the chief interest centers in the foreshortening of the forearms and of the hands. In the model's right arm the wrist is entirely hidden, and unless the arm and elbow, as seen to the left and below it, are properly rendered the unity between the hand and the arm will not be expressed. This should be very carefully studied. In the model's left arm nothing is hidden, but the foreshortening must be carefully studied and the work must be very accurate. In this position the hands appear larger than they would ordinarily, as they are from 8 inches to 12 inches nearer the eye than is the elbow. No set rule can be given for this foreshortening, but attention must be given to the proportions of all the parts in order that the foreshortening may be expressive of existing conditions.

32. The Hand.—The appearance of the hand is so influenced by foreshortening in all positions that actual measurements of its proportions are of little value. The forefinger and

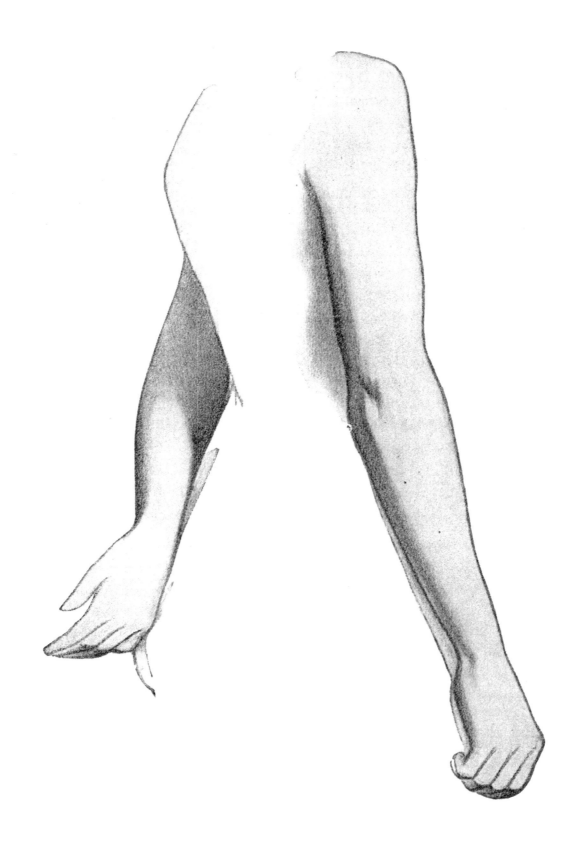

Fig. 22

THE HUMAN FIGURE

the third finger are usually of about the same length, and the distance from the knuckles of the forefinger to the joint of the wrist is approximately the same as the distance from the knuckles to the tip of the finger. The middle finger is longer than those next to it, and the little finger is the shortest of the four.

The characteristics of the hand naturally vary with the individual. In the clenched fist the forms are very similar

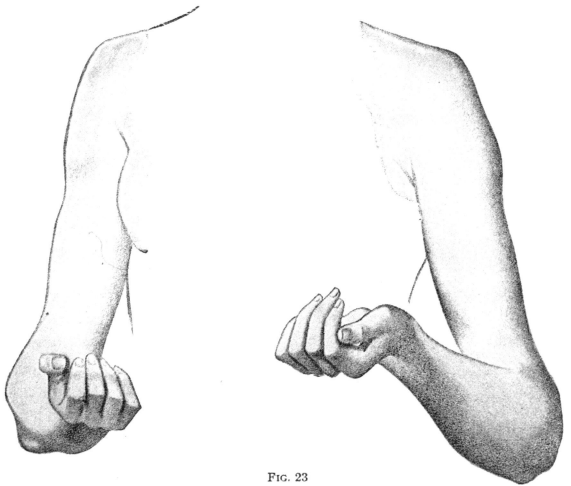

Fig. 23

to those of a plain block hand, and in drawing details of the hand the same rules apply as in drawing the head or other parts of the figure. The mind and eye seize on prominent points for starting and finishing lines. These points vary with the position of the hand, but generally speaking, the wrist, knuckles, and first and second joints of the fingers and thumb are to be located first and the construction built around them; close drawing of the contours may then follow. The shadows should be carefully modeled so that their margins will be well defined, as the solidity of appearance is dependent entirely on the accuracy with which these shadows are handled. Illustrations of hands in various positions are shown in Figs. 5 to 23, inclusive, which should be carefully studied.

THE THIGH, LEG, AND FOOT

33. Location of Principal Muscles.—When studying the thigh, it is well to know where certain muscles are placed, although this member is usually so covered with fat that it is difficult to find lines of separation between the various sets of muscles. When the thigh is made rigid by strong action it will be seen that on the outside of the upper part of the thigh a large muscular prominence forms a ridge that extends obliquely across the leg, from a to b, Fig. 24 (a), so that when it reaches a point above the knee it is on the inside of the leg. This ridge is made up of several large muscles, but their origin is difficult to trace on the figure, and consequently in rendering the thigh the eye must carefully search for shadows and their outlines in order that all may be intelligently expressed.

34. Muscles of Upper Leg.—The large muscle on the back of the thigh is known as the biceps of the leg, and has a use similar to that of the biceps of the arm; that is, to draw the lower portion of the leg upwards and toward it. Its prominence is plainly seen when the leg is viewed from the side and gives the thigh, similar to the arm, a greater depth than thickness. The upper bone of the leg is called the femur and unites with two smaller bones in the lower portion of the leg, called the tibia and the fibula.

35. Comparison of Male and Female Thighs and Calves.—Fig. 24 shows the comparative proportions of the male and female thigh and leg when viewed from nearly the same standpoint. Assuming the calves to measure practically the same in circumference, it can readily be seen that the female thigh and knee are rounder and larger than the

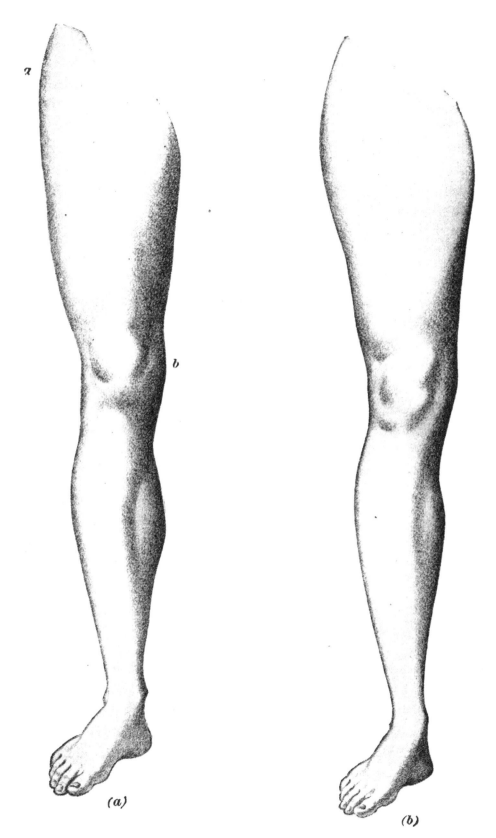

Fig. 24

male and that the lines causing this appearance are on the outside of the leg. On the outside line of the lower leg, however, the contours are nearly the same; but on the inside line the most prominent point of the calf is higher and considerably greater in the male figure than in the female. This difference of appearance is due largely to fat filling the space below the knee in the female figure, the muscular development of the male being more defined than that of the female.

In comparing these two legs one can see the characteristic difference between the male and the female figure, the former being sharply contoured and muscularly expressive, the latter being soft and undulating in its form. Study, line for line, these two legs; they will be found to possess at nearly the same points exactly the same curves and in the same directions, but the gradations from one curve to the other are much more delicate in the female than in the male leg. Here, too, can be observed the cause of the appearance of knock-kneedness so prevalent in the female figure, the outside line of the leg exhibiting a greater indentation at the knee in the female than in the male figure. If a straightedge, however, be laid along the inside of each of these legs from the ankle bone to the top of the thigh, it will be found, as a matter of fact, that neither is in the slightest degree knock-kneed, but that the female leg is a trifle the reverse if anything.

36. Muscles of Lower Leg.—The three principal muscles of the lower leg are the two large ones that form the calf, and a smaller one in front of the shin bone. Viewed from the direct front, the prominence of the calf is very marked. Its most prominent part on the outside of the leg is somewhat higher than its most prominent part on the inside of the leg, as may be seen in Fig. 24. In rising on the ball of the foot these muscles are brought sharply into prominence, and when seen from the back of the leg their form is very clearly defined. The shin muscle is brought into prominence by placing the heel firmly on the floor and drawing the foot upwards as far as possible. In profile, or side view, the shin muscle curves slightly forwards from the bone, and the greatest width of the calf is

THE HUMAN FIGURE

slightly higher than a point midway between the kneepan and the sole of the foot, as shown in Figs. 25, 26, and 27.

The position of the foot governs the appearance of the muscles of the leg in identically the same manner as the position of the hand governs the muscles of the arm. With every turn of the foot the points of muscular prominence vary.

37. The muscles on the inside of the leg are seldom as well marked in women as in men, the lines being much straighter on the inside, as a rule, and more curved on the outside. The shaping of the muscles themselves, however, is practically the same, and the difference of appearance between the male and female is due almost entirely to the filling in of fat. Owing to habitual exercise, due largely to the difference of amusements among male and female children, the male muscles become strongly developed and less fat fills in between them. In the adult's leg, the male is characterized by a development that clearly locates the position of each muscle; in the female, the curves of the leg are continuous and the delineation of the muscles can be traced with difficulty.

There is a common tendency in the male figures toward a separation of the knees giving a bow-legged appearance, while in the female figure the tendency is toward a knock-kneed appearance. This latter is intensified by the fact that the hips of the female figure are very broad, and the lines from the hips to the knees taper very rapidly. Thus, this knock-kneed appearance exists even where, as a matter of fact, the limbs are perfectly straight.

38. Characteristics of Male Lower Limbs.—Fig. 25 is a drawing of the male limbs with the weight of the body thrown forwards, thus bringing into prominence the muscle of the front of the right thigh and a fulness of the shin muscle directly below the right knee. The left leg exerts a backward pressure in this action principally on the toes and ball of the foot, and the clean definition of the thigh muscles just above the knee shows where the greatest strain comes. The muscle on the inside of the left calf also suggest pressure, and the expression of action in this figure is due entirely to the modeling

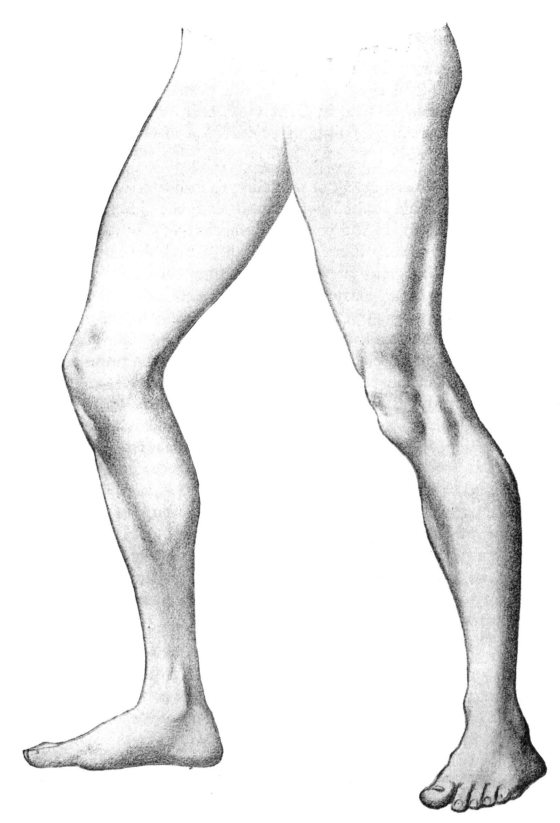

Fig. 25

THE HUMAN FIGURE

about the knees and along the sides of the legs that shows the tensity of this muscle.

In the left leg, the curve of the shin bone from the knee down is strongly indicated by the shadow on the inside of the muscle. The right foot is in full profile here, while the left foot is foreshortened in front view, and forms an excellent study in the relative points of prominence in the ankle, both outside and inside.

39. Fig. 26 is a study of modeling to indicate the muscular forms in the male limbs when viewed from the side and posed somewhat as in Fig. 25. The definition of the kneejoint and kneecap is very clearly marked here and the ankle bone stands out with great prominence, showing the point of hinge or turning at this member. The depression above the kneecap in the left leg appears here, giving fulness to the muscle above it in the same manner as in Fig. 25, but the point of view being farther to the right than in Fig. 25, the prominence on the inside of the calf is entirely lost sight of.

When studying from the model, at all times, advantage should be taken of opportunities to walk around it and notice the change of contour at each step. As one steps to the right or left of the point of view, certain muscles become foreshortened and others come into prominence, and it is only by the careful study of these that correct delineation can be given to the subtle character of the human figure. It is only by this study and the repeated drawing from the figure in these positions that the details can be impressed on the mind sufficiently to permit the correct delineation of forms in illustrative work.

40. Fig. 27 is a direct view of the prominent points on the inside and outside of the left leg when seen from behind. In the outside of the thigh, there is very slight convexity; while in the line of the inside, there is a slight concavity about midway to the knee. The point of prominence in the outside of the calf is higher than the point of prominence on the inside of the calf; the location of these points of prominence is an important detail that should be studied from the living model, as the

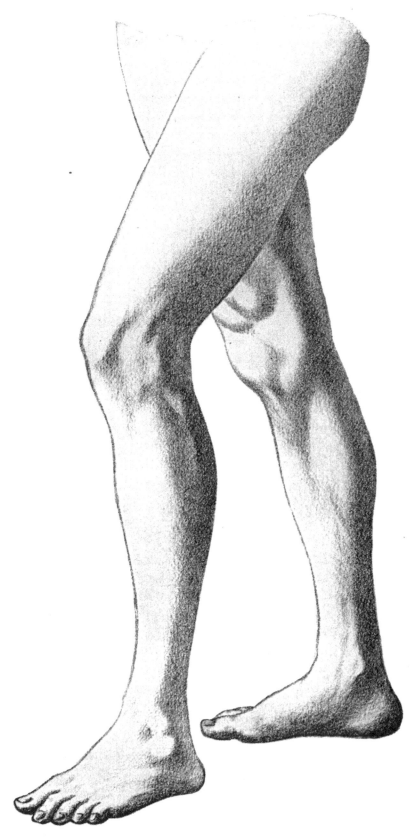

Fig. 26

THE HUMAN FIGURE

position of the feet has a strong influence in the general contour of the leg. For instance, in Fig. 27, the foot of the left leg rests at a given angle, thus causing the contours of the leg to assume a certain definite form, but the foot of the right leg is turned outwards and the contours of this leg are considerably changed. Not only is it important to establish these contours correctly in order to satisfy the eye as to the accuracy of the drawing, but the shadows indicating the planes must be well placed, or the whole composition will be incongruous and unsatisfactory.

41. Characteristics of Female Lower Limbs.—In Fig. 28 the smooth, unbroken quality of the outline is strongly indicative of the female figure. The flesh is laid so smoothly over the muscles that their characteristic prominences are almost entirely hidden. A comparison of the rounded, undulating forms here with the knotty, muscular development of Figs. 25 and 26 again illustrates the distinguishing characteristics of the male and female figure. Here, as in Fig. 24, the thigh is shown round and full, and the construction here and in the knees is almost entirely obscured by the presence of fat. The width of the hips is especially noticeable, although the figure for the most part is rather slight.

Fig. 25 showed a profile of the right foot as seen from the inside; here is shown a profile of the left foot as seen from the inside. The one being male and the other female, however, there are slight differences in contour, but the rise of the ankle from the instep and heel can be profitably studied from both points of view.

42. In Fig. 28 the comparative size of the thigh and calf of the female figure are well shown. •Owing to the anatomical character and great width of the female hips, a large thigh is a necessity in order to give grace to the leg; otherwise, the lines from the hips to the knees would be concave, giving an appearance of awkwardness and weakness. Here can also be observed another characteristic that offsets this tendency to weakness in appearance; that is, the fulness of the calf on the outside and the tendency of the same to a

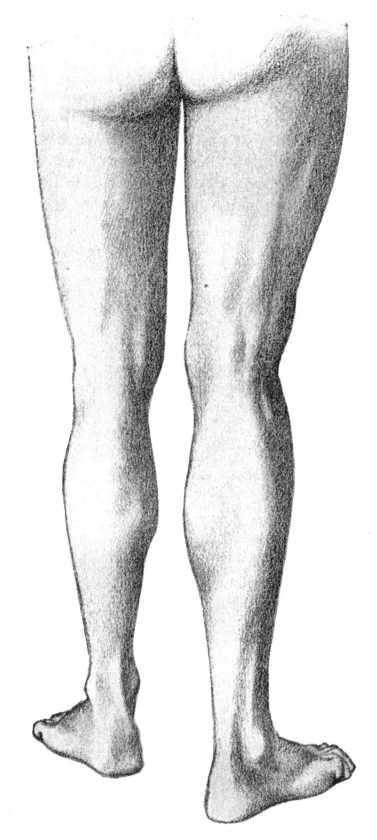

Fig. 27

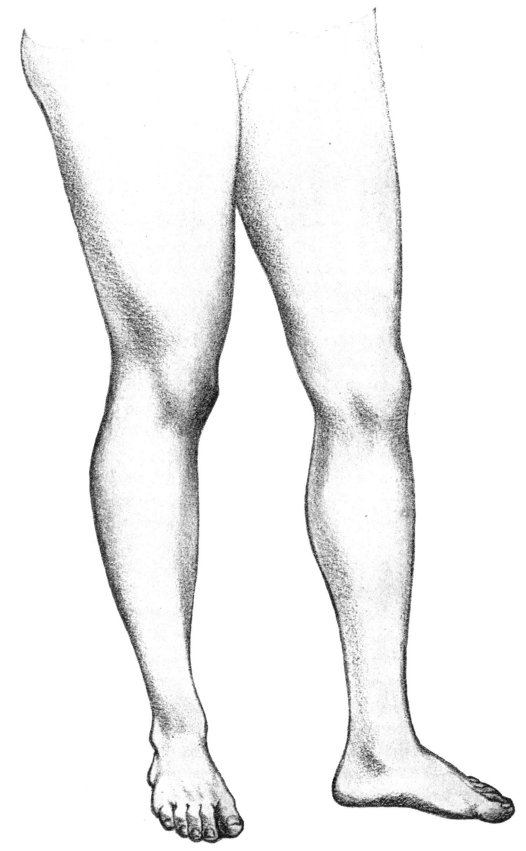
Fig. 28

THE HUMAN FIGURE

straight line on the inside. The foot here is in full front view, and the right leg is shown foreshortened, as seen from a point considerably above its level, while the foreshortened left foot in Fig. 25 was seen from a point very little above its level. In the right foot shown in Fig. 28, two prominent points of the ankle bone should be studied carefully. Whenever opportunity arises this should be studied from the living model, inasmuch as the points of prominence on the inside and outside vary constantly with changes of position.

43. The Foot.—When drawing the foot in profile, its length should be estimated by comparison with some fixed scale of measurement, such as the head, or by the proportion

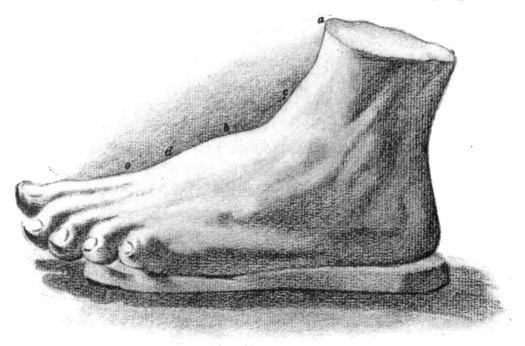

FIG. 29

it bears to the length of the leg from the knee to the sole of the foot. The contour of the instep, the position of the ankle bone, and the shape of the heel are next in importance.

Fig. 29, which is a reproduction of a charcoal drawing from a plaster cast of the foot, shows the curve of the instep, *e d b*; and the contour of the front of the ankle, *a c*. The positions of the toes as seen in profile should also be studied with great care. Views of the foot in still other positions are shown in

THE HUMAN FIGURE

Figs. 24, 25, 26, 27, and 28, and these also should be studied. In direct front view it is particularly important to observe the size and position of the toes and the relative position of the outside and inside prominence of the ankle bone.

THE FACE AND ITS FEATURES

44. Importance of Features of Face.—The most important of all the parts of the body, in the consideration of the artist and the illustrator, are the human face and its features. It is the features of the face that portray the real story of the picture; for it is the expressions portrayed on the faces of the characters that make or unmake the illustration. Expressions of the face, however, are simply the various facial features made mobile and placed in different positions and relations to one another, by the action of the various muscles. It is evident, therefore, that before expressions can be portrayed intelligently, the artist must know the shapes and positions of the individual facial features in repose and how to draw them. For instance, the eye itself, without any of its accompaniments, has no expression. But, when the muscles around the eye do their proper work under direction from the brain, all the varied expressions of love, pity, fear, grief, indignation, joy, etc., are observable and can be portrayed in illustrations.

THE EYE

45. The Eyeball.—The correct drawing of the human eye is one of the most difficult problems in figure drawing. The convex shape of the eyeball enveloped by the lids is full of subtle variety when foreshortened, while the spherical shape of the eyeball proper causes the lids and other details to be somewhat foreshortened at all times, no matter in what position the eye may be seen.

In general structure the eyeball protrudes from a socket, or *orbit*, as it is called, and is enveloped above and below by the eyelids, as shown in Fig. 30. The plane of this orbit slopes inwards as it descends to the cheek bone, as shown at *a b*, Fig. 31, and makes an angle with the plane of the forehead as the latter recedes from *a* to *d* and also with the plane of the cheek as that passes forwards, as shown at *b c*. Each detail of the eye, whether it is opened or closed, tends to preserve the direction of the plane *a b*, and the eyeball never protrudes sufficiently from its socket to disturb the slope. The upper lid extends beyond and partly covers the upper portion of the iris, while the iris slopes backwards with the plane of the orbit. The under lid is thinner than the upper and forms the base of the plane *a b*, where it intersects with the cheek plane shown by line *b c*, Fig. 31.

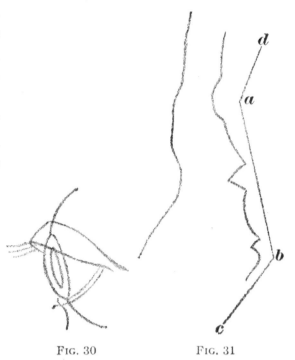

FIG. 30   FIG. 31

The eyebrows start either side of the nose just under the frontal bone and extend outwards and slightly upwards, tapering gradually toward the temple, where the growth ceases on the outside of the orbit, as shown in Fig. 32.

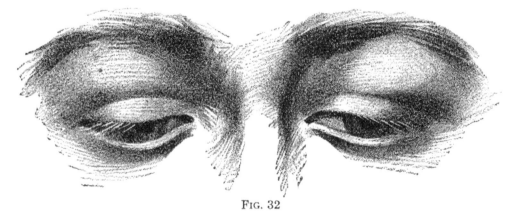

FIG. 32

46. The Eyelids—The convexity of the eyeball determines the curvature of the eyelids, but this curvature changes with every position of the head, owing to the foreshortening.

THE HUMAN FIGURE

In a three-quarter view, the upper lid makes a spiral turn that hides its thickness at the outside, as shown at *a*, Fig. 33, while in looking downwards the upper lid straightens out and the lower lid becomes more convex, owing to the fact that the eyeball is rolled into the lower lid. As the eye is turned downwards the outer corner descends slightly also, tending to straighten out the lower lid. When the eye is rolled upwards the convexity of the eyeball is emphatically marked

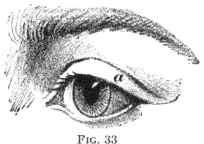

Fig. 33

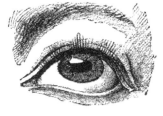

Fig. 34

by the upper lid, as shown in Fig. 34; its breadth is diminished, but its thickness is visible all the way across, while the lower lid flattens out and forms a compound curve rising from the inner corner and descending until past the pupil, when it rises abruptly to the outer corner. With most persons the upper lid is more convex on the inside than on the outside, while the lower lid is more convex on the outside. From the outside of the corner of the eye the upper lid curves slightly

Fig. 35   Fig. 36

toward the top of the iris and then descends in a more or less abrupt curve to the tear gland by the nose, while the lower curve starts straight from the tear gland, descends slowly, and returns in a rather more abrupt curve against the outer corner of the upper lid, so that lines drawn through the points of start and finish in the eye will intersect about as shown in Fig. 35. The eye very rarely composes itself into two even arcs from corner to corner, as shown in Fig. 36.

# THE HUMAN FIGURE

THE NOSE

47. Profile and Front Views.—Viewed directly in profile the nose starts beneath the eyebrows and proceeds at an angle until the tip is reached. The character expressed by it is mainly influenced by the bridge, while the terms Roman, straight, aquiline, and retrousse (turned up) are based on the degrees of convexity or concavity of the line from the brows to the tip. The upper lip joins the cartilage, or partition, between the nostrils at a point about midway between the extreme tip of the nose and the crease where the wing of the nostril joins

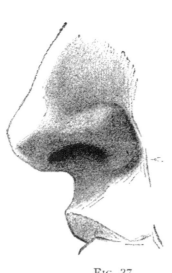

FIG. 37

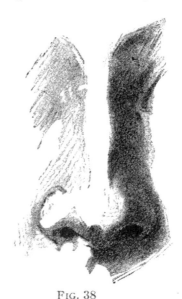

FIG. 38

the cheek, Fig. 37. When illuminated by a strong light, the margins of the shadows definitely describe and locate the planes that make up the construction of this feature.

In a full-face view, Fig. 38, the nose has its origin between and somewhat beneath the brows. At its beginning it is narrow and increases in width at the bridge; it decreases where the cartilage is reached at the end of the nasal bone, but again increases, attaining its greatest width at the tip. The nose is wedge-shaped from this view, with the edge of the wedge to the front; the sides slope gradually from the bridge to the cheeks until the nostrils are reached. The base of this wedge extends outwards from the general plane of the face, as the nose is much broader at the base than at its

THE HUMAN FIGURE

origin between the brows. If this point is not well understood, drawings of the nose are likely to look as if the nose were pressed into the face between the cheeks. A block form of the nose is shown in Fig. 39. A sharp crease marks the formation of the wing of the nostril at the base and lessens in prominence as it extends into the cheek. The greatest width of the nose is at the base across the nostrils.

FIG. 39

48. Foreshortened Views.—When the nose is seen on a level with the eye the cartilage between the nostrils extends slightly lower than any other part, Figs. 37 and 38. When viewed from below, however, the wings appear to be the lowest part, as in Fig. 40 (b); but viewed from above, the nostrils

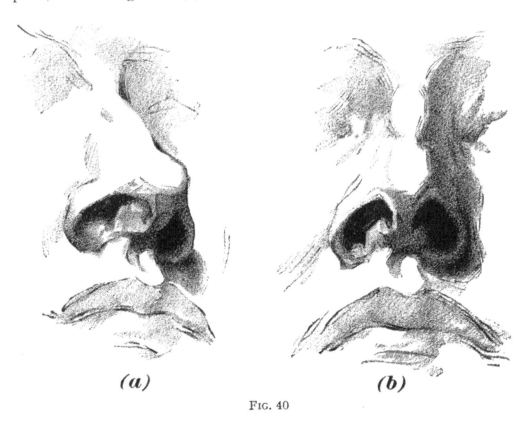

(a)   (b)

FIG. 40

are completely screened, and the lower part of the tip overhangs the upper lip, Fig. 41. When the head is thrown well back, as in Fig. 40, the formation of the nostrils and the intervening cartilage can be easily studied. The unconventionality of these

THE HUMAN FIGURE

forms makes definition difficult, and much practice in drawing them is therefore very necessary. The convex surface of the

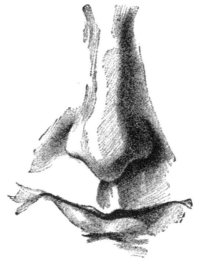

Fig. 41

wings and the end of the nose should be studied in profile, full-front, and foreshortened views. The shadows on these forms

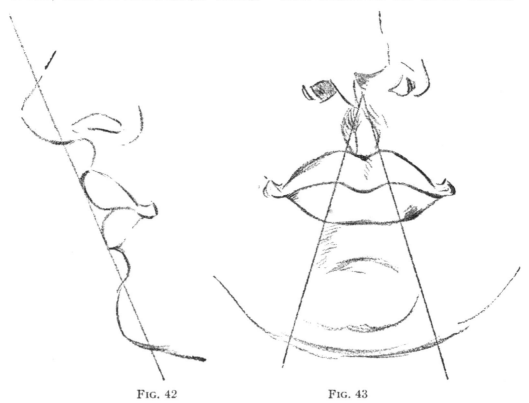

Fig. 42   Fig. 43

better illustrate their character than any verbal description can possibly do.

I L T 159B—18

THE HUMAN FIGURE

When seen from below, the bridge from the brows to the end will lose greatly in length by foreshortening, and must therefore be carefully studied in order to avoid an exaggerated appearance.

THE MOUTH

49. Profile and Front Views.—The mouth, like the eye, is one of the most difficult parts of the face to render properly, inasmuch as its form is so subtle and so greatly influenced by foreshortening that constant practice is the only

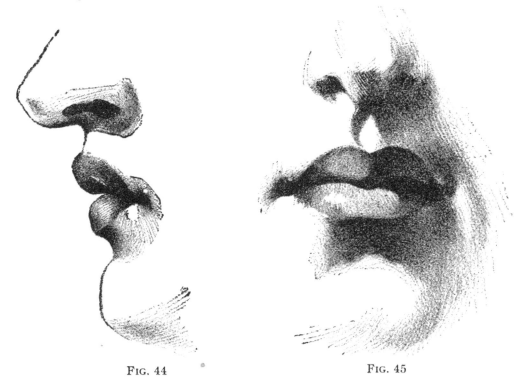

FIG. 44 FIG. 45

means by which one can successfully master its subtle curves. Viewed in profile, Fig. 42, one can study the general formation of the lips. Note the steps formed by the intersections of the nose, lips, and chin with the plane of the lips. In the full-front view, Fig. 43, the upper and lower lips are seen to be concave in their outlines from the middle to the corner. In thickness, the upper lip is much more convex than the lower one, Fig. 42, and the curves unite in a very subtle manner with adjacent curves. In the average mouth, the upper lip overhangs the lower lip slightly, and in a direct profile view, Fig. 44, the corners will be found somewhat lower than the drooping middle portion of the upper lip. In the full-face view, Fig. 45, the mass about the mouth is very convex owing to the influence of the teeth. The corners, therefore, are farther back than the middle and the concave sides become foreshortened. The red portion of the upper lip may be divided into two planes a and b, Fig. 46, while the lower lip possesses three planes, the middle one c extending each side of the center of the upper lip and the two side ones d extending into the corners of the mouth. The degree of curve and fulness in the lips is a matter of individual character, varying from a distinct bow shape to lips that are so thin and straight as to be scarcely more than a straight line across the face.

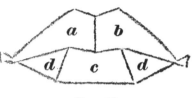

FIG. 46

50. The concavity beneath the lower lip is largely influenced by the fulness of the lip itself and the pressure brought to bear on it by the upper lip. Viewed from the front, Fig. 45, the depression that divides the upper lip beneath the nose widens as it descends toward the mouth and marks the middle of the upper lip. The little concave depression in the middle of the curve of the upper line of the upper lip seems to be duplicated in the curve of the lower line of the upper lip, both curves forming the boundary to the thickness of the lip at this point. From the middle, the upper lines of the upper lip curve downwards toward the corners, while the lower lines of the upper lip follow approximately the same direction and the two meet in the depression at the corner. In direct front view, the degrees of convexity and concavity in the form of the lips are expressed by the intensity and shape of the shadow, Fig. 45.

51. Foreshortened Views.—In various foreshortened positions in which the mouth is frequently seen, the lips assume many changes in appearance. It is plain that when observed from a low point of view, the upper lip will appear at its full thickness, Fig. 47, and the lower lip will appear thinner than when seen level with the eye of the observer. When

THE HUMAN FIGURE

seen from above, Fig. 48, the lower lip will exhibit its full thickness and the upper lip will appear thinner than when seen on a level with the eye.

In the three-quarter view, Fig. 49, the nearer side of the mouth from the middle to the corner is seen in its full dimension, losing nothing by foreshortening; the other side, however,

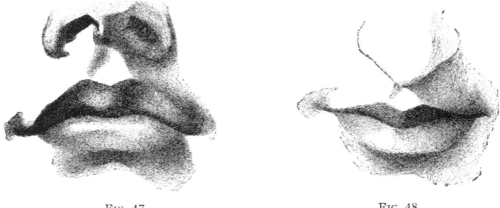

FIG. 47   FIG. 48

appears much shorter, and in some cases the space between the middle and the farther corner will be lost entirely. A three-quarter view of the mouth from below, Fig. 50, is influenced by foreshortening from two quarters, the point being to the side as

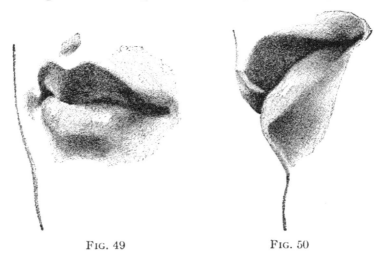

FIG. 49   FIG. 50

well as below. The curves from this position, as well as a three-quarter view from above, should be carefully studied.

The mouth and eyes combine to give various expressions to the face. When the lips are parted slightly, as in Fig. 51, the teeth show within and a half-smiling expression is given

THE HUMAN FIGURE

this feature by slightly raising the corner. In front and three-quarter views, the lips lengthen and flatten out in the act of smiling, as shown in Fig. 52. In Fig. 53 is shown the outline construction of the mouth illustrated in the previous figure.

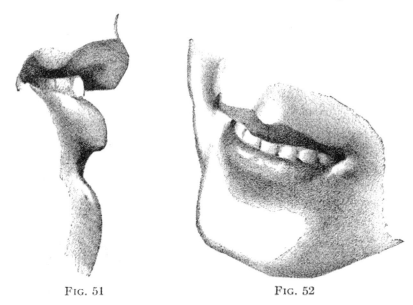

Fig. 51 Fig. 52

Note the foreshortened profile line through the center of the lips and chin. This line is identical with the profile of the nose, lips, and chin shown in Fig. 42, except that the lips are parted.

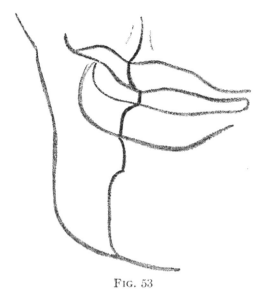

Fig. 53

If care is taken always to draw this foreshortened profile line, as shown in Figs. 42 and 53, the accuracy of profile and three-quarter-view drawings of the face will be assured.

THE HUMAN FIGURE

THE EAR

52. Viewed in profile, with the eye of the beholder on a level with the ear of the model, the top of the ear will be about on a level with the eyebrow and the bottom of the ear will be nearly on the same line as the base of the nose, although this detail varies in individuals. The ear occupies a position somewhat back of the center of the head, and in the classic figure the top of the ear rests on a line midway between the top of the head and the bottom of the jaw. The general direction of the ear is slightly at an angle, the line from its center pointing slightly toward the chin, as shown in Fig. 54. The form of the ear is decidedly unconventional, and must be studied carefully

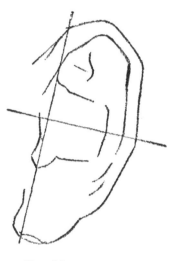

Fig. 54

Fig. 55

to be well understood. In its numerous concavities and convexities various shadows are cast, in the location of which lies the secret of rendering it properly. These shadows indicate every winding recess of the bowl and every prominence and hollow in the brim. In the front, or three-quarter view, Fig. 55, the lobe of the ear is closely attached to the head, but the upper part is much less so, as is readily seen when the ear is viewed from behind, as in Fig. 56. In Fig. 57 the ear is shown in full side view or as it appears when the head is in profile. The distinguishing characteristics of this feature should be located and their differences in the persons that are seen in every-day life noted.

THE HUMAN FIGURE

The ear is very intricate in its formation, and in the foreshortening of the head the proper placing of this feature is of the utmost importance. As said before, a line through the

Fig. 56

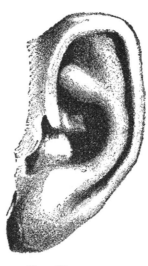
Fig. 57

head from one ear to the other forms an axis, so that the placing of the ear is a sort of key to the action of the head.

THE CHIN

53. The bottom of the chin is about one-third the length of the face below the nose when in profile. The back part of the head at its lowest extremity is about on a level with a horizontal line drawn across the head at the base of the nose. Therefore, the front of the head bears a proportion of three parts to two when compared with the length of the back of the head, and this extra third portion includes the mouth and chin.

Where the head is thrown well back, the back portion of the head is lowered and the chin raised, and great care must be exercised in order that their proper relative positions are preserved. When observed from below, the chin is more in the foreground than any other part of the face; but when observed from above, the chin is more in the background than any other portion of the face. Observance of these effects is of the utmost importance in the rendering of these details.

THE HUMAN FIGURE

FIGURE DRAWING EXERCISES

GENERAL INFORMATION

54. Required Work.—As a test to show whether or not the information given in this Section on the proportioning of the human figure has been properly absorbed and can be applied, drawing exercises in the form of plates will be required, these to be submitted to the Schools for examination.

As in previous Sections, the plates are to be of uniform size, if possible, 10 in. × 15 in., or 10½ in. × 16 in., depending on the kind of drawing paper that is used. There are to be two of these plates, which are to be arranged with the shorter dimension vertically and the longer dimension horizontally. Plate 1-2 is to be subdivided by vertical lines so as to make four narrow rectangles each about 3¾ inches wide by 10 inches high, each to contain one exercise. Plate 3-4 is to be subdivided by a vertical center line so as to make two rectangles 7½ inches wide by 10 inches high, each to contain one exercise. The plates are to be sent to the Schools one at a time for examination, as before.

55. Preliminary Practice Work (Not To Be Sent In).—No detailed or elaborate directions for methods of work need be given at this time. As the work required is simply in the nature of blocking-in sketches, no difficulty should be experienced in making the drawings. While the text illustrations should be referred to for assistance in this work, they must not be copied line for line. If possible, the blocking in and proportioning should be made direct from actual models; that is, from friends who will pose for a few minutes.

Although only two plates are required to be sent in to the Schools, all the diagrams illustrated in the text should be drawn by the student for his own practice—but not to be sent in.

THE HUMAN FIGURE

56. Character of the Plates.—As the test work in this Section is simply to give training in the correct blocking in and proportioning of the figures, there is no need of detailed rendering; therefore, the required work can be done with the simplest materials. Any cold-pressed paper, about 10 in. × 15 in., with a fine-tooth surface may be used. Two pencils are required. A rather hard one should be used for making the blocking-in lines and for proportioning the figures, and a softer pencil for drawing, in outline, the contours of the figures.

The charcoal stick may be used instead of the soft pencil, if desired; in which case all drawings must be sprayed with fixatif to protect them.

PLATE 1-2

57. Exercise A, Plate 1-2.—In the first rectangle on the plate make a blocking-in drawing in pencil about 8 inches high, of the front view of the male figure. Proportion this according to heads, using the system of horizontal lines, as in Fig. 3. Allow all proportioning lines to remain.

58. Exercise B, Plate 1-2.—In the second rectangle on the plate make a blocking-in drawing, to the same scale as Exercise A, of the front view of the male figure. Proportion this according to actual dimensions, using the system of horizontal lines for dividing upper body into thirds, as in Fig. 5. Allow all proportioning lines to remain.

59. Exercise C, Plate 1-2.—In the third rectangle on the plate make a blocking-in drawing, to the same scale as before, of the front view of the female figure. Proportion it to the male figure in Exercise B by means of the system of horizontal lines, as in Fig. 5. Allow all proportioning lines to remain. This exercise is to show the proper proportions of the female figure as compared with the male figure.

60. Exercise D, Plate 1-2.—In the fourth rectangle on the plate make a blocking-in drawing, to the same scale as before, of the figure (either male or female) seated. Show how the system of proportioning lines is applied to a seated

THE HUMAN FIGURE

figure. Allow all proportioning lines to remain. It may be necessary to have this figure slightly overlap and extend over into rectangle for Exercise C.

61. Final Work on Plate 1-2.—Letter or write at the top of the plate the title, Plate 1–2: The Human Figure; and, on the back of the sheet, the class letters and number, name, address, and date, forward the plate in the mailing tube to the Schools for examination, and proceed with Plate 3–4.

PLATE 3-4

62. Exercise A, Plate 3-4.—In the left-hand rectangle of the plate make a blocking-in drawing about 5 inches or 6 inches high of the human head and face, showing proper placing of hair, eyes, nose, lips, etc., as in Figs. 11 and 12. Make the drawing in outline only, and allow the blocking-in lines to remain.

63. Exercise B, Plate 3-4.—In the right-hand rectangle of the plate make some constructive drawings, life size, of eyes, ears, noses, lips, etc., as in Figs. 30 to 57, inclusive. Make the drawings in outline only and allow the blocking-in lines to remain.

64. Final Work on Plate 3-4.—Letter or write at the top of the plate the title, Plate 3–4: The Human Figure; and, on the back of the sheet, the class letters and number, name, address, and date, and forward the plate to the Schools for examination as before.

If any redrawn work on the first plate of this Section has been called for, and has not yet been completed, it should be satisfactorily finished at this time. Having completed all required work on the plates, the work of the next Section, in which training is given in drawing the figure in repose, should be taken up at once.

THE FIGURE IN REPOSE

DRAWING FROM SPECIAL STUDIES AND PHOTOGRAPHS

INTRODUCTION

1. Characteristics of Repose.—The proportions and framework of the human figure have now been thoroughly learned, and will serve as a necessary foundation for the work of making drawings from the human figure, which will be the purpose of the training given in this Section and the following one. For convenience the training in figure drawing will be divided into two parts; first, training is given in drawing the figure in repose, and later drawing the figure in action.

A figure is in *repose* when it is at rest and its proportions may be readily plotted, and when foreshortening need not be considered to a very great degree. Standing, seated, and recumbent, or prostrate, figures are all examples of figures in this state. A characteristic of figures in repose is that they are well balanced about a central line of support and the center of gravity is not disturbed.

2. Function of Special Studies and Photographs. Drawing from special charcoal studies of the human figure is the proper method of starting to draw the figure, because these studies are graded in such a way as to show the proper stages of making a drawing. When so understood, the use of such special studies cannot be considered as copy work, as the term is usually used, but they serve as a training in the proper method of working.

THE FIGURE IN REPOSE

3. Suggestions for Practice Work.—While no drawing plates are to be sent to the Schools until this Section is thoroughly understood, when the drawing plates at the end of the Section are to be drawn, the various studies reproduced in the text should be drawn as the description is being studied. In this way the description will be more easily understood and skill in this work will be acquired. In the practice work of this Section, charcoal is to be used as the medium. If half sheets of the charcoal paper furnished are used, the drawings will be on sheets $12\frac{1}{2}$ in. $\times$ 19 in. In all this work, the study of the figure that serves as a model should be pinned up in a vertical position, so as better to represent the living model.

STUDIES FROM CHARCOAL DRAWINGS AND PHOTOGRAPHS

4. As previously stated, the value of working first from specially prepared charcoal studies of the human figure consists in these studies being graded, showing the progressive stages by which such charcoal studies are developed. These stages, as shown in Figs. 1 to 5, are: (1) Proportioning and blocking in the contours; (2) placing the main curves in their simplest forms; (3) elaborating and detailing these curves to form all the parts; (4) plotting and shading in the blocks of shade values; (5) rendering the complete figure so as to express full modeling.

5. Proportioning and Blocking In Contours.—Let it be assumed that the female figure shown in Fig. 5 is a posed model, ready to be drawn. Therefore, it will be necessary to keep in mind, but not necessarily draw, the imaginary flexible solids in which each part of the figure may be considered as being enclosed.

The first step in the drawing of this figure is the placing of vertical, horizontal, and oblique lines to secure the proportions of the figure, as is shown in Fig. 1. The first to be drawn is the vertical line AB, on each side of which the figure is equally disposed. In this case, the short line yz should also be drawn,

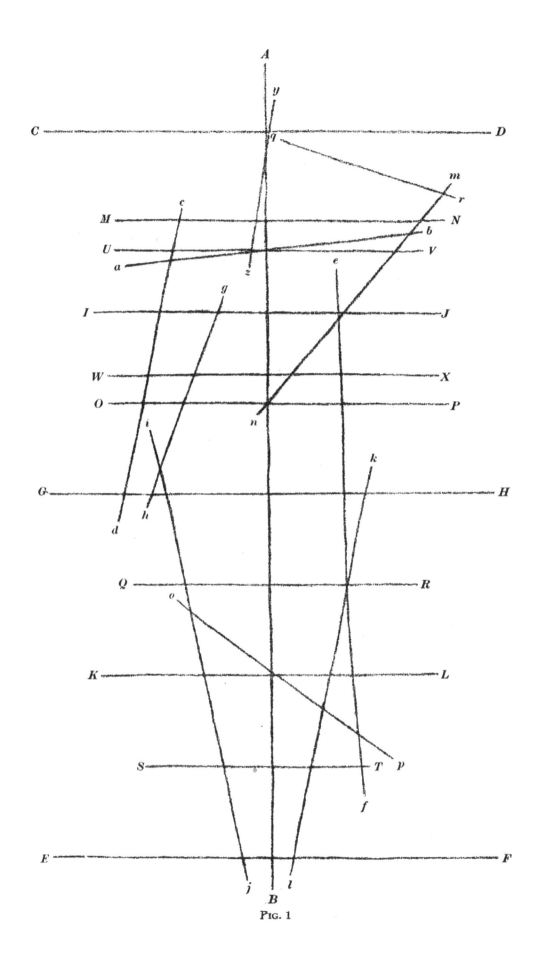

Fig. 1

THE FIGURE IN REPOSE

as this is the center line of the head, which is slightly inclined to the right. The next to be drawn are the horizontal lines CD and EF for the crown of the head and the soles of the feet. If the $12\frac{1}{2}''\times19''$ sheet of paper is used, these lines should be 16 inches apart, making the figure 16 inches high.

Next, the horizontal line GH should be drawn exactly midway between lines CD and EF, locating the bottom of the trunk, where the inside lines of the legs join it. Horizontal line IJ, midway between lines CD and GH, will then locate the arm pits; and line KL, midway between lines GH and EF, will locate the knees. Line MN, midway between lines CD and IJ, will locate the bottom of the chin, thus making the one-eighth division used as a head to proportion other parts. Line OP, midway between lines IJ and GH, will locate the navel; and midway lines OR and ST will locate middle points of the upper legs and the lower legs, respectively.

Carrying out now the division of the upper part of the body into thirds, horizontal lines UV and WX are drawn, locating the shoulders and the waist, respectively. Several of these horizontal lines must be tipped, as the line UV for the shoulders to become ab and the line KL for the knees to become op, because the shoulder and knee lines are actually tipped in the model.

6. The lateral proportions, or widths, of the figure must be obtained by means of oblique lines. Thus, line ab shows the slope of the shoulders; cd, the general direction and contour of the right arm; ef, the contour of the model's left side from armpit to hip; gh, the model's right side to hip; ij, the outside contour of her right leg; kl, the outside contour of her left leg; mn, the outside contour of the uplifted left arm; op, the tipping of the knee line; qr, the contour of the left forearm as it is raised to the back of the model's head. If all these oblique blocking-in lines are drawn with extreme care to see that their directions actually follow the contours specified, the next step, placing the main curves of the figure, will be a simple one, and an accurate drawing will result.

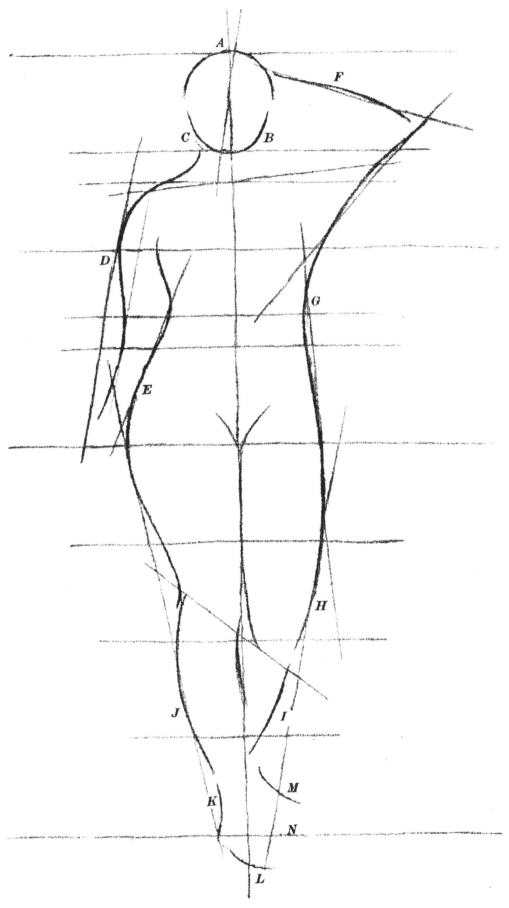

Fig. 2

THE FIGURE IN REPOSE

7. Placing Main Curves of Figure.—The next step in the drawing of the figure consists of plotting in the simplest curves or contours over the proportion and blocking-in lines used for the first step. In Fig. 2, these lines are again shown but, so as to prevent confusion, are not lettered. First, the semi-circular curve A is drawn as the general form for the top of the head; then curves B and C for the cheeks and chin, thus making an oval for the general shape of the head. Next, the compound curve D is drawn with extreme care following the blocking in line $c\,d$, Fig. 1, to show the outer contour and general direction of the shoulder and the right arm; then another compound curve E following blocking-in lines $g\,h$ and $i\,j$, Fig. 1, is drawn to express the contour of the model's right side from arm pit to knee. This must be drawn very carefully, and not simply dashed off with haste. Curve F is then drawn to contour the uplifted left forearm following the blocking-in line $q\,r$, Fig. 1; next curve G is drawn to show the model's left side from elbow to thigh, following the blocking-in lines $m\,n$ and $e\,f$, Fig. 1. The general outside contours of the lower legs are expressed by curves H and I for the left leg, and J for the right leg, following blocking-in lines $k\,l$ and $i\,j$, Fig. 1. The short curves K, L, M, and N, carefully placed to express the general contours of the feet, will then complete the main curves of the model.

These main curves must be freely and firmly drawn with the charcoal stick; they must not show any tendency to feel around for the proper positions. If the blocking-in lines have been carefully drawn, the curves can be placed with accuracy.

8. Elaborating and Detailing the Curves.—Fig. 3 shows the third step in drawing the figure; namely, the finishing up and detailing of the curves and contours so as to have a fairly complete outline drawing of the model, without any attempt at modeling or shading. While the final rendering of the figure is not to show detailed outlining, a great deal of such outlining must first be done in order to have accurate modeling. When the final rendering is prepared this outlining, made of course with charcoal, will be blended into the values,

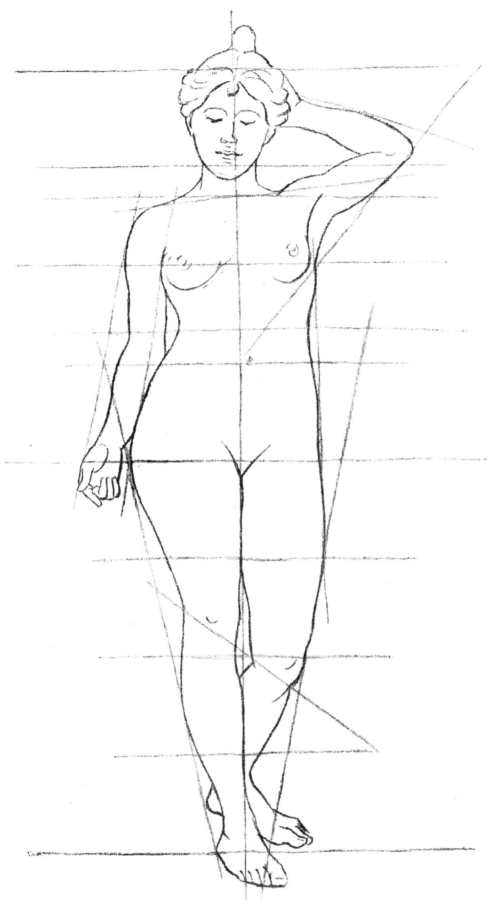

Fig. 3

THE FIGURE IN REPOSE

as was done when renderings were made from the wooden models.

To complete this part of the drawing, the features of the face and the hair, then the hands, fingers, feet, and toes, should be drawn in outline. Then should be put in the contours of other parts of the body that were not previously expressed, such as the breasts, the navel, the completion of the curves of the lower part of the abdomen, and the curves of the inner and outer contours of the arms, wrists, legs, and feet. In no case, however, should these details be drawn in a vague uncertain manner. They should be drawn according to the directions and ilustrations given in the preceding Section, which should be constantly referred to when this work is being done.

9. For instance, when the eyes, nose, and mouth in this particular figure are to be drawn these features should be placed in their relative positions as shown, and for their correct detailed drawing reference must be made to the illustrations and structural drawings of these details as given in the former Section. Thus, correct drawings will be found of the eyes looking down, just about as in the case of the eyes of the model in Fig. 5. In like manner the nose, mouth, hands, fingers, feet, toes, etc., should all be drawn in with care, and only after reference to the detailed pictures of these features. If these directions are followed there will be no reason for any inaccuracy in the outline drawing of the detailed features of the face and figure.

10. Plotting and Shading in Shade Values.—So far, the drawing of the figure has been expressed only in outline and is, therefore, only in its foundation form. Because there are no absolute outlines in nature, the figure's solidity, that is, its three dimensions of height, width, and thickness, must be expressed by means of tone values, as shown in Fig. 4. The principles governing these light-and-shade values are similar to those that govern light-and-shade values on the wooden geometric models, and can be applied readily to the human figure.

If the figure is placed in a strong light coming from one direction, the light and shade will resolve themselves into well-defined planes, while the margins of the shadows will seem to

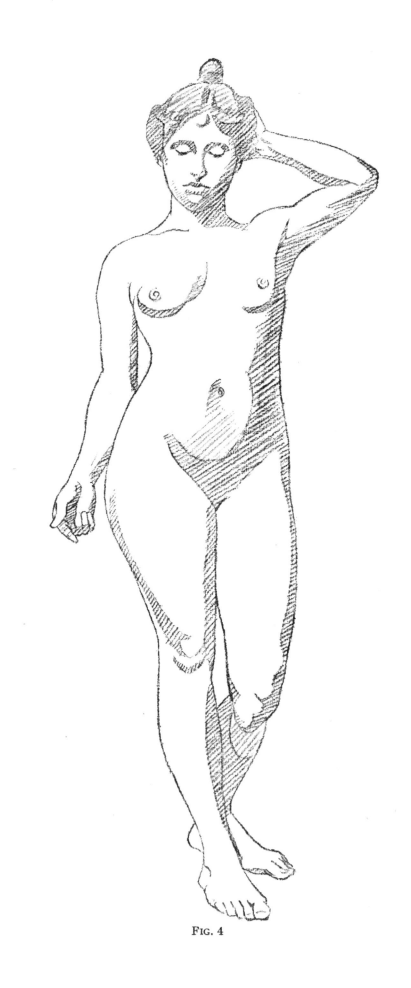

Fig. 4

THE FIGURE IN REPOSE

have a definite outline, darker in some places than the body of the shadow itself. The term *planes* of light and shade is used because that is the most convenient way of expressing these details.

Let it be assumed that the body is composed of a number of flat or flattened surfaces joined together to cover the general mass in the same manner as on the wooden geometric models. The blending of the shadows where these planes meet portrays the rotundity and completes the modeling of the figure. The simple effects of light-and-shade study in the geometrical wooden models are applicable here, and though the shadows may not be sharply defined they may be considered so and blended off afterwards. In figure drawing, the eye must search carefully for half tones of shades in order to express them in their proper values.

11. When drawing from the figure, the first thought should be to search for the definite margins of the main shade values. Accents that are strong in some portions of the margins are lost in others, and in other places the margins of the tones appear to blend with the lights forming the half tones. Careful search, however, will disclose the fact that the half tone itself has a definite margin. Looking at the figure as a whole, different planes of tone, the full light, the half tone, and the full shade should be sought. With practice it is possible to distinguish and draw the outlines of these three tones accurately and then to lay in the tones themselves. Thus, the effect of solidity is certain, because the blending of one tone with another is a very simple matter.

When the limits of the planes of shades have been located by outlines, they should be tinted in with flat values by drawing light diagonal lines with the point of the charcoal stick, as shown in Fig. 4. If the model is looked at with partially closed eyes, these darker shade values assume distinct forms, and can be readily contoured and shaded. In this model, the very darkest shades (aside from the dark value of hair itself) are noticeable on the model's left cheek and chin, on left side of her neck, under her left arm, along her left side, in

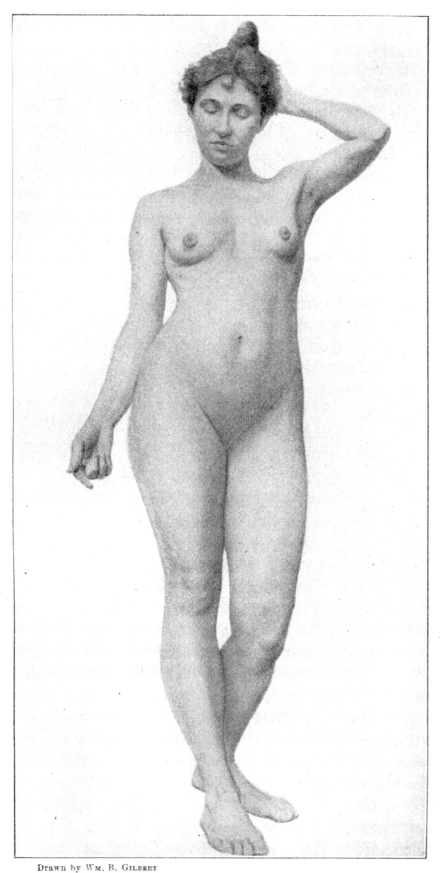

Drawn by Wm. B. Gilbert
COPYRIGHT, 1903, BY INTERNATIONAL TEXTBOOK COMPANY
ENTERED AT STATIONERS' HALL, LONDON
ALL RIGHTS RESERVED

Fig. 5

THE FIGURE IN REPOSE

the hollow made by the rounding portions of the lower part of the abdomen where it meets the legs, along the inner side of the right leg, and on the left lower leg. These darker shades are accompanied by other distinct shades not so dark, as over the front of the abdomen, along the left side, on the arms, legs, etc. By training himself to see these shade values, preferably through half-closed eyes, a person will soon become accustomed to locating them in any figure.

12. Rendering the Figure to Express Full Modeling. Fig. 5 shows the fifth and last stage of drawing the human figure. It consists of so blending the blocked-in shade values of the previous stage as to soften off their edges and make a gradual transition from the lightest values, through the semitones, to the darkest values, in all parts of the figure. When this has been done the figure will then be completely rendered to show proper rounding, or modeling, of all its parts, and proper texture of flesh. The method of making a realistic charcoal drawing of the human figure is similar to that used when drawing from the wooden models.

13. To complete this drawing, search the study of the model, Fig. 5, for places in the blocked-in planes of shade where the margins of the shade values are not sharply defined, or are altogether lost. At such places, the shade values melt into the lighter tones. There will be other places where the margins are accented by a greater depth of tone and a more distinct edge. In the case of both kinds of margins, the dark values and the lighter values must be pulled together so that they blend softly. The sharp lines of the edges of the blocked-in shades may be lifted off (partially or entirely) with the kneaded eraser and, first by oblique parallel lines and then by a blending of these lines by slight rubbing, the tones may be gradually fused one into the other. The rubbing of the charcoal lines must be done very lightly, with the tip of the finger or with a piece of chamois skin, so that the charcoal lines will be blended but the surface of the paper will not be spoiled. The kneaded rubber can always be used to advantage in lightening any value that seems too dark, or for securing more brilliant high lights.

THE FIGURE IN REPOSE

No hard-and-fast rules for rendering light-and-shade values and flesh textures can be given, for every one must find out by experiment just how to handle the charcoal to get the desired effects. However, certain general suggestions, applicable to the securing of various effects, may be of special value in the rendering of figure studies.

14. Hints on Use of Charcoal for Figure Studies. 1. When rendering the face, the general tint may first be placed by light oblique lines close together and afterwards lightly rubbed to make a flat tint. The shaded portions of the face may be portrayed in the same way with darker strokes afterwards blended. The lighter portions of the flesh tint may be rubbed off with the stomp or lifted off with the kneaded rubber. The details of the eyes, nose, mouth, etc., may be placed by means of lines made with the sharpened charcoal stick, these lines afterwards being softened with the tip of the stomp.

2. Transparency of tone, to express the texture of flesh, is secured by first placing a tint over the desired portions in the usual way lines lightly rubbed) and then, with the point of the sharpened charcoal stick, placing other lines over this ground work tint, cross-hatched and curved, or straight, allowing the lines to show crisp and clear, and unrubbed.

3. Transparency must also be expressed even in the deepest shadows. Simply because a shade value or shadow appears to be the darkest spot in the study is no reason for making it black by rubbing the lines hard. How far it is from being absolutely black may be seen by placing next to it a piece of perfectly black cloth, cardboard, or paper, and noting how light, by comparison, is the shade or shadow value.

4. The edges of the planes of shade or shadow may be blended off softly into the lighter values by gentle touches with the end of the finger, the chamois skin, or the stomp, the deeper shadows being added later by lines and worked over as before.

5. When very small or narrow planes or values are to be expressed, as the planes to express the fingers or toes, the edges of muscles, etc., powdered charcoal can be made by scraping

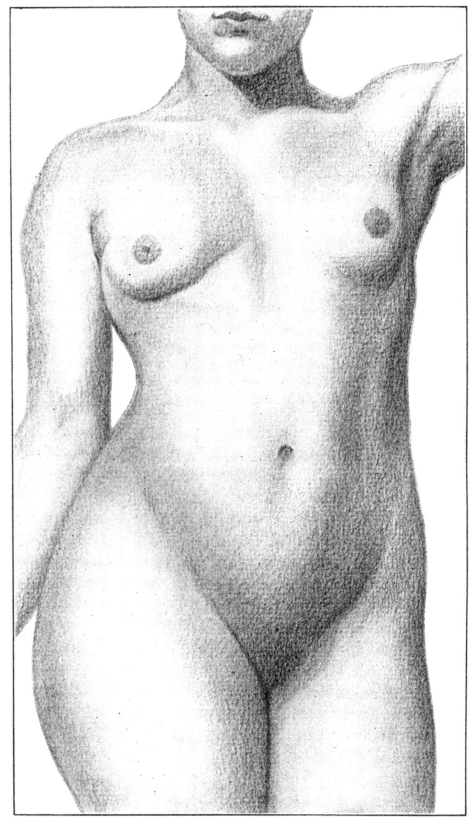

Fig. 6

THE FIGURE IN REPOSE

some from the sticks of charcoal and then applying it with the tip of a small stomp at the desired places.

6. Rubbing with the stomp should be done only when necessary; that is, on small details where the finger would be too clumsy. If the stomp is used to excess for rubbing, the paper will be spoiled, and the tone value will be hard and muddy.

7. After most of the modeling has been secured in the manner just explained, it is perfectly allowable to accent portions by means of lines made with the sharpened charcoal stick. These must be carefully placed, however, and must be used sparingly, otherwise the roundness of the body and limbs will be destroyed.

Fig. 6 shows a reproduction of a portion of a charcoal drawing of the model shown in Fig. 5, made at an enlarged size so that the texture of the charcoal paper and the manner in which the charcoal is applied are plainly seen. This reproduction in Fig. 6 should be studied with extreme care.

EXAMPLES OF CHARCOAL STUDIES AND PHOTOGRAPHS

15. The illustrations shown in Figs. 7 to 18 are reproductions of charcoal drawings made direct from male and female models. These charcoal drawings were prepared as part of the regular work of students learning to draw the human figure, and show not only proportions and postures of various types of figures, but reveal the steps by which the student drew and rendered the figure after he had blocked in its proportions, contours, and planes of light and shade. These illustrations will reveal much more than would mere photographs of a single model.

16. Preliminary Charcoal Study of Blocking-In Lines.—The reproduction in Fig. 7 shows the entire figure lightly blocked in, and a complete rendering, or modeling, of the face and neck started before rendering in detail the other parts of the body. The manner in which the student should swing in the long main contour lines in a broad way, before starting the detailing, is clearly illustrated.

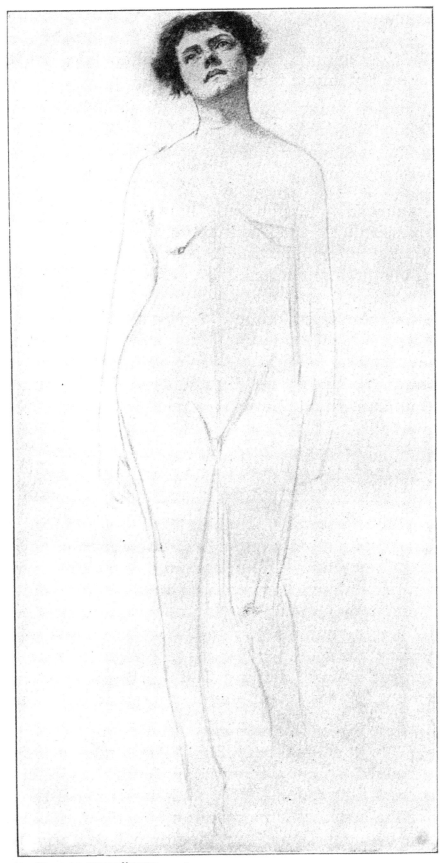

Drawn by Melvin Nichols

COPYRIGHT, 1903, BY INTERNATIONAL TEXTBOOK COMPANY
ENTERED AT STATIONERS' HALL, LONDON
ALL RIGHTS RESERVED

Fig. 7

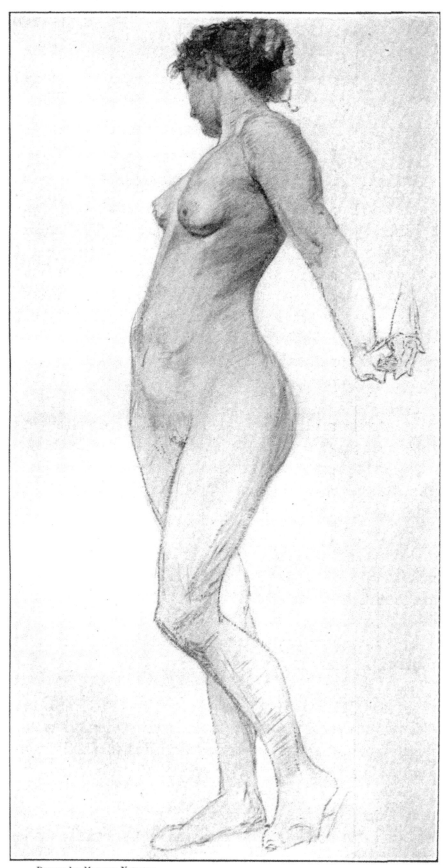

Drawn by Melvin Nichols
COPYRIGHT, 1903, BY INTERNATIONAL TEXTBOOK COMPANY
ENTERED AT STATIONERS' HALL, LONDON
ALL RIGHTS RESERVED

Fig. 8

THE FIGURE IN REPOSE

17. Study Showing Main Contours Blocked In. Fig. 8 shows a rendering fairly well contoured and more parts detailed in modeling than in the example just given. The hair, cheek, breasts, left side, etc., have been partially modeled, indicating that the study has been carried somewhat farther than that of Fig. 7. In this figure, the pose reveals the beautiful curve in the female back, as well as the profile of the breast and upper portions of the body.

The general direction of the right leg gives the line of support; and the relative points of prominence in this entire figure in profile, may be compared with the relative points of prominence studied in connection with the other illustrations. The outside of the thigh in the left leg is slightly convex, while the corresponding line on the inside of the thigh has a tendency to be concave. The positions of the feet govern the appearance and points of prominence of the leg. In the left leg, the foot rests at an angle; but in the right leg, the foot is turned in profile and is flat on the floor, thus changing the contours accordingly. From the back of the neck to the hollow of the back is an even, graceful, convex curve; at the back it becomes concave and swells again to the thigh. The left arm, extending to the ring that is grasped by the hand, exhibits some of its muscles in prominence; here the muscles swell out to form a tangential union with the curve from the back of the neck to the back of the body. The muscles of the forearm are necessarily prominent, owing to the weight that is thrown on the wrist. The fulness of the chest is shown above the left breast, and a nearly straight line extends from the under side of the right breast to the navel.

18. Study Partially Completed in Full Modeling. Fig. 9 shows a drawing of the male figure when viewed from behind, in which the rendering is carried still farther, as the entire upper part is completely modeled. The shadows are strongly marked, showing the prominence of the shoulder blades and the relative positions of the elbow and waist line, as previously pointed out. Attention is especially called to the shadows at lower part of back.

Drawn by Melvin Nichols

COPYRIGHT, 1903, BY INTERNATIONAL TEXTBOOK COMPANY
ENTERED AT STATIONERS' HALL, LONDON
ALL RIGHTS RESERVED

Fig. 9

THE FIGURE IN REPOSE

As this figure is rather thin, the points of bony prominence are readily seen. The left elbow is clearly indicated by a plane of shade and a high light in the center of the arm, while the right elbow is brought into prominence by means of the position of the arm. The bony construction of the hips beneath the flesh is shown by the fulness on the right side of the figure above the buttocks, and the curve from this point to the broadest point of the hips and thence to the back of the knee is plainly indicated. It can be easily studied here how the line of the waist is affected by the position of the hip and the amount of fat thereon.

In this figure, the weight is thrown on the right foot, but the curve in the waist line here is flat because in this example there is little flesh on the hips and consequently the line is straighter. Were the hips fuller, the fleshy portion would cause them to appear higher and thereby emphasize this curve at the waist.

19. Study Showing Broad Simple Method of Modeling.—Fig. 10 shows another view of the male figure as seen from behind, and is an example of a very simple form of rendering. The hands clasped behind the back are simply indicated, and in this position give considerable prominence to the shoulder blades. There is no attempt at variety of tone here, except where the high lights fall on the shoulders and elbows. The hair is increased in tone somewhat, in order to contrast with the flesh, and a few strong lines are placed throughout the figure in order to express the direction of the planes. Although the hands are incomplete and roughly blocked, their position and pose can be readily felt; this shows the importance of expressing details well in mass. In the legs, there is no attempt at precision of outline, yet they are drawn in with a bold, free sweep that shows the artist had a definite idea of points of start and arrival; the position and direction of each line was determined before the crayon was placed to the paper. For instance, at the juncture of the right thigh with the abdomen, a point of start was established and the line sweeps boldly and freely to the knee, which is the definite point of finish or arrival, and from here to a point above the instep another line

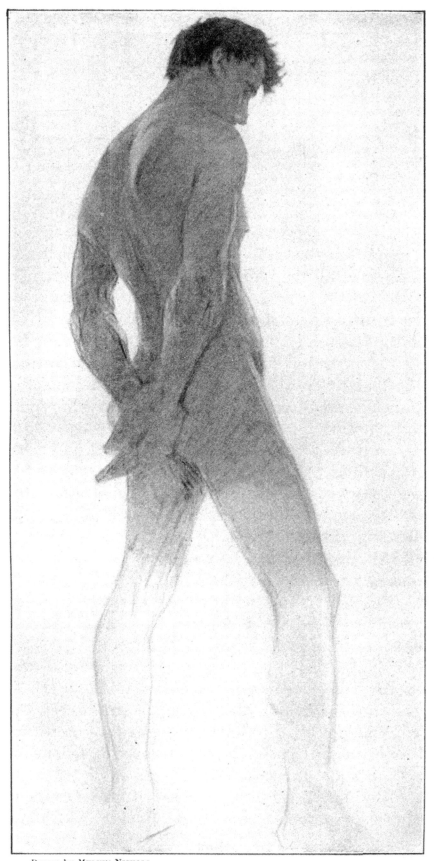

Drawn by Melvin Nichols
COPYRIGHT, 1903, BY INTERNATIONAL TEXTBOOK COMPANY
ENTERED AT STATIONERS' HALL, LONDON
ALL RIGHTS RESERVED

Fig. 10

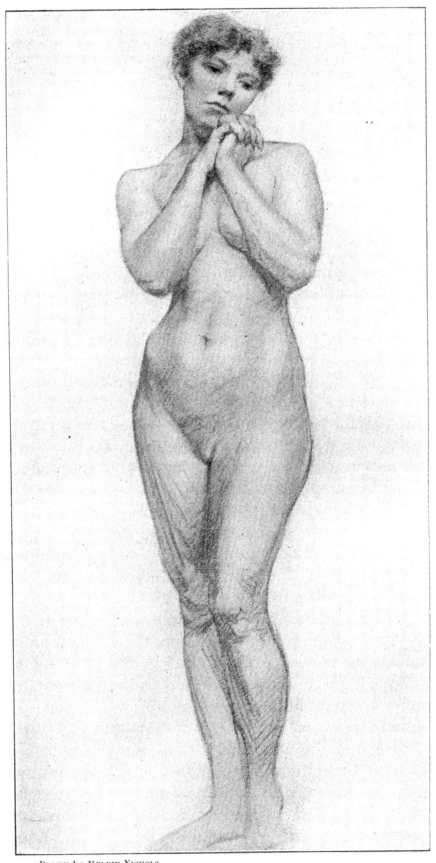

Drawn by Melvin Nichols

COPYRIGHT, 1903, BY INTERNATIONAL TEXTBOOK COMPANY
ENTERED AT STATIONERS' HALL, LONDON
ALL RIGHTS RESERVED

Fig. 11

THE FIGURE IN REPOSE

is boldly drawn. Similar points can be found on all the parts of the figure, showing that the mind grasped the problem and the hand executed the work with mutual understanding.

The determination of these points is acquired only by practice and careful study, but when the ability to place these lines correctly is once gained this method of procedure will instil into the drawings that feeling of action that is so important in all figure work.

20. Study Almost Entirely Completed.—Fig. 11 shows a front view of another female figure, in which the rendering has been carried somewhat farther than in previous examples. The details of the face have been softened one into the other by means of the point of the stomp, touched lightly here and there to remove the darker color and to blend off the lighter shade where the planes of shadow fade into one another. The hair, although indicated in masses, possesses no detail, but a few strongly placed shadows assist in bringing its main features into prominence. The position of the arms throws the shoulders rather squarely across, and the clasped hands cause the muscles of the forearm to swell into prominence near the elbow. The raising of the shoulders in this position also draws out the waist and causes a hollow appearance at the elbows, while the weight of the body on the right leg throws the pelvis on that side in a higher position, showing a prominence of the bone above on a level with the navel and a prominence of the thigh muscle immediately below it. The fulness from the thigh to the knee is caused by the strain on the right leg; also, the fulness of the shin muscle, as in Fig. 8. Here the kneecaps and knee joints are clearly defined, and in the outside of the left leg there is a depression above the kneecap similar to that referred to in the previous figure. The planes of shadow on the outsides of the arms express the muscles drawn into action, and the deep shadows under the clasped hands and the elbows cause the body to appear to recede at that point and give it the proper roundness and other characteristics.

21. Study Completed in Full Modeling.—A good example of a fully modeled female figure, of still a different

I L T 159B—20

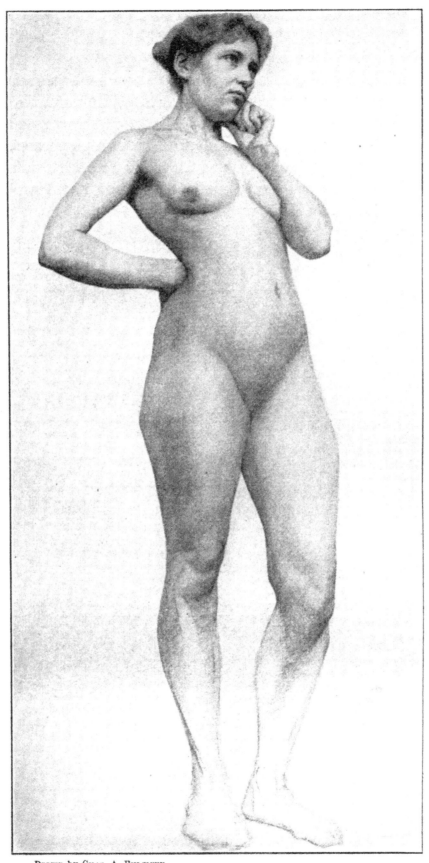

Drawn by Chas. A. Pulcifer

COPYRIGHT, 1903, BY INTERNATIONAL TEXTBOOK COMPANY
ENTERED AT STATIONERS' HALL, LONDON
ALL RIGHTS RESERVED

Fig. 12

THE FIGURE IN REPOSE

type, is shown in Fig. 12. The outlines are clear, the shadows are softly blended, and the whole drawing is rendered to give a finished effect of light and shade as it existed in the original. Note, however, that no matter how dark the deepest shadows may appear, they possess a transparency free from all muddiness.

The body rests, as before, on the right leg, throwing the right hip somewhat above its normal position. The back of the right hand rests above the hip, causing a depression of the flesh at this point, and the line of the upper portion of the body should be nearly straight from the arm to the intersection of the wrist and the waist. This line is not straight, however; it is concave at the beginning and ending and convex in the middle, because of the prominence of the muscles of the back. The muscles of the forearm are rather full, but neither the upper arm nor the forearm is perfectly straight but both are slightly curved. The convexity of the upper arm and the concave contour of the inside of the arm consist of a number of delicate curves and not one even curve.

Note carefully the lines bounding the planes of shadow down the entire right side of the body, and that these planes blend into the high light on the front of the abdomen. The accented shadow under the right breast outlines this feature, while the left breast is crushed into the forearm, causing a depression in the left forearm from the wrist half way to the elbow. This must be carefully rendered in order to prevent a distorted appearance in the left arm.

The line from the intersection of the body with the left arm to the prominence of the thigh, appears at first to be composed of two concave curves with one convex curve between them. Careful study, however, will show that between the convexity of the abdomen and the prominence of the thigh, the line is rather convex and not flat. The knee on the left leg is sharply defined, and the fulness back of the knee is decidedly prominent. The right leg is in full front view, showing the points of prominence on the inside and outside of the calf, the fulness of the ankle bone, and the general trend to concavity from the bottom of trunk to the ankle bone, caused by the curvature of the bones in this member.

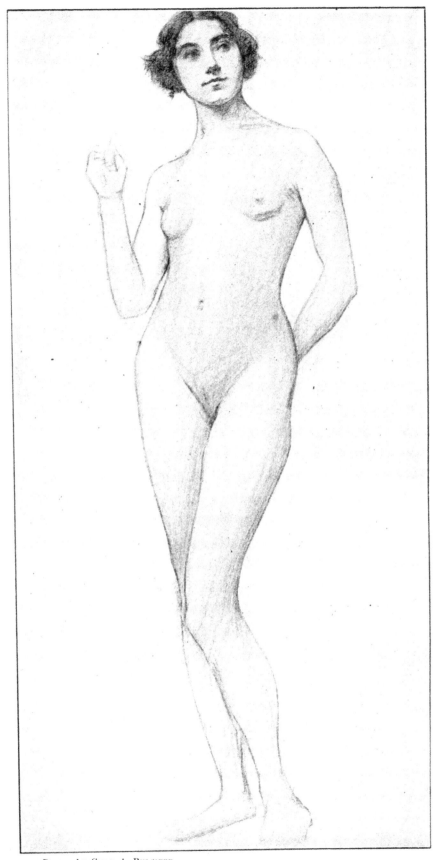

Drawn by Chas. A. Pulcifer
COPYRIGHT, 1903, BY INTERNATIONAL TEXTBOOK COMPANY
ENTERED AT STATIONERS' HALL, LONDON
ALL RIGHTS RESERVED

Fig. 13

THE FIGURE IN REPOSE

The modeling on this study is completed almost entirely by the use of the stomp. The shadows, being generally placed and their planes well defined, should be blended off softly into the high lights by gentle touches with the end of the stomp, the deeper shadows being added and worked in with the smaller stomp where required. Where the contours of the muscles are to be emphasized, as in the knuckle, under side of the right arm, and about the knees, careful touches of the crayon-charged stomp will express the planes and can afterwards be flattened off into the surrounding planes where required.

22. Study of Slender Female Figure.—Fig. 13 shows a fully (but lightly) rendered study of the figure of a somewhat tall and thin person, and a study of it will reveal certain marked differences in it from the characteristics of the rather more fully developed female figures studied so far. The figure is somewhat less than eight heads in height, but appears tall because largely above the eye level. The head, however, is not thrown so far back as in some previous cases, and although the under side of the brows and nose as well as the chin are distinctly visible, none of these features become very much foreshortened.

The figure is turned somewhat away from the observer, and the weight, though thrown on the right leg as before, causes the body to sag somewhat so that the breasts are not on the same line. The figure being of a rather thin person shows the prominence and depressions rather clearly; the lines are angular and in no place show the full curves of maturity, and therefore this figure forms a good subject for study. Attention is called to the shoulders, the elbows, the prominence in the upper part of the hips, the knees, and the heels.

23. While none of the lines in this figure are absolutely straight, none possess a continuous curve. The model's left shoulder starts nearly horizontally across the chest, but the horizontal line marking the line of the collar bone is depressed at each end and high in the middle. The opposite shoulder is composed of a series of flattened curves that disappear behind the upturned arm, and from the shoulder to the neck the curves prevent the general contour from appearing stiff and monotonous.

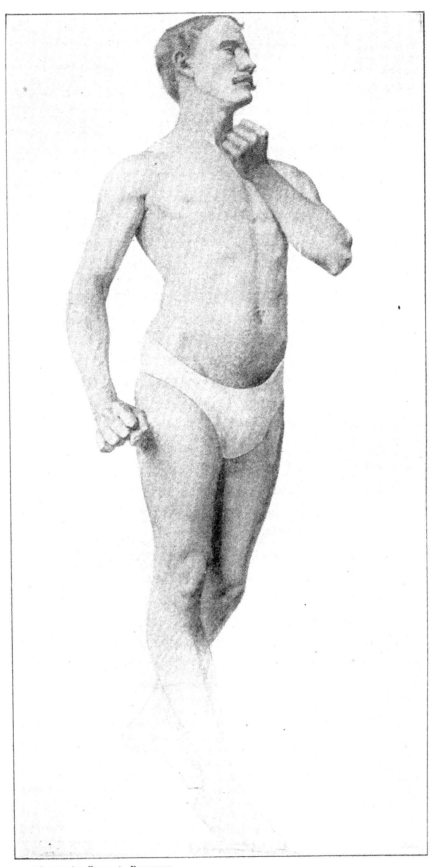

Drawn by Chas. A. Pulcifer
COPYRIGHT, 1903, BY INTERNATIONAL TEXTBOOK COMPANY
ENTERED AT STATIONERS' HALL, LONDON
ALL RIGHTS RESERVED

Fig. 14

THE FIGURE IN REPOSE

The points to be particularly noted in the rendering are the depression in the left kneecap, the ankle bone, and the position in which the model is posed so that it throws the weight of the body forwards and causes a prominence of the muscle in the right thigh as well as a certain fulness in the shin. The backward pressure of the left leg calls the thigh muscles into action; first, just above the knee, where most of the strain comes, and after, farther up on the inside of the leg. The calf of the left leg is rounded and full, also suggestive of this pressure, and the entire trend of the modeling should be to express this action with the fewest possible lines. Here the right foot is seen in profile, and the left foot is sharply foreshortened and nearly on a level with the eye.

24. Three-Quarter Front-View Study of Male Figure.—Fig. 14 shows a very carefully modeled study, fully rendered (except the lower legs), of the male figure, and one that will bear long and careful study. The figure is posed in such a manner that it brings the principal muscles of the upper portion of the body into prominence. This light graceful figure is an admirable one for study, for the sweeping lines are not cut by excessive muscular development nor rounded off by fatty tissue. The median line from the pit of the throat to the navel is clearly marked, and is of the greatest assistance in drawing, inasmuch as one could easily build upon it the relative proportions of the figure.

The entire outline is made up of short, straight lines, as for instance in the right arm, from where it joins the shoulder to the inside of the elbow; and in the forearm, where the inside contour is composed of a series of short, broken, straight lines. Observe, too, the general curvature of the right leg, throwing the right foot well under the center of the body. The feet as sketched here appear abnormally large, but this is due to the fact that the figure is almost entirely above the eye and the feet are much nearer the point of view than is any other portion.

25. Side-View Study of Male Figure.—Fig. 15 shows the male figure in a good pose. The interest is centered in the head and right arm, the muscles of the neck giving a clear idea of the

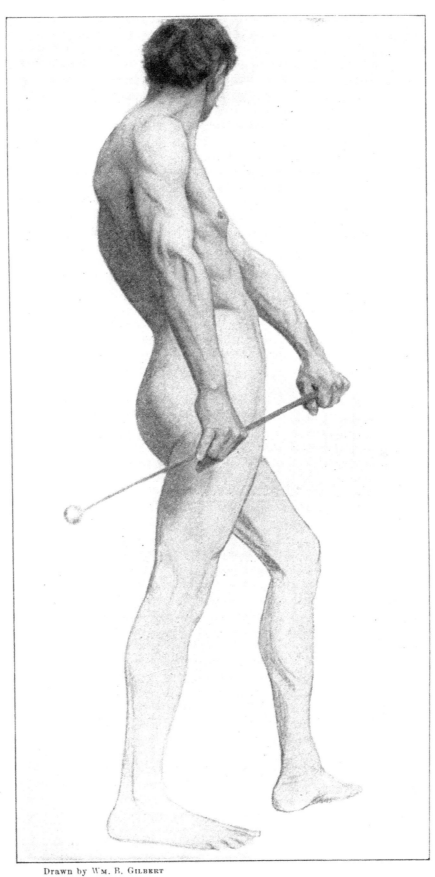

Drawn by Wm. B. Gilbert

Fig. 15

effect of turning the head, while the muscles of the arm are thrown into prominence by the pose of the figure. The left shoulder appears considerably below the right owing to the fact that the figure is seen from below. The hands are well brought out, as the knuckles catch the light and form points that must be carefully located in order to preserve the proper construction. While the front of the body is mainly composed of a single sweep from the neck to the ankle, an analysis of it will show that it consists of a series of convex lines subtly joined to one another so as to mark prominences due to muscular development. The deep shadow on the back contrasted with the high light on the upper arm, and the darkened hands profiled against the high light of the hip, tend to throw the right arm into prominence and give the figure a feeling of depth and solidity.

26. Rear-View Study of Male Figure.—Fig. 16 shows a rendering of still another type of male figure, in a pose that reveals new features in the modeling of the figure. Most of the figure is expressed in monotone with a few high lights placed to give modeling an occasional deeper shadow to emphasize the form. Attention is called to the transparency of the shadow over the back; there is no feeling of deadness there, but simply of partial shade. If the eyes are slightly closed, the planes of light and shade become very strongly marked. These planes of light and shade should be carefully studied and an effort made to outline them before the shadow tone is placed on the drawing. Care must be taken not to overwork the shadow to make it too dark; also where two shaded portions are in contact the high lights in the deeper shadows must be well placed in order to emphasize the outline. For instance, the left hand placed in the hollow of the back is rendered in practically the same tone as the back itself, but the small high light on the upper part of the hand and the deepening shadow under the wrist, gives it outline and permits it to contrast with the tone against which it is placed. The upper side of the thumb, however, receives no high light, and as a matter of fact merges into the shadow of the back; but the eye feels the

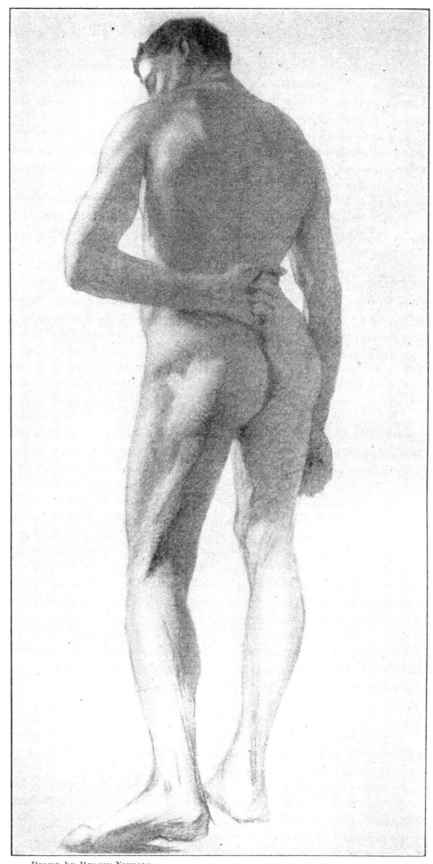

Drawn by Melvin Nichols
COPYRIGHT, 1903, BY INTERNATIONAL TEXTBOOK COMPANY
ENTERED AT STATIONERS' HALL, LONDON
ALL RIGHTS RESERVED

Fig. 16

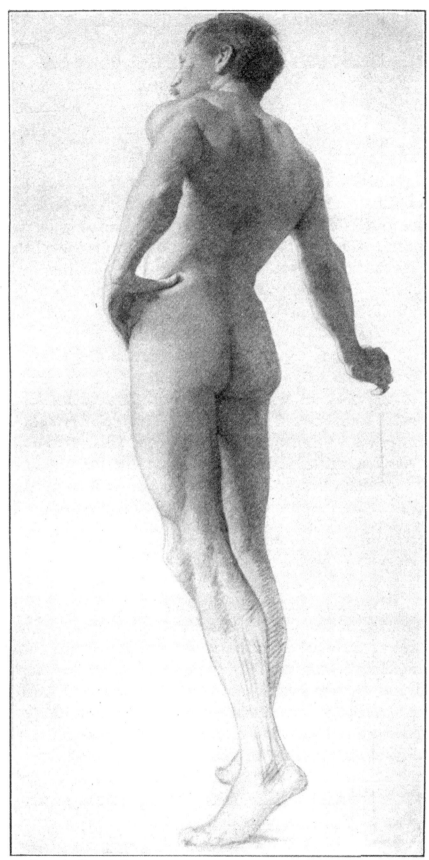

Drawn by Chas. A. Pulcifer

COPYRIGHT, 1903, BY INTERNATIONAL TEXTBOOK COMPANY
ENTERED AT STATIONERS' HALL, LONDON
ALL RIGHTS RESERVED

Fig. 17

THE FIGURE IN REPOSE

presence of the outline, as also of the ends of the knuckles, yet all that is placed there to convey that impression is the simple shading between the fingers. The whole solidity of this figure is based on a keen sense of light and shade and a clear understanding of where one begins and the other ends.

27. Three-Quarter Rear-View Study of Male Figure. Fig. 17 shows another light graceful pose of the male figure. The point of interest in this figure lies in the study of the foreshortening. The eye of the artist was about on a level with the ankle of the model, and as the figure leans slightly forwards, parts of it are materially foreshortened. The left elbow becomes very prominent, while the forearm tapers rapidly to the wrist owing to the fact that it is more distant. The right arm is similarly drawn, the taper of the muscles of the elbow to the wrist being even more conspicuous here. The vigorous treatment of the outlines where a series of simple lines block out the general form should be studied. The high light under the left arm tends to throw the left arm into the foreground apparently and increase the effect of foreshortening. The lines across the shoulders and hips are at such an angle that one readily feels the height of the figure above the eye.

28. Study of Slender Male Figure.—Fig. 18, the last of the series of charcoal studies, shows the figure of a rather thin person, and though the bones are well covered with muscles there is not much prominence given to any one set, nor any development of fat. The lines, however, remain practically the same as those of a muscular figure, but not so prominent. The modeling is carried out with great nicety, and the effect of contrast between light and shade in order to show foreshortening properly is well studied. There is not a great variety of tone here, and the simplicity with which the effect is obtained is readily illustrated in the plane of shadow that extends the full length of the left leg, particularly the part of the leg from the knee to the ankle. The union, or intersection, of this plane, of shadow with the plane of light marks the intersection with the shin bone, while the contrast of the pale light with the deepest shadow on the right leg gives the full contour of the left

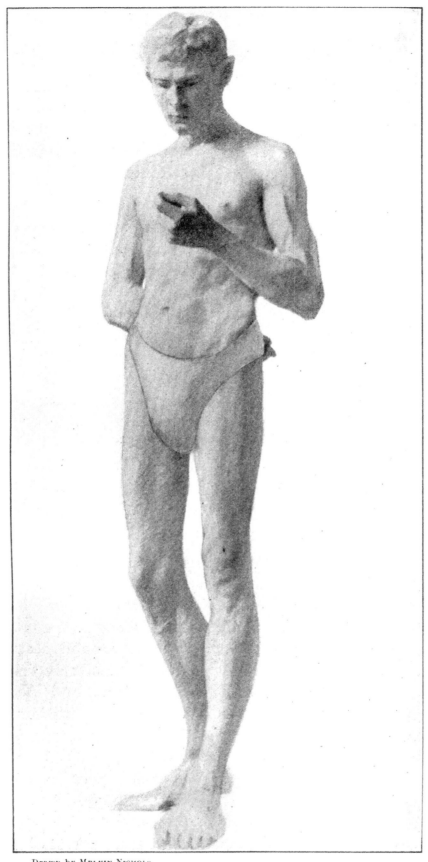

Drawn by Melvin Nichols

COPYRIGHT, 1903, BY INTERNATIONAL TEXTBOOK COMPANY
ENTERED AT STATIONERS' HALL, LONDON
ALL RIGHTS RESERVED

Fig. 18

THE FIGURE IN REPOSE

leg, without individual outline. The enormous size of the left foot is due to its being thrust well forwards and much nearer the eye than the rest of the figure. The careful modeling of the left hand and the deep shadow on its under side tend to throw it well forwards of the high light on the chest; and the muscles of the chest and abdomen, though but slightly expressed, all make their appearance felt, although the outlines are very elusive.

29. Photographs of Female Figure in Various Postures.—Figs. 19, 20, and 21 are reproduced from photographs of the same female model, and are introduced here to show certain postures of the figure not covered by the reproductions of charcoal studies just illustrated. A further purpose of these photographs is to show, in rather more detail than can be shown in a charcoal study, the drawing, modeling, and flesh texture of certain parts, as the face, hands, fingers, breasts, feet, toes, etc.

In Fig. 19 is shown a side view of the figure in a rather conventional position in order to indicate the relative position of the various members, as compared with previous figures where the model was standing. Here the position of the arm hanging by the side in profile, and the curve from the under side of the chin to the breast can be studied. It will be noted that the line of the back disappears entirely behind the arm, but this illustration is of importance to show the effect of relaxation on different muscles. The breasts, relieved of the lifting tendency caused by the arms in previous cases being thrown above the head, now fall to their natural positions and the line of the abdomen flattens out, as the muscles in the upper part of it, being in repose, no longer support the under part. The contours of the calves of the legs, the instep, and the foot in profile are illustrated here.

When drawing the side view, convenient points for bounding the outlines, in the pit of the throat, nipples, juncture of the abdomen with the legs, the knees, ankles, and toes must be found. The planes and subtle curves that indicate the contours of the various parts must be carefully studied.

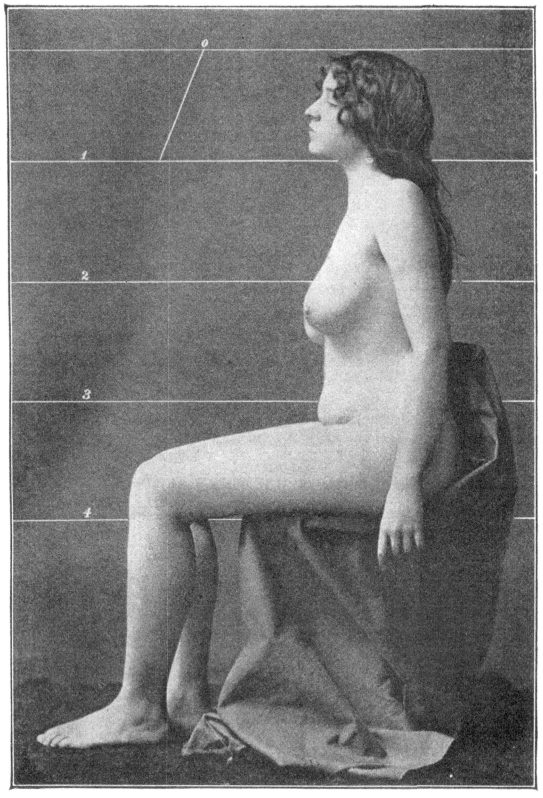

Fig. 19

THE FIGURE IN REPOSE

30. In Fig. 20 is shown another seated posture in which the parts are more foreshortened. In this case, the proportions of the parts of the body from the top of the head to the base of the trunk, from the base of the trunk to the knee, and from the knee to the ground should be compared. The head as a scale of measurements is indicated here by lines, those on the left leg being indicated in a diagonal direction in order to be at right angles with the member.

In Fig. 19, it should have been noted that the elbow falls just above line *3* and that the waist line does not appear distinctly, but the shadow on the inside of the arm would indicate it to be very nearly at the level of the elbow, thus showing that the waist line has been pushed up somewhat in the seated posture. In Fig. 20, the waist line is distinctly visible just above the elbow, and proves that this change of posture has produced a change in the relative positions of waist and elbow.

In Fig. 20, considerable attention should be given to the location of the shadows. The face is divided by a distinct line through the center; beneath the chin as the shadow falls on the throat and shoulder it becomes diffused, but when viewed with partially closed eyes its margin is distinctly discernible and its characteristic shape can be studied. A triangular mass of shadow marks the turn of the breast into the side, and beneath the breast a small patch of deeper shadow shows, by contrast, the general form and contour of the breast. On the thigh and down the side of the leg the shadow is very diffused, but its margin becomes sharp near the knee and on the ankle and can be indicated if carefully studied. The right foot, as it turns under the knee of the left leg, is a difficult piece of foreshortening. The under side of the foot is partially visible here, although in deep shadow.

31. In Fig. 21, the sinuous and serpentine character of the figure is well illustrated by the pose. All of the parts are much foreshortened, but the beautiful outlines are sharply profiled against the background and indicate the margins of the planes distinctly. There is scarcely an angle to be observed. From the waist to the shoulder and from the shoulder to the

Fig. 20

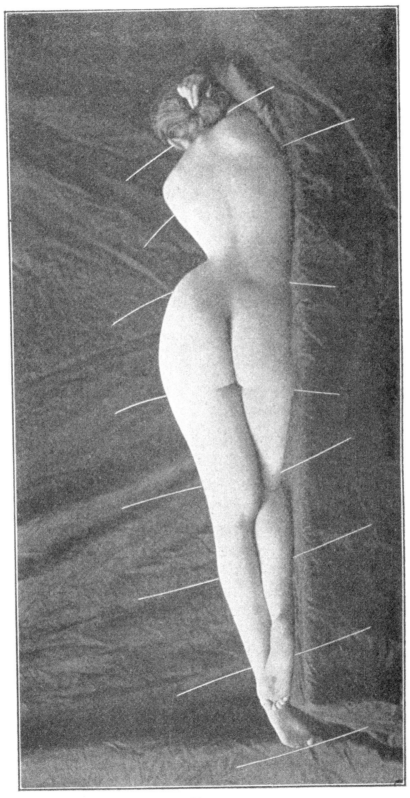

Fig. 21

THE FIGURE IN REPOSE

neck are two nearly straight lines, and an angular mass of shoulder and back where the left shoulder is profiled against the background.

Attention is especially called to the sagging appearance of the upper leg where it rests against the lower one, and the droop of the left foot over the end of the sofa. The appearance of weight in different parts of the body is thus represented clearly, as wherever the flesh is given an opportunity it sags into a natural and comfortable position. This is again indicated in the calf of the right leg, where it is flattened by the weight of the leg above it. The left hip in this pose is made more than usually prominent because the whole body is leveled on the lower side on account of the unyielding character of the sofa on which it is posed.

The white lines crossing the backgrounds in Figs. 19, 20, and 21, indicate that, no matter what the position of the figure may be, the height may be divided into eight equal parts, or heads, as previously explained.

DRAWING FROM CASTS

INTRODUCTION

32. Function of Casts.—Any one who has made figure drawings from reproductions of charcoal studies made by others, or from photographs, will have become familiar with the height and width of the human figure, but the thickness, or rotundity, will have been left largely to the imagination. Plaster casts of the figure and its parts are therefore used to enable the art student to see and feel the effects of roundness and solidity. A knowledge of these effects will not only aid a person drawing the figure in repose to so render it as to depict the lifelike appearance of the human body, but this knowledge will also help a person to appreciate the positions of the parts of the body and the alterations that each part undergoes when the figure is in action.

THE FIGURE IN REPOSE

The aim in drawing from casts should be to get the best general effect with the fewest number of lines and the least amount of work. A drawing that is constantly fussed over and changed loses character, and it is better to spend more time studying the subject and less time putting it on paper than to hastily sketch some detail that must be almost immediately rubbed out because insufficient thought was given to that detail before the drawing of it was commenced.

33. Suggestions for Practice Work.—The casts that will be described and studied, and which are provided with this Section, are a full-length cast, or statuette, of the female figure in fully modeled form, and almost life-size casts of the head, hand, and foot. As in the case of preceding studies, it is expected that drawings will be made from these casts as their descriptions are being studied, but these drawings are only for practice work and are not to be sent to the Schools for examination.

When these casts are studied, they should be so placed upon a table, or hung against a wall or other surface, as to be conventionally lighted. The practice drawings are to be made with the materials and by the methods already described, but in addition, the plumb-line is to be used to note the points that fall below one another on the cast. This line consists simply of a string with a weight at one end, and may be held between thumb and finger at arm's length between the eye and the cast from which the study is being made. By means of it various details may be recorded to give points from which to work.

The process of making the drawings from the plaster casts should consist of the same five progressive stages as were followed in making figure studies from reproductions of charcoal studies and photographs.

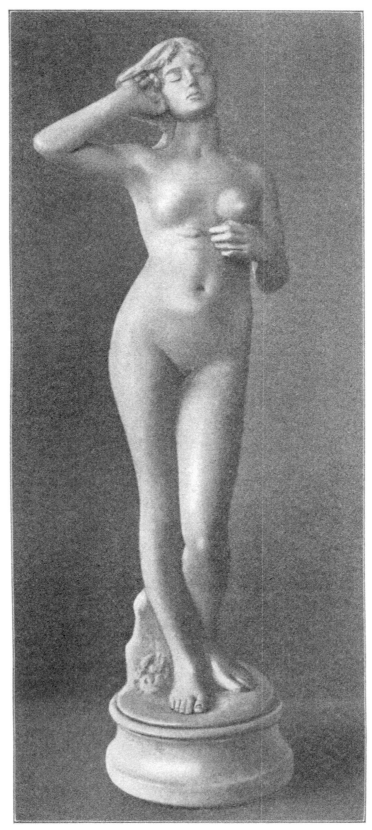

Fig. 22

THE FIGURE IN REPOSE

rendering aims to secure broad effects, and in the blocking in of planes of shade values nothing should be represented but a series of flat planes that join each other to make up the characteristics of the human form. When their position and form is once understood, these planes may be easily varied and softened into one another so that the general softness and characteristics of the individual figure can be represented in close portrayal, or, if it is the face that is being drawn, in exaggerated portrayal, as in caricature work. It is important that the flat, plain surfaces of the forms be well understood before the subtle curvatures of a finished form are attempted.

36. Profile and Three-Quarter Views.—Studies from this cast of the female figure in other positions should be made, as, for instance, side views (that is, right profile and left profile), three-quarter views, first one side then the other, and a rear view, proceeding with the drawing and rendering in the five stages as previously described. The drawing, and the arrangement of the blocks of shade values on these profile, three-quarter and rear views, will be quite different from those shown in Fig. 23, but the practice in making these drawings of various views of the figure will make one very familiar with the modeling of the human figure and its parts and will serve as an excellent preparation for the work of actually drawing from the living model, which comes later.

CAST OF HEAD

37. Full Front View.—The cast of the block form of the head is provided so that practice may be had in drawing the entire head, face, and individual features, approximately full size. In this way a familiarity with the placing, proportions, and foreshortening of these features may be secured and they can be drawn readily in the full figure. The description of the proportions and contours, as well as of the planes of light and shade, of this block form of head, and the directions for making drawings from this cast, are somewhat detailed on account of the importance of the treatment of the human head and face in illustrating work.

THE FIGURE IN REPOSE

38. When studying it, the cast should be hung in a good light so that the shadows will fall below and toward the right side as shown in Fig. 24. If it is hung near a window, the lower part of the window should be shaded slightly and the drawing

Fig. 24

table placed with the window to the left and the cast in front of the worker and not more than 6 or 8 feet away, so that, when the arm is extended to get the pencil measurements, the full length of the head from the crown to the chin will measure approximately 3½ inches. The width at its widest portion will

THE FIGURE IN REPOSE

then be about $2\frac{3}{4}$ inches. These measurements should then be doubled so that the drawing of the head will, by pencil measurement, be about 7 inches high. These proportions should be determined by pencil measurements and the measurements here given should not be adhered to unless the proportions by pencil measurement vary so greatly that the block drawings cannot be contained within the confines of the drawing sheet. In this case, the drawing table should be moved farther away, so that the head may be drawn within the limits suggested.

39. Proportions of Head.—Although all proportions should be laid off by pencil measurement, it is well that the general proportions of the features to the rest of the face should be understood. In the first place, from the chin to the roots of the hair is four-fifths the height of the entire head. Therefore, in the present case, should the drawing of the entire head be 7 inches in height, it will be a little more than $5\frac{1}{2}$ inches from the chin to the roots of the hair. The face from the roots of the hair to the chin may be divided approximately into three equal parts, the uppermost marking the lines of the eyebrows, the next the end of the nose, and the last the chin. The entire width of the head may be divided into five equal parts, each part being equal to the width of one of the eyes, and the space between the eyes, and the spaces on each side, each being equal to the width of the eye.

The general lines of this block form of head in full-front view should first be laid in, after the usual proportioning and blocking in, as shown in Fig. 25. The general outline given to the eyes is in the proportion previously explained, the eyebrows being flattened and more angular toward the outside edges in the block form than in the free rendering. The indentation from the line of the eyebrows to the top of the nose casts a small shadow, and this should be carefully outlined, while two nearly straight lines mark the sides of the nose down the center of the face. The end of the nose is broader than the middle, or bridge, and the two side lobes, where the nose itself enters the cheeks, extend on each side and mark the broadest part of the nose.

Fig. 25

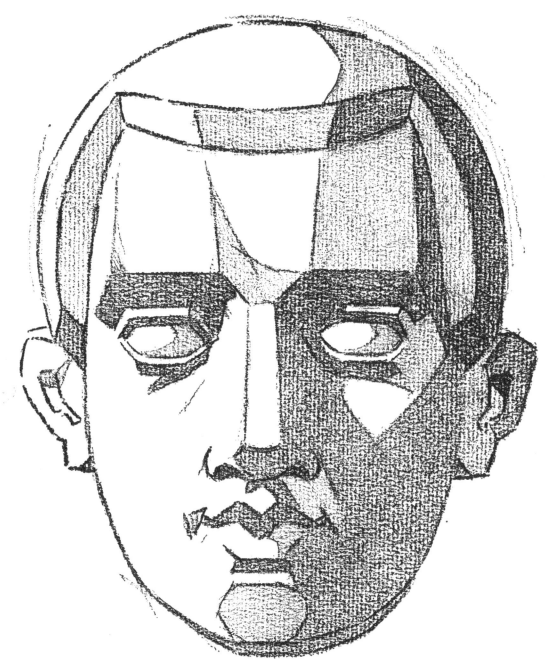

Fig. 26

THE FIGURE IN REPOSE

The mouth should then be outlined, great care being taken that it is properly proportioned, as can be determined by pencil measurement; and the line under the lower lip marking the indentation of the chin so located that it would form, if continued, a slightly flattened circle where it joins the under curve of the chin.

40. By closing the eyes slightly, so that the cast can be observed between the eye-lashes, a great contrast between the lights and shades of the cast will be observed, and the forms of the shadows caused by the various features can be outlined, as shown in Fig. 25, and the shaded surfaces rendered as shown in Fig. 26, although they may appear to be more varied, as shown in Fig. 24. However, it is better at present to render all values in an even tone and leave the gradation of tones until later. If the cast is hung somewhat above the eye, the line marking the roots of the hair will be almost straight, but if nearly on a level with the eye, this line will curve upwards. Slightly curved lines mark the hair on the sides where it rounds down to the tops of the ears. The ear extends from the line of the eye to the bottom of the nose, and in the full front view appears somewhat as shown in Fig. 27. In shading the various flat surfaces of which this cast is composed, it is important that an even tint should represent each part of them. Softness and detail are not desired in this drawing, as a simple block representation is all that is required.

FIG. 27

41. Profile View.—A second position in which to study the cast of the head is in profile, as shown in Figs. 28, 29, and 31. When drawing the cast in the position shown in Fig. 28, a line should first be drawn approximately representing the angle of the forehead, as shown in Fig. 29, and the relation of the line of the nose to this construction line should be carefully studied. Another line from the end of the nose, touching the chin, should be carefully drawn, the angle being studied from the cast itself. The outline of the profile should now be carefully sketched

Fig. 28

Fig. 29

THE FIGURE IN REPOSE

and the edges of the shadows indicated thereon, while the eye and mouth are carefully rendered in accordance with the suggestions made. The ear in this drawing will appear more as shown in Fig. 30, but the back part and inside will be the only parts that are in strong shadow. The line of the hair at the forehead will curve upwards or be straight, as in the previous case, according to the position of the cast, but the line should curve out toward the temple and fall slightly below the top of the ear at the side. The shaded drawing of this profile view will appear as in Fig. 31, where the planes are sharply outlined. The planes are not so clearly defined and the cast must be studied for these lines of limitation.

FIG. 30

42. Three-Quarter View. — The third and last position is the most difficult of these three studies, and will vary from the illustrations given in the text in connection with it, according to the amount the cast is turned from the last position. It should be hung, as shown in Fig. 32, so that rather more of the full face than the profile is seen, and the best guide is to turn it away from full face so that the corner of the farther side of the mouth is not quite visible. This will bring the mouth in the cast, and one eye, in the position previously illustrated. The line of the forehead will not now be continuous down the bridge of the nose, but will reach to the outer visible extremity of one of the eyebrows, and a portion of the eyelids of that eye will appear. All the features possess the foreshortened aspect, and each should be carefully studied before attempting to outline it on the drawing sheet. First draw the outlines of the planes of shadow, as shown in Fig. 33, and then work in the even tones that represent these planes, as shown in Fig. 34.

When working on this figure, each feature should be considered for a while as a separate problem in itself. Sometimes it will be found desirable to make separate studies of the eye, nose, and mouth before attempting to draw same in the face, but when thoroughly understood there should be no

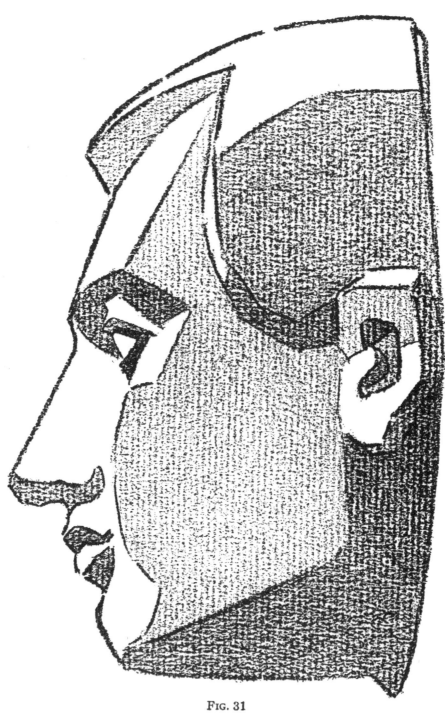

Fig. 31

Fig. 32

Fig. 33

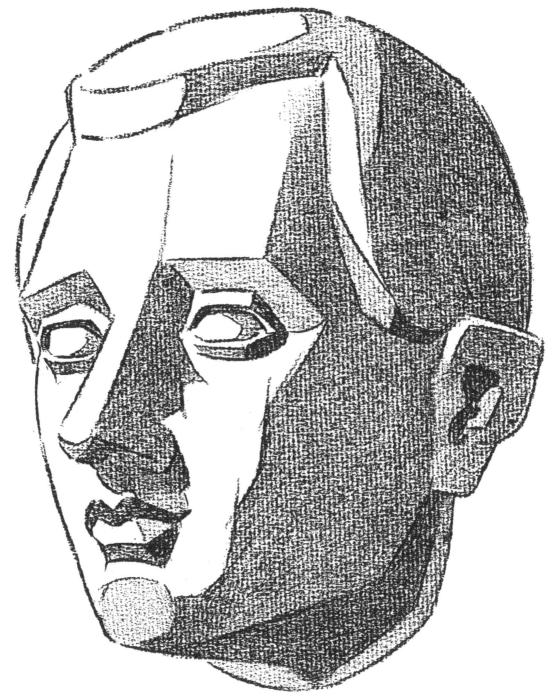

Fig. 34

hesitation to draw them in with bold lines, making pencil measurements wherever necessary to locate the features. Also, from time to time, the drawing should be compared with the cast, to see that the renderings approach as closely as possible to the form. The outline of the shadows should not be attempted until all the features are properly in place; then the shades may be rendered lightly in an even tint, to finish the study. There is nothing extremely difficult about the rendering of this position, if the two previous ones have been carefully studied and executed.

CAST OF HAND

43. Next in importance to a detailed study of the head and face is the necessity for being familiar with the life-size hand and its detailed modeling. The cast that is provided was made from an impression taken from the hand of the living model and not from the hand of a statue, which makes a study of this cast, with all its detailed modeling, extremely valuable.

When it is being studied, the cast should be stood or hung vertically, and conventionally lighted, as shown in Fig. 35. The system of measuring and proportioning with pencil and plumb-line (as used in the studies of the head) and then doubling the dimensions secured may be used, or, the full-size dimensions may be laid off at once on the drawing sheet. In this case the height from extreme tip of middle finger to limit of wrist line will be 10 inches, and the extreme width from the side of the little finger to the tip of the thumb will be 7 inches. When drawing this cast, if desired, the supporting slab need not be shown; this is placed on the cast simply to prevent the outstretched fingers from breaking off. It will be sufficient simply to draw and render the hand itself and put in a tinted background and arrange to have the shadows of the thumb and fingers fall upon this tinted background just as they fall upon the plaster supporting slab.

44. When proportioning and blocking in the parts of the cast, curved guide lines may be drawn to locate the positions

THE FIGURE IN REPOSE

of the points of the fingers, middle joints, and knuckles. Then the main curves of the wrist and of the fingers may be drawn in, and all the fingers and the extended thumb drawn carefully in outline. Special care must be taken to get the contours properly drawn where the inside of the thumb joins the hand and first finger. Before proceeding with the blocking in of the

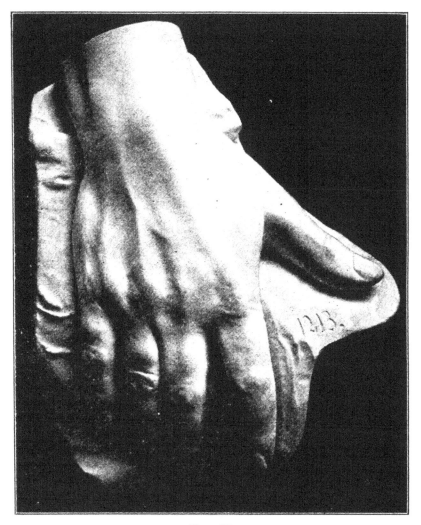

FIG. 35

shaded values, the contour drawing should be carefully compared with the cast and any necessary corrections made.

The system of blocking-in shade values has already been explained fully. If the cast is looked at with half-closed eyes, it will at once be noticed where the deepest shadows and shade values fall, namely, in the hollow of the thumb and side of hand, on the sides of the fingers, and in the little valleys or channels on the back of the hand caused by the tendons and muscles running to the fingers. These require particularly careful observation. When the main shadows and shade values

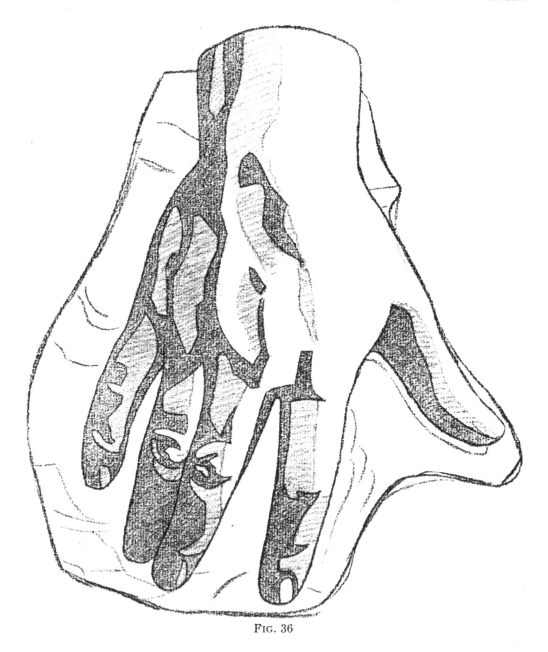

Fig. 36

have been blocked in, the subordinate ones can be indicated as they appear next to the high lights. The blocking-in and tinting of the shade values on the drawing will appear as shown in Fig. 36.

THE FIGURE IN REPOSE

The process of blending off the blocks of shade so as to make a finished drawing is by this time a familiar one, and the rendering should now be completed as indicated in Fig. 37. While it is not expected that the rendering of this cast shall be done

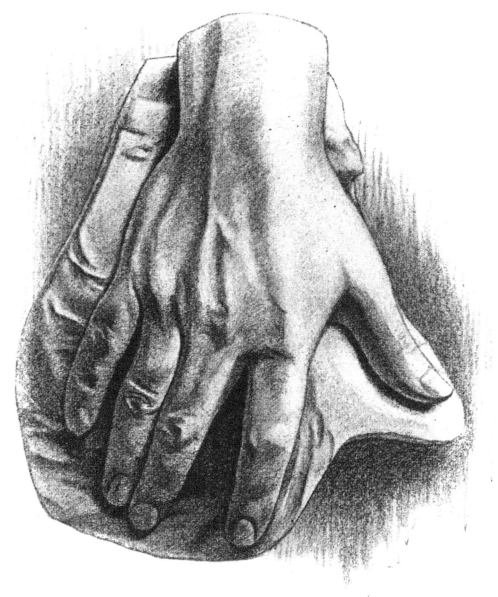

Fig. 37

with such fidelity of modeling that every little ridge and every depression are shown, yet the rendering should be sufficiently complete to show the general modeling of the wrist, hand, fingers, and thumb, and the surface modeling, so as to portray a typical hand.

THE FIGURE IN REPOSE

CAST OF FOOT

45. In illustrating work, even when drawing from life, there will be fewer occasions to render the naked foot than the hand. It is necessary, however, to be familiar with the shape and characteristics of this detail, so as to better appreciate the form when rendering feet enclosed in shoes or sandals, as is more often the case.

When drawing the foot in its first block form, as shown in Fig. 38, the cast should be placed on a table, slightly below the eye, at such a distance that the pencil measurement will make

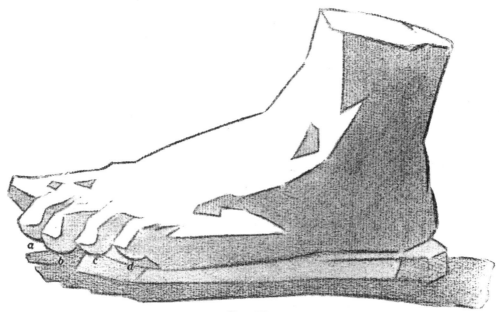

Fig. 38

it about 4½ inches long, which can be doubled to 9 inches if desired. The height should then be located, and the base on which the foot rests. If desired, the dimensions for the drawing of the cast of the foot may be taken direct from the cast, as was suggested in the case of the cast of the hand.

The ankle, instep, and heel should be indicated by a few bold lines, greater care being used to outline the subtle curves from the height of the instep to the point of the great toe. The positions of the other toes, relative to the block on which the foot rests, should then be indicated by a series of small curves, as shown at a, b, c, and d, Fig. 38, and the outlines of

THE FIGURE IN REPOSE

the toes then drawn carefully to where they join the top of the foot. The outlines of the shadows should be indicated as shown in Fig. 38, and all the shaded surfaces rendered in an even tone to express the dark side of the cast.

46. When finishing up this rendering, great care should be given to the outlining of the front of the ankle and the top of the

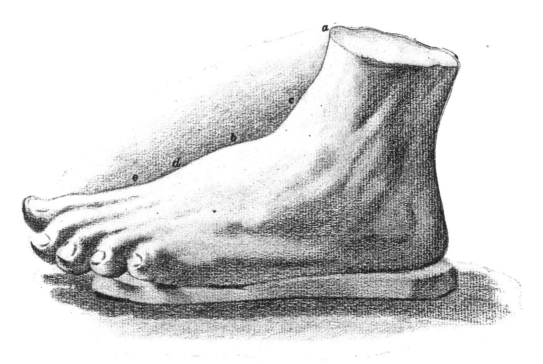

Fig. 39

foot. The straight, bold lines that in Fig. 38 characterize the work may be subdued into gentle curves, but these curves should be studied carefully in the cast, and it will soon be seen that the sweep from *a* to *b* in Fig. 39 is not an even, unchanging curve, but a combination of curves, and that at the point *c* it is nearly flat and in contrast with the other curves appears almost convex, and at *b* and *d* it comes into fulness again.

THE FIGURE IN REPOSE

DRAWING FROM LIVING MODELS

INTRODUCTION

47. Function of Living Models.—While drawing from charcoal studies, photographs, and casts familiarizes a person with the proportions of the human figure and gives valuable training in the rendering of the human form, the art student must be able to draw from the living model before he can successfully portray human beings in his illustrations. But the fact that he is not able to draw from professional models should not be considered a disadvantage, for usually it is quite easy to induce friends to pose for short periods of time, and it is sometimes possible to sketch persons who are not aware that they are serving as models.

For general practice it is well to have the model elevated somewhat above the level of the eye. To accomplish this, the model should stand on a box or platform, while the effect of elevation may be still further increased by the student working in a sitting posture as low as possible. A convenient easel can be made by inverting an ordinary kitchen chair, as shown in Fig. 40, which is a photograph of the life class of a typical resident art school and their usual method of working. The drawing board can thus be rested at a convenient angle with its lower edge upon the rounds of the chair, and at the same time the student can plainly see the model.

48. No one should undertake to make finished drawings from a living model without having first had considerable practice in drawing from the plaster casts. There is no harm, however, in making sketches from the figure that require no longer than 15 or 20 minutes' time, if full and proper attention is given to the direction of the lines and the position of the masses.

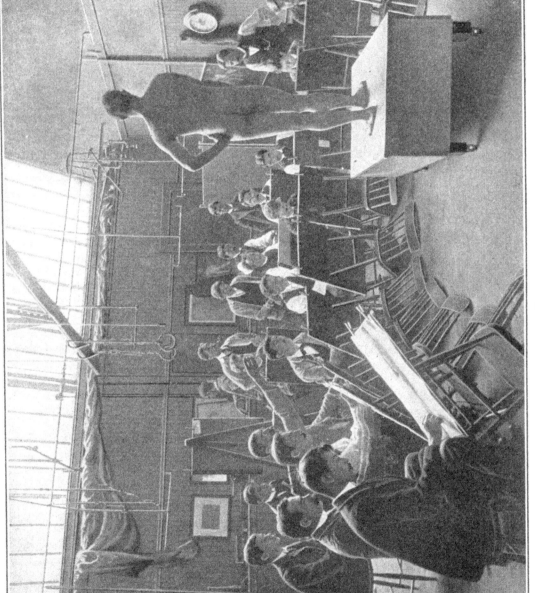

Fig. 40

THE FIGURE IN REPOSE

But the student must be familiar with the forms of the different parts of the body as they appear in the plaster casts before he can successfully draw from the living model. No matter how steady it may be, the living model will unconsciously change its posture under growing fatigue, and unless familiar with form and construction the student will draw one part of the figure as it first appears and another part as it appears after the model has sagged from fatigue.

49. Suggestions for Practice Work.—While the exercises on the drawing plates at the end of this Section require figure drawings made direct from the living model, it is necessary for the student to do a certain amount of preliminary practice work in drawing from living models as he studies the following pages. This practice work is not to be submitted to the Schools. Detailed suggestions for various groups of figure postures, and the making of studies from them, will be given later.

STUDIES MADE DIRECT FROM LIVING MODELS

50. Groups of Subjects for Sketching.—In order that he may acquire skill in drawing from living models, the student is expected to make drawings of some of the subjects suggested in the five groups that follow. In no case are these figures to be drawn in action and all are to wear their ordinary dress. The poses called for are not tiresome; therefore, the student should have no difficulty in securing his models.

GROUP 1.—Some senior male member of the family, as grandfather, father, older brother, husband, uncle, etc., as the case may be, talking over the telephone, full figure showing; reading a book or newspaper; writing at a table or desk; standing, at window or in front of fireplace, smoking cigar or pipe. Or, if practicable or desirable to make partially draped or undraped studies, in running trunks or gymnasium suit, ready to exercise; in bathing suit, ready for dip in lake or ocean; or in any other natural and easy posture in repose.

THE FIGURE IN REPOSE

GROUP 2.—Some senior female member of the family, as grandmother, mother, older sister, wife, aunt, etc., as the case may be, engaged in occupations or occupying postures as follows; the costume or dress in each case being such as is ordinarily worn for such occupation or posture: Sewing or knitting at window or by lamplight; rolling dough at kitchen table; leaning on fence or gate talking to some one; seated in rocking chair with hands in lap. Or, if practicable or desirable to make partially draped or undraped studies, in gymnasium suit, ready for gymnasium exercise or basketball game; in bathing suit, ready for dip in the water; or any other position in repose.

GROUP 3.—Some junior male member of the family, as younger brother, son, etc., as the, case may be, standing, cap on head, books on strap, ready for school; sitting on bank of stream, fishing; flying a kite; building a snowman; or other erect position. Or, if practicable or desirable to make partially draped or undraped studies, on bank of stream, disrobed, ready for a swim.

GROUP 4.—Some junior female member of the family, as younger sister, daughter, etc., as the case may be, in street dress, with hat, gloves, etc., ready for a walk; seated, reading or writing; standing at a window, looking out, profile showing. Or, if practicable or desirable to make partially draped or undraped studies, in bathing suit, ready for a dip in the water.

GROUP 5.—If he is not living at home to take advantage of groups 1, 2, 3, and 4, that is, if boarding or living among strangers, the young artist can secure some acquaintance—as for instance, a room mate or other associate—to pose; or if not to pose specially may make sketches from this acquaintance (or even from strangers) in any of the following positions: Man, or woman, reading book or newspaper; man resting at noon hour eating his lunch; woman resting at noon hour; policeman standing on corner; newsboys, bootblacks, or other characters, in repose. If practicable or desirable to make sketches from the partially draped or undraped figure, a visit to the

THE FIGURE IN REPOSE

gymnasium or swimming pool of the local Y. M. C. A. or Y. W. C. A., and a tactful talk with the physical director, will doubtless result in permission to make at least a hasty time sketch from the partially draped figure of some one in gymnasium costume or swimming suit.

51. Studies From Undraped Figures.—While the figures used in the great majority of illustrations are draped, or costumed, it is necessary first of all to imagine and draw the figures under the drapery, or clothing. Practice must, therefore, be had in drawing the undraped figure. While many people consider the studying and drawing of the undraped figure a most delicate subject, such studying and drawing must not be considered from the standpoint of sentiment or morals. A knowledge of the proportions, contours, muscles, textures, etc. of the human figure is absolutely essential to the art student who desires to perfect his training in figure drawing. Advantage should therefore be taken of every opportunity to study and make drawings from the undraped figure in various postures, and of individual parts of the figure.

FIGURE DRAWING EXERCISES

GENERAL INFORMATION

52. Required Work.—As in the case of former Sections, the required work here will consist of drawing exercises arranged as plates. These five plates will be of uniform size and prepared and forwarded according to a systematic plan. Each plate will be $12\frac{1}{2}$ in. $\times 19$ in., being one-half of the regular $19'' \times 25''$ sheet of charcoal paper. The first two plates will be undivided, so as to contain the drawing of the figure as large as possible; the next three will be divided across the shorter dimension by a vertical line so as to make (on each plate) two rectangles each $9\frac{1}{2}$ in. wide by $12\frac{1}{2}$ in. high. The plates are to be sent to the Schools one at a time for inspection, as in preceding subjects.

THE FIGURE IN REPOSE

The work on these plates will carry out the well-rounded method of training in figure drawing: namely, from studies and photographs, from casts, and from living models in repose. Therefore, Plates 1–2 and 3–4 will be made from other artists' charcoal studies of figures, and from photographs of figures reproduced as text illustrations; Plates 5–6 and 7–8 will be made direct from the plaster casts or text illustration; and Plate 9–10 made direct from the living model in repose.

53. Preliminary Practice Work (Not to Be Sent In). When drawing and rendering the plates required, practice work should first be done in drawing the various figure studies in charcoal outlines. Then, on each plate, the study should first be blocked in with charcoal outlines, and later worked up in charcoal tones, properly placed and graded,—charcoal outlines being eliminated. Certain plates will each show one fully rendered figure, and certain others will show the blocking-in on the left side and the finished rendering on the right side of the sheet.

54. Character of the Plates.—The most important of the materials to be used are the plaster casts from which the studies should be made if possible, and be made in charcoal on charcoal paper. In connection with the work in previous Sections a sufficient quantity of charcoal sticks, charcoal paper, and other materials for working were doubtless secured to do not only the work in those Sections but also the work of following Sections. However, should the supply of any material become exhausted, a new supply should be purchased at once.

55. In general, the methods of working followed in the preparation of drawings made in previous Sections are to be used here. Reference should therefore be made to the previous directions for methods of placing the object to be drawn, taking freehand proportions, blocking in, tests for accuracy of drawing, and particularly the directions for rendering the drawing in charcoal, where are described practice strokes, practice

THE FIGURE IN REPOSE

in flat and graded tones, and the four graded steps of rendering a drawing in charcoal.

Although these methods are to be supplemented by certain concrete practices and plans particularly adapted for properly portraying figures in repose, yet they must be borne in mind as fundamentals when drawing work of any kind is undertaken. To these general directions for methods of work must be added the specific methods of portraying the figure in full modeling, the texture of flesh, etc., that have been given here. When the drawings of the plates are made these specific directions should be referred to, and the drawings made in accordance therewith.

PLATE 1-2

56. Blocking-In and Rendering for Plate 1-2. Make a blocking-in drawing from the charcoal study of the female figure shown in Fig. 12, first carrying the drawing as far as those in Figs. 1, 2, and 3 are carried, using proportioning lines and guide lines. Make the drawing about 16 inches high and make all parts of the figure in proportion. Use charcoal lines lightly placed. Then, upon these blocking-in outlines as a basis, make a finished charcoal rendering of the female figure shown in Fig. 12, completing the modeling and the portrayal of flesh values as shown in the methods illustrated in Figs. 4 and 5.

57. Final Work on Plate 1-2.—Letter or write at the top of the plate the title, Plate 1-2: The Figure in Repose, and on the back of the sheet the class letters and number, name and address, and date. Forward the plate in the mailing tube provided; after which proceed with Plate 3-4 at once.

PLATE 3-4

58. Blocking-in and Rendering for Plate 3-4. Make a blocking-in drawing from the charcoal study of the male figure shown in Fig. 14, first carrying the drawing as far as those in Figs. 1, 2, and 3 are carried, using proportion-

THE FIGURE IN REPOSE

ing lines and guide lines. Make the drawing about 16 inches high and make all parts of the figure in proportion. Use charcoal lines lightly placed.

Then, upon these blocking-in lines as a basis, make a finished charcoal rendering of the male figure shown in Fig. 14, completing the modeling and the expression of flesh values as shown in the methods illustrated in Figs. 4 and 5. Spray with fixatif as usual.

59. Final Work on Plate 3-4.—Letter or write at the top of the plate the title, Plate 3-4: The Figure in Repose, and on the back of the sheet the class letters and number, name and address, and date. Then forward the plate in the mailing tube to the Schools for examination, after which proceed with Plate 5-6, if all required redrawn and rerendered work has been completed.

PLATE 5-6

60. Exercise A, Plate 5-6.—Exercise A is to occupy the left-hand $9\frac{1}{2}'' \times 12\frac{1}{2}''$ rectangle of Plate 5-6. To do this exercise, make a blocking-in drawing either from the cast or from text illustration, of the statuette of the female figure, arranged as a front view of the figure, showing the upraised right arm. This position agrees with that illustrated in the text. Make the drawing about 10 or 12 inches high and all parts in proper proportions. Follow the methods of lighting and working that have been described. Use charcoal or a soft pencil as desired.

61. Exercise B, Plate 5-6.—Exercise B is to occupy the right-hand $9\frac{1}{2}'' \times 12\frac{1}{2}''$ rectangle of Plate 5-6. To do this exercise, make a finished charcoal rendering, direct from the plaster cast, of the statuette of the female figure blocked in in Exercise A. Have cast in same position, and make drawing of it same size, as in Exercise A. Follow method of modeling and expressing values by means of charcoal as previously described. Suggest in the rendering a neutral background,

THE FIGURE IN REPOSE

and allow a margin of white paper all around the rendering. Spray with fixatif as usual.

62. Final Work on Plate 5–6.—Letter or write at the top of the plate the title, Plate 5–6: The Figure in Repose, and on the back of the sheet the class letters and number, name and address, and date. Forward the plate, in a mailing tube, to the Schools for examination and proceed with Plate 7–8, unless there is some work to be redrawn on previous plates.

PLATE 7–8

63. Exercise A, Plate 7–8.—Exercise A is to occupy the left-hand $9\frac{1}{2}'' \times 12\frac{1}{2}''$ rectangle of Plate 7–8. To do this exercise, make a blocking-in drawing, either from the cast or from text illustration, of the cast of the block form of head, arranged as a three-quarter view, so that the sides of face and of nose show. This position agrees with that illustrated in the text. Make the drawing about 7 inches high and all parts in proper proportions. Follow the methods of lighting and working that have been described. Use charcoal or a soft pencil.

64. Exercise B, Plate 7–8.—Exercise B is to occupy the right-hand $9\frac{1}{2}'' \times 12\frac{1}{2}''$ rectangle of Plate 7–8. To do this exercise, make a finished charcoal rendering, direct from the plaster cast of the head shown blocked in in Exercise A. Have cast in the same position, and make the drawing the same size as in Exercise A. Follow the methods of rendering in charcoal previously described and used. Suggest a background and include the usual $\frac{1}{2}$-inch margin of white paper all around the rendering. Spray with fixatif as usual.

65. Final Work on Plate 7–8.—Letter or write at the top of the plate the title, Plate 7–8: The Figure in Repose, and on the back of the sheet the class letters and number, name and address, and date. Forward the plate, in a mailing tube, to the Schools for examination, and proceed with Plate 9–10, unless there is some work to be redrawn on previous plates.

THE FIGURE IN REPOSE

PLATE 9–10

66. Exercise A, Plate 9–10.—Exercise A is to occupy the left-hand $9\frac{1}{2}''\times 12\frac{1}{2}''$ rectangle of Plate 9–10. To do this exercise, make a fully-rendered charcoal drawing direct from the living model; that is, from some one in the family or from some friend who will pose for a few minutes, of a male figure in some typical attitude. Suggestions for various attitudes and actions of male figures, costumed and partially draped or undraped, are given in the text, and any one of these (or some other selected one) may be used. Follow the method of working described in the text, and make the drawing fit conveniently into the rectangle, say about 10 inches high. If more convenient to make the drawing on a separate, smaller, piece of paper (as the page of an $8''\times 10''$ sketch book) this may be done, the smaller page then being pasted in the proper rectangle. Spray with fixatif as usual.

67. Exercise B, Plate 9–10.—Exercise B is to occupy the right-hand $9\frac{1}{2}''\times 12\frac{1}{2}''$ rectangle of Plate 9–10. To do this exercise, make a fully-rendered charcoal drawing direct from the living model, that is, from some one in the family or from some friend who will pose for a few minutes, of a female figure in some typical attitude. Suggestions for various attitudes and actions of female figures, costumed and partially draped or undraped, are given in the text, and any one of these (or some other selected one) may be used. Follow the method of working described in the text and make drawing fit conveniently into the rectangle, say about 10 inches high. If desired, the drawing may be made on the page of a sketch book, detached, and then pasted in the rectangle. Spray with fixatif as usual.

68. Final Work on Plate 9–10.—Letter or write at the top of the plate the title, Plate 9–10: The Figure in Repose, and on the back of the sheet the class letters and number, name and address, and date. If these drawings from the living models are made direct on the $12\frac{1}{2}''\times 19''$ sheet, they

THE FIGURE IN REPOSE

may be rolled and mailed to the Schools in a tube, as usual. If sketch-book pages have been used and pasted in the rectangles, the sheet should be folded once (making it $9\frac{1}{2}$ in. $\times 12\frac{1}{2}$ in.) and then mailed flat to the Schools, stiffened by a sheet of cardboard.

If any redrawn work on any of the plates of this Section has been called for, and has not yet been completed, it should be satisfactorily finished at this time. Having completed all required work on the plates of this Section, the work of the next Section, in which training is given in drawing the figure in action, should be taken up at once.

THE FIGURE IN ACTION

ACTION

1. Action Contrasted With Repose.—It has been learned that the chief characteristic of the standing figure in repose is the manner in which it is disposed about a vertical center line of support, this center line remaining stable and undisturbed. When the stability of this vertical line of support becomes disturbed the figure makes an effort to regain its equilibrium; this effort is termed **action.** The action may be involuntary; as stumbling, falling, etc.; or it may be voluntary; as walking, running, gesticulating with the arms, etc.; but in either case it is the result of disturbing the equilibrium of the figure, or, as expressed in mechanics, disturbing the center of gravity.

That point in a body in which the body, when acted on by gravity or other parallel forces, is balanced in all positions is the **center of mass,** or, as more commonly called, the **center of gravity.** The nearer this point is to the ground or other supporting object, the more stable is the body; that is, the more difficult is it to upset or tip the body.

2. In the case of the human figure, the center of gravity is in the upper part of the trunk, midway between the shoulders. As a result, the human figure is not as stable as many other figures and objects. That such is the case is well illustrated by the necessity for a person to brace himself with legs and feet when a heavy wind is blowing, or to lean against the wind when walking in the face of it. If a vertical line $x\,y$, Fig. 1 (a), is dropped from the center of gravity, when the figure is standing erect, it will be in the median line of the body, and, passing

THE FIGURE IN ACTION

down through the body and between the legs, will touch the ground near the heels, as shown in (*a*) and (*b*). Even though a weight, or pull, is applied to one side of the figure, as when the figure is carrying a pail of water, the other side simply leans away from the weight, or the other arm is stretched out away from the weight, and the center of gravity is not seriously disturbed, for it is kept at a point exactly above the point between the heels of the standing figure. As long as this condition exists; that is, when the center of gravity is not

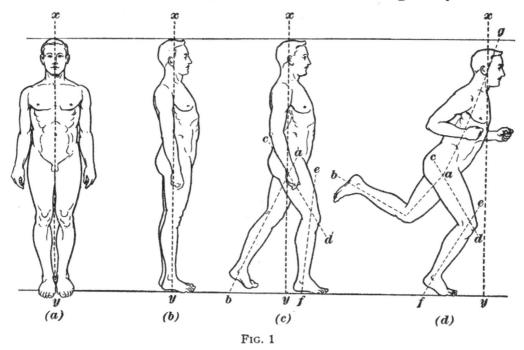

Fig. 1

seriously disturbed, the figure is said to be **in repose;** and it is the figure in repose that has been studied so far.

3. When this center of gravity is so seriously disturbed that it requires quick and violent action to restore the body's equilibrium, as when walking or running, or if it is entirely overthrown, as when falling, then action is shown in the truest sense of the word. Walking and running simply consist of starting to fall forwards on one's face, and then suddenly recovering one's balance by thrusting one leg and foot forwards. Note in Fig. 1 (*c*) that the upper part of the body is pushed slightly in front of the line of balance $x\,y$, and would fall if it were not for the right foot being thrust quickly forwards.

THE FIGURE IN ACTION

In (d), the attitude of running portrays this still more plainly; the center of gravity at the bottom of the throat is then thrust violently forwards, the trunk of the body becoming inclined as shown by line *g a*. If nothing else were done the figure would fall flat on its face, but it is saved from doing so by thrusting first one leg *a f*, and then the other *a b*, forwards and thus restoring balance. Observation will show that when a man stumbles or trips over some obstruction he takes little running steps to keep from falling.

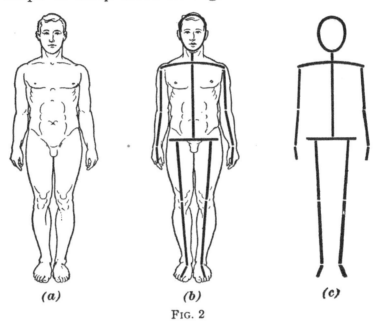

FIG. 2

4. **Expressing Typical Attitudes of Action.**—As has been suggested, when the human figure is being drawn it may be considered as a number of flexible hinged solids, which in turn may be reduced to the simple form of an egg-shaped outline for the head and flexible hinged pipes, or lines, for the trunk, shoulders, pelvic bones, arms, hands, legs, and feet. The position of these lines is shown in Fig. 2. View (a) shows a front view of the figure. In (b) the figure is shown with the heavy black lines placed over it to show the framework; an ellipse is drawn for the head, a slightly curved horizontal line for the shoulders, a straight horizontal line for the hips, and straight vertical lines—properly placed and hinged—for the neck, trunk, arms, hands and legs. In (c) is shown this heavy line framework by itself.

Fig. 3

THE FIGURE IN ACTION

5. With the human figure in this simplified form, it is easy to block in any form of action. A few typical forms of action and the method of expressing them by framework forms are shown in Fig. 3. In (*a*) is shown the front view of the figure in repose; its framework lines are shown in (*b*) directly beneath it. In (*c*) is shown the familiar pose of a man making a speech; his right arm is extended, his left hand is in his coat pocket, and his right knee is slightly bent. The framework of this figure is shown in (*d*) directly beneath. In (*e*), the figure is reaching the arms up over the head as if to place some books upon a high shelf; and in (*f*), directly underneath, the framework lines show these actions clearly, the bent spine, the back tilted head, the upstretched arms, etc.

6. In Fig. 4, examples of more violent action are shown. In (*a*) the figure is jumping. Not only does the position of legs portray this action, but the arms, drawn up tightly, assist largely in showing such action. In (*b*), directly below, the framework lines give a very clear idea of how the action of jumping can always be expressed. In (*c*), two men are boxing; the framework lines, in (*d*), directly underneath, show clearly the bent back and legs and upcast arms of the one and the vigorous forward lunge of the other, and thus give a graphic idea of the leading lines in a drawing of two figures boxing or fighting. In (*e*), the man starts to run rapidly; in (*g*), he is in full flight and covering the ground rapidly; and in (*i*), he stumbles and falls, or pitches forwards from exhaustion. These forms of violent action are expressed by the framework lines of (*f*), (*h*), and (*j*), respectively. In (*f*), the framework lines show the head thrust forwards and the back bent forwards; the left arm is stretched forwards and the right arm backwards; the legs are crouched to give impetus to the first spurt or dash in the run. In (*h*), the framework lines show the head kept vertical, although the back is nearly horizontal and curved backwards; the upper and lower legs in each case make right angles with each other; one foot is on the ground and the other is in the air nearly as high as the body; the arms are outstretched. In (*j*), the framework lines show the action

Fig. 4

THE FIGURE IN ACTION

of running violently arrested by a tumble; the arms are outstretched to save the runner; the back is again bent forwards, and the upper and lower legs are still at angles with each other because the impetus of running has not entirely ceased. These examples of action by no means cover all, nor a great proportion of, the forms of action observable in men and women every day, but the principle of the framework lines and their method of placing can be readily applied to any form of action.

7. Limitations of Movement.—When drawing the figure in action it is very necessary that no expression of movement on the part of the entire figure or any portion of it should exceed the bounds of possibility. Each part of the body has a limit to its power of turning; therefore, when a part is drawn beyond such limit, the drawing is not only thrown out of construction but it oversteps the real purpose of legitimate illustration. It is true that the caricaturist takes many liberties, not only with the face, but with the actual construction of the figure and its parts and their movement. But the present consideration is with the normal and correct drawing of the figure and its action; these must first be learned before one can take the liberty to distort them and make caricatures.

These limitations of movement can be learned only by careful study and close observation. Sketches should therefore be freely made of all possible positions of the body and its members and these sketches kept for reference. The charts, books, etc., published by the makers of athletic goods, showing exercises with chest weights, dumb bells, etc. should also be procured and studied, for their diagrams and pictures give, with great accuracy, the principal movements and their limitations.

8. A few of the limitations of movement are as follows:

1. The forearm bends at the elbow only forwards from the rigid upper arm. If the arm is rotated from the shoulder the forearm may be directed to various positions, but its movement is only a forward one, as if on a hinge.

THE FIGURE IN ACTION

2. The lower leg bends at the knee only backwards.

3. The hand and foot bend at the wrist and ankle, respectively, in a rotating manner over arcs not exceeding 180°; the motion is freer than that of the hinge movement of the elbow and knee.

4. The entire arm can rotate at the shoulder in every direction with the ball-and-socket movement, like the spoke of a wheel on the hub; it can also turn sidewise (back and front) being stopped only by the body.

5. The leg has the same general ball-and-socket rotation but with not so much freedom as the arm.

6. The head can bend forwards, backwards, to the right and to the left, and can also roll around, or rotate. In turning the head, however, the large neck muscles prevent its turning around very far, so care must be taken as to how much profile of the face is shown when the body is drawn in full-front view.

7. The trunk can be bent forwards quite far, like a jack-knife, but its backward movement is quite limited in normal persons. The side and rotating movements are also limited.

DRAWING FROM PHOTOGRAPHS

INTRODUCTION

9. Function of Snapshot Photographs.—It is extremely difficult to be able to sketch, from life, figures in rapid or violent action, expecially when one is untrained in such sketching. Usually, by the time he has decided upon the main action lines or framework forms, the subject has gone or the action and movement have been concluded. The best way, therefore, to start drawing figures in action is to take simple snapshot photographs of typical examples of action. These photographs may then be carefully studied and the positions of the different parts of the body and their relation to the ground and the line of balance learned; the drawing, too, can then be made at one's leisure. But these photographs

THE FIGURE IN ACTION

are to be used only as records of typical action forms and must not be slavishly copied. There are many forms of action, especially if violent or rapid, that are caught by the eye of the camera that are not caught by the human eye. For this reason, a snapshot of a rapidly running horse is quite likely to show the legs in a somewhat cramped or stiff position, because the rapidly acting lens and shutter of the camera have caught the rapidly moving legs in a small fraction of a second when they were passing from one position to the next. However, when the human eye sees motion it registers upon the retina a succession of images, not simply one isolated one, as does the lens of the camera. Therefore, when making drawings from snapshots of figures in rapid action, allowance must be made for this phenomenon, and the constraint or stiffness must be eliminated from those parts that appear stiff and awkward. In snapshots of mild action this stiffness, or appearance of arrested motion, is not particularly noticeable.

10. Suggestions for Practice Work.—It is understood that no drawings are to be sent to the Schools until this Section has been carefully studied and understood; but the student is expected to make, for his own practice, action sketches from snapshot photographs as he proceeds with the study of the text. These studies (made in charcoal) may be from the snapshots reproduced in this Section or in current magazines, from snapshots made by friends who have cameras, or from snapshots made by the student himself.

USE OF CAMERA

11. Necessity for Using Camera.—Every student is supposed to have a camera and to use it freely. This camera need not be an expensive one, however, for cameras that sell for $2 to $10 take suitable snapshots of most subjects. The rapidly acting lenses and shutters of the higher-priced cameras, though, greatly enlarge the scope of one's work and increase the number of rapid movements that can be photographed and, consequently, studied.

THE FIGURE IN ACTION

The actual operating of the snapshot camera and the taking of pictures requires no especial study or training. Explanatory booklets accompany the camera; and, furthermore, the local dealer who sells the camera to the customer is always ready to give any needed explanation as to its use, the method of loading it with the film, using the finder, etc. At first, it may be advisable to have the films developed and the prints made by a reliable photographer, but the processes of developing and printing are easily learned and the work may be readily done by any one who is willing to devote the necessary time to it.

12. Subjects to Photograph.—When beginning to study movements by means of snapshot photographs, a definite course of procedure should first of all be planned. Then the subjects should be carefully chosen and the exposure made when the movement wanted is within the field of the finder. At first, only the simpler forms of action should be photographed; for example, a man walking, a man running, a horse and wagon jogging leisurely along the street, laborers working, a man gesticulating as in making a speech, two persons boxing, two persons conversing, a man riding a bicycle or a horse, etc. As one becomes familiar with taking such photographs, more violent or rapid motion may be photographed; for example, a horse running rapidly, a man on a motorcycle, an automobile at high speed, a motor boat plowing through the water, etc. Then groups of people in action may be taken, in so far as the field of the picture will accommodate them.

SPECIMEN PHOTOGRAPHS OF ACTION

13. As specimens of the kind of snapshot photographs of the figure that should be made, there are reproduced in Figs. 5 to 14 snapshot photographs, all made with the Graflex camera, of various forms of action. These photographs not only serve to suggest subjects that may be photographed as action studies, and how they may be arranged, but they also show some interesting things as to the positions into which

THE FIGURE IN ACTION

the human body places itself when in violent action. A careful study of each one will show the characteristic positions of the body in its various forms of action. These photographs were taken with a rapid-action lens and shutter, and the student cannot expect to duplicate, with an ordinary camera, some of the most violent actions shown.

14. Walking.—Fig. 5 shows a body of men walking. It should be noted that the opposite arm to the leg is the one that swings forwards; that is, when the left leg moves for-

Fig. 5

wards the right arm moves forwards and when the right leg moves forwards the left arm moves forwards, thus preserving balance. It should also be noted how straight are the legs in all the figures, and that the foot on the leg that moves forwards is turned up to such a marked degree that a great part of the sole of the shoe shows.

15. Catching and Batting.—Fig. 6 shows characteristic positions of the batter who has just hit the ball and the catcher

Fig. 6

Fig. 7

THE FIGURE IN ACTION

who is all ready to catch it in the event of the batter failing to hit it. Attention is especially called to the manner in which the batter checks his tendency to be whirled around by bracing himself with the outstretched left leg and the toe of the right foot. The crouching position of the catcher and his manner of holding arms and hands at just the right level to receive the ball are typical.

16. Boxing.—Fig. 7 shows two young men boxing. The attitude of the one on the left in delivering his left-arm

Fig. 8

blow and at the same time using his right arm for protection is clearly shown. The slight motion of drawing backwards, on the part of the right-hand figure, to break the full force of the blow, is also plainly expressed. A careful study of the various expressions of joy, fun, and enthusiastic enjoyment of the boxing bout, on the part of the crowd of spectators, reveal many forms of action and facial expression, which will be of great value in future work. This photograph

THE FIGURE IN ACTION

illustrates, to a marked degree, how very valuable may be made a collection of photographs of typical forms of action.

17. Running.—Fig. 8 shows typical attitudes of boys in a relay race. The near runner was photographed when his body was practically free from the ground. The forward thrust of the left arm and the clenching of the hand are

Fig. 9

plainly shown. The typical attitudes of interest, other forms of action, etc., in the spectators should also be noted.

18. Putting the Shot.—Fig. 9 shows a young athlete putting the shot, and is particularly valuable for study. Here again is shown the action of checking the body's impetus to dash forwards, by means of the firmly planted and braced right leg and the balancing left leg and left arm.

THE FIGURE IN ACTION

19. Playing Tennis.—Fig. 10 is an excellent example of a tennis player's high jump and backhanded stroke; here also the ball is seen just after it has been hit. The man's body is entirely free from the ground and balanced by the outstretched left arm. Every muscle and nerve is exerted with the greatest vigor so that the player not only can leap high enough to get the ball but also can return it by a vigorous backhand stroke.

20. Jumping.—Fig. 11 portrays violent action in its most active form. The young man was photographed right

FIG. 10

in the midst of his vigorous running jump. It will be noted that his body is not only entirely free from the ground but considerably above it. The forward thrust of the right arm as the left leg comes forwards and the backward thrust of the left arm as the right leg extends backwards is very plainly shown. The muscles of the legs and chest are so vigorously brought into play that they plainly show through the clothing and cause it to be stretched and strained at places, as shown.

Fig. 11

Fig. 12

THE FIGURE IN ACTION

The facial expression of the jumper leaves no doubt that he is undergoing extremely violent action; which is a point that should be remembered, for such facial expression, in greater or less degree, always accompanies violent action.

21. Pole Vaulting.—Fig. 12 shows the young athlete doing the pole vault, just as he has cleared the bar, let go of

Fig. 13

the pole, and is about to drop down gracefully on the other side. The position of the arms and hands of the standing figure who is about to catch the pole should also be noted. This photograph shows, in a marked degree, the gracefulness of the human figure in any form of action, no matter how violent.

THE FIGURE IN ACTION

22. High Diving.—Figs. 13 and 14 show divers jumping from an elevated diving platform. Here again is revealed the apparent ease and gracefulness of the human figure, even in attitudes of unusual action. These divers are falling gracefully toward the water, but are ready on the second to alight properly on the surface of the water. It will be noticed, in

Fig. 14

Fig. 14, how the two lower divers are already getting their hands, arms, and head into the proper position for entering the water.

23. Use of Moving-Picture Scenes and Magazines. Moving pictures, and the magazines devoted to moving pictures, are of great value to the art student. Not only do they give him an opportunity to study facial expressions but they enable

THE FIGURE IN ACTION

him to study a wide variety of forms of action. They are of advantage because they are actual illustrations, and the types of action are purposely made dramatic and graphic, just as should be the action of the figures in a newspaper, magazine, or book illustration. These actions should therefore be studied with the greatest care and hasty memoranda sketches made in a convenient notebook. This can be done readily, for most moving-picture theaters are now partly lighted, while the moving pictures, very brilliantly lighted, are being thrown upon the screen.

The magazines issued by the producers of motion-picture films are profusely illustrated by very clear reproductions of photographs from the films shown on the screen. These are practically snapshot photographs, and record in permanent form a wide range of forms of action of all types of men, women, and children.

MAKING SKETCHES FROM PHOTOGRAPHS

24. While a collection of snapshot photographs of human figures in action will prove of value simply as memoranda, the purpose of preparing such snapshot photographs in this connection is that preparatory practice may be had in blocking in the leading lines of action of the figures, and then filling in the other details. The method of making such action sketches has already been discussed, but further instruction will be given in connection with the making of time sketches and rapid-action sketches direct from the figure.

After the films have been developed and prints have been made, the photographs should be carefully studied and the characteristics of each form of action sought. Then enlarged charcoal drawings, properly blocked in and rendered, should be made by the methods used when drawing from the charcoal studies of the human figure.

First of all, the framework of action lines that express the head, body, and limbs of every figure, or animal, in the picture should be carefully placed. Then the proportioning and blocking-in lines should be drawn and then the figures modeled with a fair degree of completeness. These drawings will very forcibly acquaint the student with typical forms of action and how to express them.

25. The photographs and the drawings may be mounted in a scrapbook, properly arranged and indexed. The general title of the scrapbook might be Typical Forms of Action of Human Figures. One section or group of pages may be headed Walking; another, Running; another, Climbing Stairs; another, Carrying Loads; and so on. In this way a book will be formed, the pages of which will be of inestimable use in a practical way at a later period. As a matter of fact, scrapbooks and memoranda of this kind are prepared and used by the most practical and businesslike of the present-day successful illustrators.

The distinct advantage in practicing on the snapshot photographs is that, in them, the action is recorded in permanent form and cannot get away, and therefore action sketches in soft pencil or charcoal. may be made therefrom at leisure.

DRAWING FROM LIVING MODELS

INTRODUCTION

26. Function of Living Models.—A realistic drawing of the human figure in action can be made only after training and experience have been had in drawing the figure in repose from special studies and photographs, from casts, and from the posed figure, and after making drawings of action studies from photographs. One who has done such preliminary work is ready to draw direct from the living model in action. Nothing will serve for this purpose except the living models themselves, in action. For time sketches, these models may be posed; but for action sketches, one must be constantly on the alert and in readiness to make sketches from men, women, and children that are seen every day, walking, running, jumping, etc.

THE FIGURE IN ACTION

27. Suggestions for Practice Work.—Detailed instructions are here given for making sketches of action from living models; these are illustrated with time sketches made in charcoal. It is expected that the student will prepare similar sketches as he studies, not only as a preparation for the rendering of the drawing plate work but as a necessary preparation for the portrayal of action in his illustration work later. These practice sketches are not to be submitted to the Schools at this time.

MAKING TIME SKETCHES

SKETCHES FROM THE UNDRAPED FIGURE

28. To make a faithful portrayal, direct from living models, of figures in action requires careful training and experience. The first step in this training is the making of quick *time sketches* from models in arrested action; that is, quick sketches from a model posed in such a position as to express action but remaining stationary. For instance, a man might be posed as if throwing a ball, having arm up above head, holding ball, the other arm balancing, and a leg raised to give impetus to the throwing of the ball. Even if the lifted leg is steadied by resting it on a stand or chair, the model will find it quite difficult to hold that position for more than a few minutes. For that reason, only a sketch that will quickly but accurately portray the action of the model, without any detailed rendering or modeling, can be made.

29. Method of Making Time Sketches.—The method of making time sketches is the same as when sketching from a model in repose, except that in time sketching some of the stages are not actually placed upon the paper. As the work must be done quickly and as the proportions and blocking-in lines of the figure are now known, it is only possible to suggest, roughly and lightly, the direction of the framework action lines, and then to clothe them by putting in, quickly but carefully, the main curves of the figure.

Fig. 15

THE FIGURE IN ACTION

30. The procedure can best be illustrated by examples of such time sketches, as shown in Figs. 15 to 25, made direct from models by the artist Violet Roberts, and used here with her permission. In Fig. 15 is shown a time sketch of an action pose, the model being represented as fencing. First the usual points were quickly established; these are the top of the head, soles of the feet, and the bottom of the trunk, then the bottom of the chin, the shoulders, armpits, and knees were located.

FIG. 16

Then the action lines were lightly put in, and finally (and that which shows most plainly in the drawing) the main curves of the figure were drawn quickly but carefully. In doing such work one must feel one's way and should not use heavy lines, for these may be incorrect; only light accurate lines should be drawn. The different parts of the figure must be constantly compared with one another, and with the figure as a whole, as the drawing proceeds. It is of primary importance that the

THE FIGURE IN ACTION

equilibrium of the figure be properly maintained and expressed, the center of gravity and line of balance being placed as previously explained.

31. Figs. 16 and 17 are also excellent examples of the simple manner in which a time sketch of a figure in arrested

Fig. 17

action is started, and they will bear very close study, for they will reveal to the student the proper way to start such

Fig 18

Fig. 19

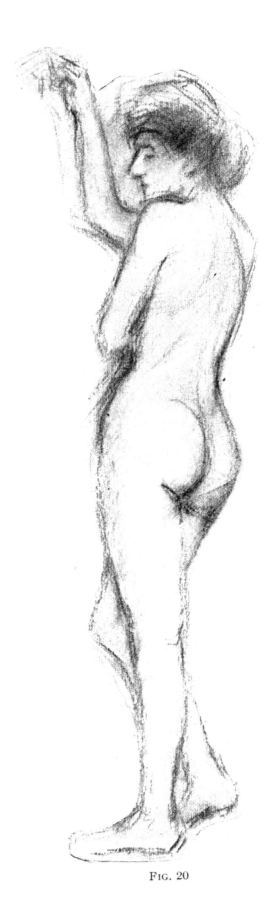

Fig. 20

Fig. 21

THE FIGURE IN ACTION

a sketch. The next step in the treatment (all worked very rapidly of course) is to put in with good bold lines clearly-fixed contours at places where a muscle or bony structure comes, thus giving solidity to the figure. This is well shown in Figs. 18 and 19.

When making time sketches from the female model the angular lines used for the male model should be abandoned and softer, more delicate, and gently curving lines should be used. The female figure is less muscular (at least the muscles are better clothed with fat) than the male figure. Figs. 20 and 21 are good examples of time sketches from female models and have been worked up in the stages previously described.

32. Technique for Time Sketches.—The reproductions of time sketches from nude figures just illustrated, show not only lines but also an even blurring, with high lights taken out. This effect is obtained by using for the rough blocking-in lines the point of the charcoal stick, getting the swing of the figure by using long lines. Then the lines are rubbed lightly with a piece of chamois skin, thus softening the lines and placing a slight tone over the space occupied by the drawing. The necessary lightening of the spaces on the limbs to express roundness is done with a clean part of the chamois skin and the brighter high lights are lifted off with a kneaded rubber. The most prominent shadows, and the crisp accents and the lines to give modeling to the figure are then placed. The tint, or tone, produced by rubbing the drawing, serves as a slight background and also as a half tone on the figure, thus relieving the high lights.

Studies of this kind are not made on regular charcoal paper, or even on water-color paper, for these are too rough; they are made on "Steinbach" paper or board, or what is known as *illustrators' board*, the surface of which is even and regular with a slight tooth, like bond paper, but not smooth and polished.

FIG. 22

Fig. 23

Fig. 24

Fig. 25

THE FIGURE IN ACTION

SKETCHES FROM COSTUMED FIGURE

33. The next step in practicing drawing from the living model in action is to make time sketches from costumed models in arrested action. It would be very unwise to attempt to draw costumed figures; that is, figures wearing everyday clothing, without first knowing how to draw nude figures. When drawing any costumed figure, one should always know just the shape and modeling of the body and limbs under the clothing.

Figs. 22 and 23 show the rough but accurate blocking in of the leading lines of the costumed figure. It is perfectly evident that the one who made these time sketches had a full appreciation of the solidly modeled body underneath. The method and technique of preparing such time sketches is the same as that employed in making time sketches of the undraped figure. These two reproductions should be carefully studied and note made as to what lines are considered the main ones, and which can therefore be properly drawn in the short time allowed.

34. Figs. 24 and 25 show time sketches of costumed figures carried still farther by means of tone values suggested on the clothing. In Fig. 24, the values are only lightly indicated but in Fig. 25 the modeling is carried quite far, so that not only are the finished values expressed but, to a degree, the actual textures of the material are shown.

MAKING RAPID-ACTION SKETCHES

35. Quick Sketching from Unposed Subjects.—It is one thing to make studies and sketches from posed figures, but quite another to make sketches from figures in rapid and violent action when these figures make no effort to pose for or in any way accommodate the one who is sketching. Before a person can make a sketch of a figure in violent action that is even fairly acceptable, he must spend a great deal of time observing how figures move and act. For instance,

THE FIGURE IN ACTION

if he expects to make sketches of men walking or running he must first watch them actually walking or running, as at a baseball game, or on the street. As he watches them he must carry is his mind what he has learned about the proportions of the human figure and the relations of the head and limbs to the trunk, and how these members move, and their limitations of movement. He must be able to see, just as if painted in bold black or white lines upon the clothing of the figures, the framework action lines previously described. By closely observing men walking or running he will form mental pictures of these actions so that he will think of them and see them in composite form. In this way his idea of a man walking will be an image that shows a combination of the various motions through which the man goes as he walks. By thus having observed, he knows exactly what he is going to draw before he touches his pencil to his paper.

36. Making Action Sketches.—Let it be supposed, then, that such careful and thorough observing of various forms of action has been done. To do the sketching, the art student should always carry with him a small sketching pad or book of bound sheets of drawing paper, say, 3 in. × 5 in. or 4 in. × 6 in. (which will easily fit into the pocket) and several well-sharpened soft pencils, HB, B, 2B, etc. Let it be assumed that the sketching is being done at a ball game, and it is desired to make a quick sketch of the pitcher, or perhaps of the catcher who is trying to throw a runner out at second base. It is evident that the player will not hold such an unstable position for 10 or 15 minutes for the accommodation of the student who is trying to sketch him. The artist's pencil must move rapidly under such circumstances, but as he knows just what it is he wants to sketch his procedure is simple and direct. He will first put in, with great rapidity, the action lines, as shown in Fig. 26 (a), by the heavy black lines. He already knows the relative proportions of these lines from his previous study of this subject, and all he needs to do, therefore, is to observe the direction and angles of these lines. After these action lines are placed, the general curves

Fig. 26

Fig. 27

THE FIGURE IN ACTION

of the body may be sketched in lightly, as also shown in (*a*). The pitcher will certainly again assume a similar attitude and the general contours of his baseball uniform may then be sketched in as in (*b*). If the attitude is not again assumed, it may be sketched in from the general knowledge and observation of baseball uniforms. In like manner, the rendering of the light-and-shade values may be worked up into a completed sketch, as in (*c*). There will, of course, be only one sketch when the student makes his drawing on the sketching pad; the three separate drawings shown are simply to illustrate three distinct stages of the same sketch.

37. In like manner, sketches of any other forms of action may be made with great accuracy. Fig. 27 shows the stages of making an action sketch of one of the fielders at the ball game running sidewise to catch a fly ball. In (*a*), the framework action lines are shown in black and the main contours of the figure lightly sketched in over these action lines. In (*b*), the general contours of the baseball uniform are put in; and in (*c*), the completely rendered pencil sketch is shown.

38. Sketches of Violent Action.—When the action of the subject to be sketched is still more violent, so that the subject will pass from the field of view in a few minutes or even seconds, the procedure of sketching is the same, only the powers of observation must be still more alert and keen and the pencil must move still more rapidly. Suppose that a sketch is to be made of a runaway horse attached to a wagon with the driver attempting to check the flight of the animal. The main framework action lines of the runaway horse can be blocked in in a few seconds, and—in even shorter time—the action lines of the standing and tense figure of the driver as in Fig. 28 (*a*). The position of the wheels and body of the wagon can be lightly suggested, to be afterwards detailed at leisure. Perhaps there will even be time, before the rapidly moving vehicle has passed, to hastily plot in the general forms of the horse and driver, as are also shown in (*a*) and (*b*). However, even if the subject has passed out of view, these can be put in from general knowledge of the proportions of

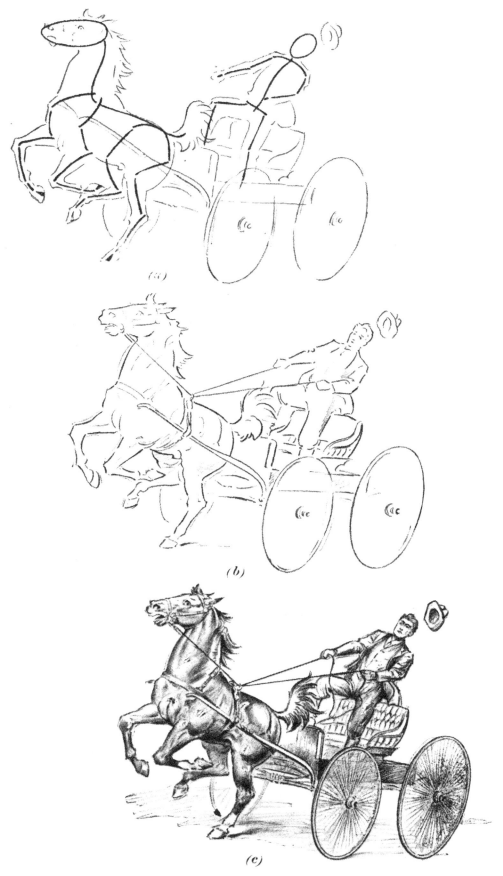

Fig. 28

THE FIGURE IN ACTION

a horse and a man. Similarly, from his observation of the color of the horse and how the man was dressed, the sketch may be finished up as in (c).

39. These directions for making rapid action sketches are simple and will be found usable. They are the methods employed by professional artists and may be relied on. However, the young artist must remember that frequently he will make his sketches in crowds, where people will be looking over his shoulder and perhaps commenting (not always favorably) on what he is doing. He must not therefore become confused but must concentrate his attention and efforts on the securing of a correct sketch of the figure or figures in action.

In like manner, he must not allow the dramatic element of the situation to distract his attention. It is quite natural that a runaway team will excite the onlooker; but if the student is trying to get an action sketch of a horse running away and the driver trying to check him, he must make his drawing as quickly and as accurately as possible and let some one else stop the runaway.

MAKING SKETCHES FROM MEMORY

40. Function of Memory Drawing.—It is not enough for a person desiring to become a newspaper or general illustrator to be able to draw from studies, photographs, casts, or living models the human figure in repose and in action. He must become so familiar with the proportions and modeling of the human figure and its typical forms of action that he can draw from memory the figure in repose or in action. There will be many times when the illustrator will have no one to pose for him, and he must depend on his memory. Therefore, he should be so familiar with drawing the figure that he can use it, singly or in groups, with just as much ease and freedom as he uses the letters of the alphabet. If the instruction that has been given has been carefully studied, and practice work done as advised, there should be no difficulty in drawing from memory the human figure in any desired position.

THE FIGURE IN ACTION

41. Suggestions for Practice Work.—In the following pages full instructions are given for cultivating the ability to draw from memory, and suggestions as to tests for such ability. One can never secure this ability unless he actually prepares drawings from memory and does the practice work in connection therewith. The student, therefore, will be expected to do such practice work, but the practice drawings are not to be sent to the Schools for criticism.

The best plan, when cultivating one's ability to make action sketches from memory, is first to make mental studies; that is, to observe carefully the figure in its various postures and actions, and then to attempt to draw these poses or actions (one at a time, of course) without looking at or referring to the original. This drawing should then be carefully compared with the original, and all points of difference should be noted, and should be carefully remembered. Another memory sketch of the same pose or action should then be made, and again compared with the original, and also with the first attempt, to see how close to actual conditions this second study has come, and whether errors and points of difference in the first study are corrected in the second one. This process should be repeated, and corrections made again and again, until one is able to make a correct memory study of the figure in repose or in action, without alterations or corrections being necessary. In addition to training the memory, this process develops the perceptive faculty because it forces one to observe everything more closely. The tests, or series of studies and corrections, should be made and remade from figures in all conceivable positions and actions.

42. A few of the postures and actions from which these memory drawings may be made are as follows:

A man ascending a flight of stairs.
A man leaning upon a gate or fence.
A man sitting in a chair, legs crossed.
A man walking or running.
A man on horseback.
A man pulling on a rope.
A man using a pick or a shovel.

THE FIGURE IN ACTION

A woman sweeping with a broom.
A woman carrying a bucket of water.
A woman throwing corn to chickens.
A woman combing her hair.
A woman leaning down in front of a stove.
A woman hanging clothes on a line.
A woman pulling weeds from a garden.

This list could be extended almost indefinitely, but the student will find that the making and correcting of memory sketches of these positions and actions will give him a very thorough training in drawing the figure from memory.

DRAWING EXPRESSIONS AND DRAPERY

INTRODUCTION

43. Importance of a Knowledge of Expressions. Although the positions and proportions of the features of the face have been studied, they have been considered only as parts of the entire human figure and as related thereto. As long as these facial features remain immobile they can serve no purpose whatever in an illustration. However, as soon as the human figure gets into action, the facial features also get into action, and there results **facial expression.** Closely connected with facial expression is **portraiture,** which is the depicting of those facial expressions of a person that distinguish him as an individual. Connected also with the consideration of the figure in action is the matter of **gesture;** and also that of **drapery,** because, in the practical application of figure drawing to illustrative or decorative work the figure is most frequently portrayed as being in action and as being draped; that is, clothed.

44. Suggestions for Practice Work.—Typical forms of facial expressions and gesture and how to draw them, and the principles of drapery and how to draw it, are here given. For the purpose of better understanding the descriptions given,

THE FIGURE IN ACTION

and as a preparation for the drawing plate work, the student will be expected to practice drawing facial expressions and gesture, and drapery, from the text illustrations and from life. A pocket sketch book and pencil, carried about with one at all times, will be useful for making such practice sketches. These practice sketches are not to be sent to the Schools.

FACIAL EXPRESSIONS

45. First of all, typical facial expressions must be recognized by careful and intelligent observation, after which they can be portrayed properly, if successful illustrations are to be made. Every illustration of any importance will require, on the face of one or all of its characters, expressions appropriate to that which is being illustrated. For instance, if the picture of two men engaged in a fierce hand-to-hand encounter shows their facial expressions in mild repose, as if they were sitting for their portraits, the whole effect of the picture as an illustration would be spoiled. The proper facial expression must be suited to the action of the figures or to the context of the quoted passage. Further, proper facial expressions must underlie any successful caricature or cartoon work. For the present, however, it is only the normal facial expressions that will be discussed. Later, training will be given in distorting and exaggerating these expressions so as to make caricatures.

A knowledge of all the typical facial expressions of emotions comes only after careful and extended observation of these expressions on the faces of persons that one sees every day in the home, on the street, in the office, and in other public places. Here, above all places, is needed on the part of the student the faculty of observation. Once observed, most of these typical expressions can be carried in the mind, but snapshot photographs or simple pencil sketches to serve as memoranda will be helpful.

Certain expressions that are characteristic of well-known emotions may be readily classified and their characteristics

Fig. 29

Fig. 30

Fig. 31

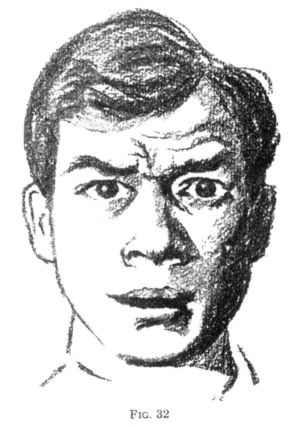
Fig. 32

Drawn by THOMAS PALMER
Used by Permission

THE FIGURE IN ACTION

easily remembered. In Figs. 29, 30, 31, and 32 are shown various expressions on the face of the same person. If, when studying the descriptions of these expressions, it is observed just how the effects of various expressions were secured in the illustrations, no difficulty will be met when depicting similar expressions in the drawing of faces and figures.

46. Repose.—When the facial features are in repose they are drawn just as has been described; they occupy their normal positions and the muscles are at rest. If the person is in good health there is no particularly marked expression on the face, although the eyes will probably have a glitter or snap to them, showing good health and plenty of life. Fig. 29 is a crayon drawing, direct from life, of the face of a young man with the features in repose.

47. Laughter or Smiling.—In laughter, or when smiling, the lips and the angles of the mouth are separated to a very marked degree and the teeth are shown. The corners of the eyelids wrinkle and turn up slightly, the eyes gleam, the sides of the nose are wrinkled, the corners of the mouth are raised and extended, and the upper parts of the cheek are raised so as to partly close the eyes. This last motion gives a pull on the muscles at each side of the mouth, thus making at those places very pronounced vertical curves, like parentheses, thus ( ). Fig. 30, showing the expression of smiling or mild laughter, is another crayon drawing of the face that, in Fig. 29, was shown in repose. If it were desired to portray violent laughter the mouth would be widely opened.

48. Joy, Cheerfulness, Contentment.—As far as outward visible expression is concerned, joy, cheerfulness, and contentment might be termed mild varieties of laughter and smiling. When expressing these emotions, the eyes have a brilliant gleam; the mouth is slightly open and its corners somewhat turned up, so that the teeth show slightly.

49. Sorrow, Dejection, Melancholy, Pity.—When depicting sorrow, dejection, melancholy, and pity, the following expressions, with variations, are noticeable: The muscles

THE FIGURE IN ACTION

of the face are greatly relaxed, and almost flabby. Sometimes the head is bent forwards. The eyebrows are extended upwards toward the center of the forehead. The pupils of the eyes are slightly raised and the eyelids droop. The corners of the mouth are sometimes lowered. The normal length of the face between the eyes and the mouth is considerably increased. In Fig. 31 is shown the expression of sorrow on the face shown in repose in Fig. 29 and expressing laughter and smiling in Fig. 30. On this particular type of face, which is strong and kept under good control, the feeling of sorrow does not so easily affect the muscles of the lower part of the face but it does affect the eyes and forehead. On a face whose features are more mobile, the appearance of sorrow would be more pronounced.

50. Grief, Pain, Anguish, Despair.—Grief, pain, anguish, and despair are all strongly allied with the preceding group. In grief, vertical wrinkles are produced between the brows. The cheeks and angles of the mouth are drawn downwards. The lips are slightly parted and the eyelids and the lower jaw droop.

In pain, there is some frowning. The mouth is tightly closed, the lips or teeth being pressed tightly together; in some cases the mouth is slightly opened.

In anquish and despair, the muscles of the face all droop and relax, and the eyelids droop.

51. Astonishment, Fear, Terror, Horror.—The typical expressions of astonishment, fear, terror, and horror are similar but they vary in intensity. The most noticeable parts affected are the muscles about the eyes and about the mouth. In fear the eyes, which are opened wide and show whites, stare directly at the person or the object that has caused the emotion. The mouth is partly opened; the forehead wrinkled horizontally; the eyebrows are raised; and, frequently, the hair has a tendency to raise itself from the scalp, although it does not actually stand on end as is sometimes described in fiction.

In terror and horror, in addition to the foregoing, the pupils of the eyes are greatly dilated. In Fig. 32 are shown the expressions of astonishment and fear on the same face on which the other expressions have been shown in Figs. 29 to 31.

52. Anger, Fury, Rage, Hatred, Revenge.—A typical outward expression characteristic of anger, fury, rage, hatred, and revenge, when expressed, is that the head is raised and the muscles of the face are rigid; the lips are compressed; the eyebrows contracted; the eyes are glaring; and the veins of the head are noticeably swollen.

53. Scorn, Disdain, Contempt, Sneering.—The common expression of scorn, disdain, contempt, and sneering, is a slight elevation of the sides of the nose; a raising of one side of the mouth and thus slightly exposing the sharp side tooth. This is a somewhat "sneaky" expression, for it can easily be turned into a smile. Sometimes the chin is lifted and the face is partly turned away from the person or the object that excites the emotion; the lips are raised at the corners and the nose is wrinkled; the eye is half-closed, and the pupil lowered and directed toward the cause of the emotion.

PORTRAITURE

54. Portraiture, or the drawing of portraits of individuals, is dependent on the ability to see and draw the distinguishing features of a person. It therefore requires the ability to depict correctly the various facial expressions. The power to see the distinguishing features of a person is acquired by the concentration of the mental as well as the visual powers. But before he can do this a person must have a thorough knowledge of the shape of the head and the face, the shapes of the eyes, nose, mouth, lips, chin, ears, etc., and their proportions in relation to the whole face and to each other, and their proper placing on the face. The habit of thus observing features should become as much second nature as are the ability to recognize the letters of the alphabet and the ability to write. The standard forms and proportions that have been given should be made the basis of any portrait that is to be drawn.

THE FIGURE IN ACTION

55. Portraiture requires the observing of all points in which the features of the individual being sketched differ from the standard forms. In some faces, all the features of the face are crowded toward the center of the face, the eyes being close together, the nose small, the mouth close to the nose, and all the features surrounded by a large area of face. There are other faces in which the features are widely separated, the eyes being far apart, the nose long, the mouth far from the eyes, and the lips long. Some faces show thick hair coming rather low on the forehead, while others show thin sparse hair above a high forehead. Some faces show mustache, beard, whiskers, etc., and other faces are smooth shaven.

56. These distinguishing features must be carefully portrayed in the drawing. But first of all the main features of the face must be blocked in, as has been described, and the main lights, shade values, and shadows broadly expressed. Then the distinguishing characteristics that mark the individual must be drawn in as observed. It is not the purpose here, however, to train the student to make portrait studies. The methods of preparing portrait studies will be presented and practice given in making portraits when the various mediums and techniques for rendering are studied.

GESTURE

57. The facial expressions are always accompanied by movements of all parts of the body; these movements are termed *gesture*. By this term is not meant those studied movements made by orators and elocutionists to emphasize certain passages in their speeches and declamations, but rather the natural, spontaneous movements of the body, or some parts of it, that accompany the expression of emotion. For instance, laughter is often expressed not only by the facial movements but by a gesticulation with the arm and hand, slapping the knee, throwing backwards the head, etc. Fear or terror are shown by both the facial expressions described and a shrinking backwards of the body, and holding out the hands before one as a sort of protection.

THE FIGURE IN ACTION

58. There are certain emotions or feelings that are expressed more by gesture than by facial expression; some of these are as follows:

Doubt and **indecision** are characterized by shrugging the shoulders and a slight toss of the head.

Candor and **honesty** are shown by the head being held erect and by a direct fearless look.

Shyness is expressed by turning not only the face but the entire trunk to one side, or from side to side, as if to avoid facing directly what should be faced.

Self-consciousness and **bashfulness** are expressed by having the eyes looking downwards, a continual movement of the limbs and sometimes blushing.

Self-appreciation is shown by holding head and body erect, and a firm, decisive, confident walk.

Deceitful humility is expressed by a lowering of the head, a shifting of the eyes, rubbing of the hands and a shuffling walk.

59. Sources for Observing Expressions and Gestures. It has already been pointed out that these expressions should be observed in the faces and figures of people that are to be seen every day; this is, of course, the best method. Sometimes these opportunities are not of the best on account of the hasty and flitting view one gets of his subjects; therefore, one must be able to study them more at leisure. For this purpose, there is no better way than to observe the expressions of the actors in the legitimate drama or (for this purpose) in the just as valuable productions to be seen in the motion-picture theaters, familiarly known as moving-picture shows. Indeed, the pictures thrown on the screens are so large, clear, and distinct as to offer to one better opportunity to observe the various expressions at close range than in any other way; and the beginner is advised to make use of this excellent opportunity for this purpose.

There are also published monthly, by producers of the moving-picture films, magazines that give the stories of the newest films, illustrated by photographs from the actual motion plays. These are also valuable to the art student, for here the emotions depicted are stable and permanent and can be studied at leisure. The ambitious beginner will see the advantage of keeping in touch with these motion-picture magazines.

DRAPERY

60. In order that successful studies of living models may be drawn, not only must the proportions of the figure and its parts, in repose, be understood, but one must be able also to draw drapery and costumes, because the models will be draped as a general rule. By drapery and costumes is meant simply the clothing worn day after day by men, women, and children.

It might be thought that there is nothing particularly difficult about the drawing of clothing; that all one needs to do is to draw what one sees. But the untrained eye does not usually see the draping of clothing correctly and therefore the young artist is not successful in depicting it.

61. Influence of Kind of Material.—In the study of drapery, the appearance of the folds and creases is dependent largely on the weight, thickness, and general texture of the fabric, and the way in which it is made up into a garment, as well as on its age and the uses to which it has been put. In an old coat sleeve, for instance, the folds or creases about the elbow will produce, as a rule, a repetition of themselves when the arm is again placed in the same position after having been changed. This is due to the repeated foldings in the same place. But in fresh cloths, the folds will arrange themselves differently, even though the cloth is placed approximately in the same position in which it was before. The study of drapery is therefore important, in order to observe the general directions of the folds under certain conditions and the representation of the texture of the material by the characteristics of the folds as well as by its light and shade. Heavy fabrics will hang in larger folds than lighter ones and will be blunter at the angles. Generally, however, the fold has a definite structure common to all fabrics under similar conditions.

THE FIGURE IN ACTION

62. In the case of an ordinary coat sleeve, which is practically a cylinder of cloth with an arm inside, the general trend and direction of the folds at the elbow will be practically the same in most cases even though the fabric is new; whereas, in a broad and loose sleeve, usually termed the Bishop sleeve, a more extensive range is likely to be observed and no set characteristics can be determined. In the same way, any tight-fitting garment will fall naturally into repetition of old creases. A tight-fitting pair of trousers will crease in much the same way each time the knee is bent; whereas, Zouave or bloomer trousers will display a great variety in the folds. It is a study of this variety of creases that gives character to the goods and the garment. Old clothes will naturally possess numerous creases; new clothes but few.

The gloss and smoothness of silk and satin cause them to catch the light and add another complication to the appearance of these folds. The reflection of light from one brilliant surface to one that is practically in shadow renders the shadow more transparent, and detail in the shadows much more clearly defined than with goods that do not reflect the light. Again, in semitransparent fabrics, such as cheese cloth and veilings, the effect of drapery is very complex, as the light is seen shining through one thickness, giving it a transparent effect, but beyond this it appears opaque owing to the fact that one or two thicknesses lie so close together as to form a solid material through which the light cannot pass.

63. In opaque fabrics with dull surfaces, such as woolens, the laws of light and shade are not influenced by the gloss or reflections from shiny surfaces; the appearance of these goods is then brought out by the modeling, in the same manner that one models the shadows on the human figure. All the convex portions of the folds receive high light, and the shadows cast from them on the concave portions are very dark. These numerous complications make it necessary to work always from the draped figure or model when rendering draperies, as the true characteristics cannot be expressed from mental conceptions until one has had great experience in this direction.

THE FIGURE IN ACTION

64. Supporting Surfaces for Folds of Drapery. In this study of drapery, the point of chief interest is the drapery that clothes the human figure; especially where and how it is supported and how it falls away from the supporting points and hangs in folds. The main supporting points or surfaces are those from which the drapery usually hangs, as the shoulders, or, in the case of a head-piece or shawl, the crown of the head; the subordinate supporting points are such places as obtrude or push out against the drapery,

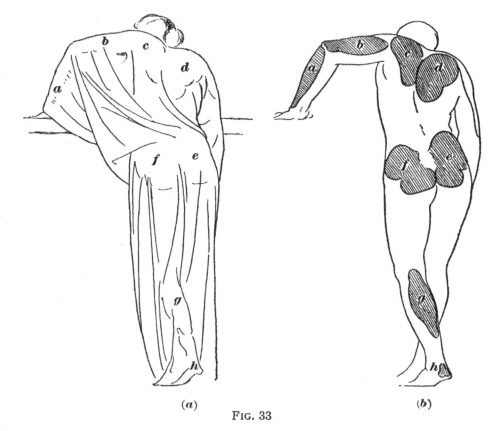

(a)   (b)

Fig. 33

as the hips, the breasts, etc. A very convenient and practical method is to outline the supporting surfaces to be afterwards left plain, and then draw the folds as falling away from these surfaces. This is shown in Fig. 33, where (a) is the rear view of a draped figure leaning forwards, as if looking over a wall, and with the left hand and arm raised as if resting on the wall. In this case the drapery is supported at the left forearm a, left upper arm b, left shoulder c, right shoulder d, right hip e, left hip f, back of left leg g, and left heel h. At these places the drapery is smoothed out as shown, and from them the folds fall away and hang in lines. In (b) is shown the general appearance of the figure under the drapery, and at the supporting points a, b, c, d, e, f, g, and h, the surfaces are contoured and shaded in, to show just where the drapery rests. The positions of these supporting surfaces will, of course, shift somewhat as the pose of the figure changes; but this principle of supporting surfaces should always be used where drapery of any kind is to be portrayed on a figure.

65. Folds Hanging From Supporting Surfaces.—The folds fall away from the supporting surfaces in gracefully curved lines that radiate like the flutings in a sea shell. The higher edges radiate and spread farther and farther apart

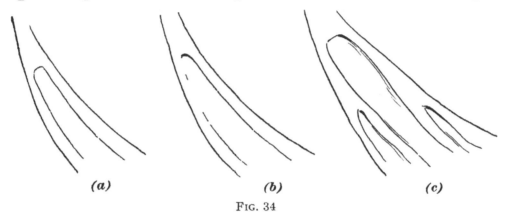

Fig. 34

until they become lost in the body or surface of the drapery. Between the raised edges of these flutes the drapery sags in a concave manner; this concave surface is usually shaded when making a drawing of drapery. In Fig. 34 (a) and (b), the beginning of the two raised edges of the flute is shown and, between them, the sunken or concave part. When the fold is long, the tendency is for each raised edge to again divide, making two more valleys or concave sags, as shown in (c). This system of subdivision may continue still further, and in fact the folds, or creases, do extend across transversely, but the general direction of the main ridges or folds falling from the point of support will be maintained.

66. It must be remembered that these groups, or systems, of folds frequently come together after having started from several supporting surfaces. Where they meet, a sag or series of sags results. This sag, in its simplest form, is shown in Fig. 35 (a). It should be noted that the surface distance from x to y appears to be considerably less than from a to b and c to d; yet this distance is the width of the goods, which

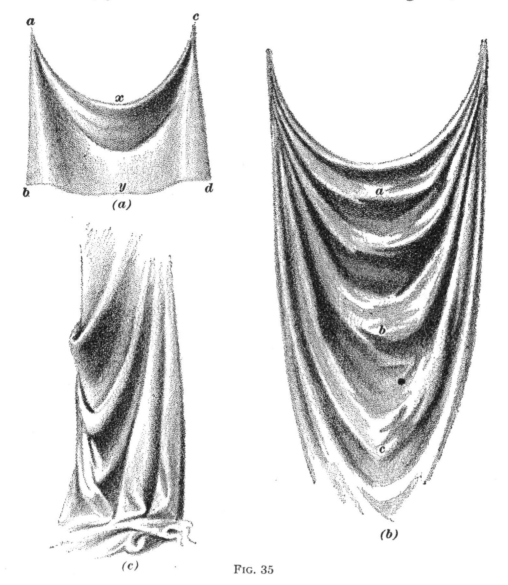

Fig. 35

is the same throughout. The part at x in Fig. 35 (a) simply sags downwards and forwards and pushes the part beneath it downwards and backwards.

In hanging drapery there is, of course, more than one sag, as is shown in (b), where a second, third, etc., follow below the first one. The first, or higher, ones have a tendency to

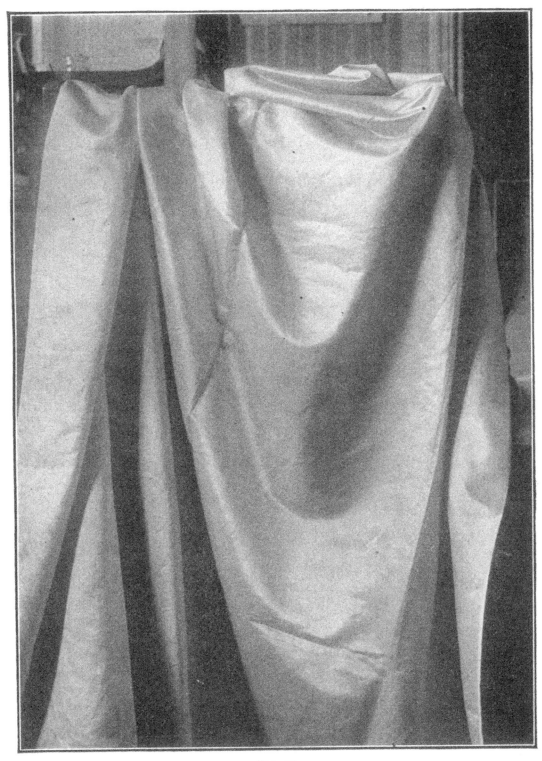

Fig. 36

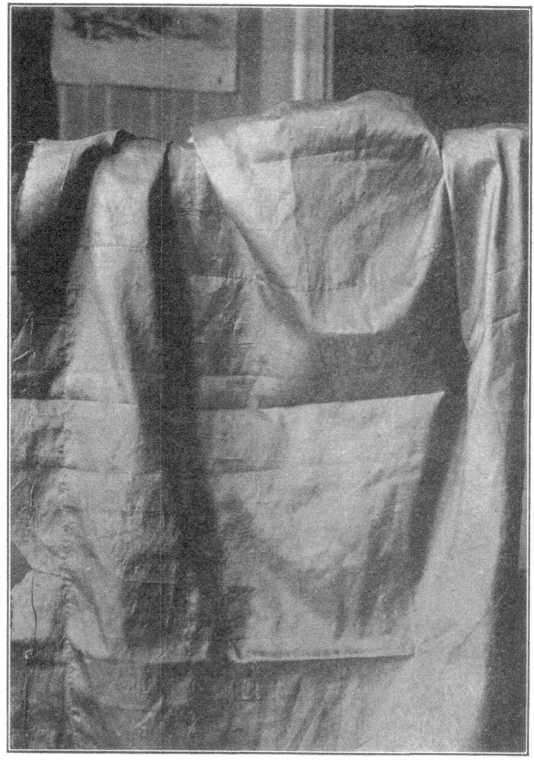

Fig. 37

Fig. 38

Fig. 39

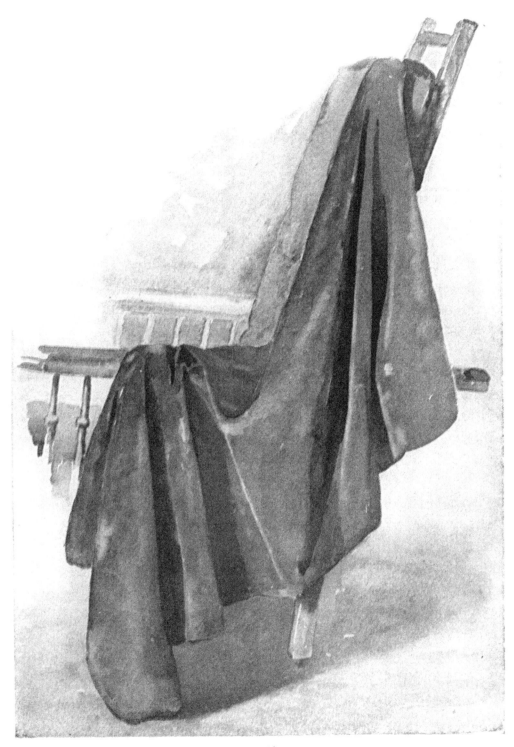
FIG. 40

THE FIGURE IN ACTION

be evenly curved, approaching the semicircle; the lower ones become more pointed, as is shown by the folds *b* and *c*. These duplex, triple, quadruple, etc., sags do not always hang so regularly as in (*b*), but, depending on the weight and quality of the goods, break up into sharp angular folds, sometimes transverse, especially when they reach the floor, as shown in (*c*).

67. Texture of Drapery.—When depicting drapery, the characteristic texture of the cloth must be shown in addition to the appearance of the folds. Both of these points are brought out in Figs. 36 to 42; the first four of these are reproductions from photographs of different fabrics. In Fig. 36 is shown a piece of satin, which approaches nearest to a polished surface in quality; it sharply reflects the light and the various regions of light and dark are clearly marked. This characteristic makes this texture much less difficult to render than some others, the boldness of its planes being much easier to perceive and to record than the subtle gradations of tone in the cotton goods. The silk, Fig. 37, has somewhat the same qualities as the satin, but is softer and more pliable and is broken up into smaller planes, which are apt to be angular and sharply defined. Velure, Fig. 38 (also velvet and plush), has a peculiar shininess, which comes not where one would naturally expect to find it—in the direct light—but on the planes that are partly turned away from the light and on the edges of the folds, where the light strikes the sides of the masses of silken threads forming the long pile. The planes turned directly toward the light are apt to be very much darker; the blotchy effect is due to the nap being disturbed in places, the surface being brushed in different directions. The light and dark regions are sharply defined, but the edges are more softly blended than in the silk or satin. Cotton goods, shown in Fig. 39, hang in rather limp folds; the masses are large and simple and the contrast not great. Starched cotton goods exhibit more sharply defined and angular planes.

68. Fig. 40 represents a piece of old, blue velure, in which the pile has been disturbed by considerable handling. In addition to studying this figure, if possible, a piece of goods of similar texture (not necessarily of the same color), should be draped on a chair somewhat in the same manner; a small piece will answer even if it is in the form of a garment. In fact, this should be done with all the different textures, and all the points brought out carefully studied.

Fig. 41 shows a piece of delicate pink satin draped in large folds that hang somewhat like a lady's skirt. The ripple of light and shade, like reflections in moving water, should be carefully noted. It should be observed that all edges are not softened, many being clearly defined, while others disappear altogether. The folds lying on the floor, in the horizontal plane, appear darker than the upright folds.

69. The example shown in Fig. 42 is a piece of cotton drapery (cheese cloth), of a light, violet hue, arranged on a model; the figure is arranged in a sitting posture in order to give greater variety of planes. The three large divisions should be noted first: (1) From the neck to the hips, a vertical plane; (2) from the hips to the knees, a horizontal plane; (3) from the knees to the feet, a vertical plane. As the large mass of light falls on the horizontal plane, it should be observed how the interest centers in this spot and how the eye unconsciously comes back and dwells on that centered high light. The upper part of the figure fades gradually into the background, both in color and in tone; this, with the soft, greenish, reflected light on the right side and the shadowy suggestions of arms at the sides, gives a peculiarly realistic effect, so that one cannot help but feel that it is an object of three dimensions. It should also be noticed how the dark increases as it approaches the lights toward the bottom, lightens and becomes redder in the reflected light on the inner plane of the fold, and gradually melts into the deeper shadow again, changing into greenish gray. These soft gradations are characteristic of the shadowy parts of soft cotton drapery.

70. Application of Laws of Drapery to Modern Clothing.—While the principles underlying the folds and textures of drapery, as they have been learned, so far, apply to classic

(a)

(b)
Fig. 43

THE FIGURE IN ACTION

draperies and to the modern dress of women, the cloth ordinarily used for men's clothing is so stiff and heavy and the cut of the garments of such a character, that many new points must be observed. One has only to look at the magazine or street-car advertisements of men's suits, overcoats, etc., or at the actual garments themselves as displayed on forms in the clothier's windows, to see that every fold or wrinkle has been carefully pressed out of them until they resemble nothing so much as painted sheet metal. But when the clothes are worn by the average man they quickly acquire folds and wrinkles typical of these garments. The most common and noticeable are those at the elbows of the coat, and at the knees and thighs of the trousers.

71. In Fig. 43 (*a*) and (*b*) are shown typical examples of the wrinkling of coat sleeves and trousers legs. These two views represent two positions of a man when bowling. In (*a*), he thrusts his right arm quite far back, as when getting ready to throw the ball; this causes numerous wrinkles in the upper part of the coat sleeve where it is attached to the coat, and across the front of the coat from the place where is it buttoned in front. These wrinkles are due to the backward pull that is exerted on the entire right side of the coat when the arm is drawn back. As the coat is buttoned about the body, it must be the fairly loose part; that is, the upper sleeve, that will give, and therefore the wrinkles appear as they do, diverging lines from the point that receives the greatest strain, namely, the under and front side of the sleeve hole.

In (*b*) the wearer of the coat extends his arm as when actually delivering or throwing the ball when bowling, and, as will be observed, quite a different set of wrinkles appear. The pull or strain is due to the same causes as in the preceding case, but here the wrinkles start from the back and under side of the arm hole and run across the upper part of the sleeve and the side and back of the coat itself. There are also characteristic wrinkles at the inner side of the elbow where the cloth folds upon itself.

72. The same principles of wrinkling appear in the case of the trousers, as also shown in Fig. 43 (*a*) and (*b*). When the left leg is bent to nearly a right angle, as in (*a*), and the weight is put upon it in the position of bowling, numerous wrinkles appear in the trousers that do not appear when the leg is vertical. The pull is tightly over the kneecap, and the wrinkles are numerous under the knee and above the shoe top. The wrinkles in the left leg in the bowling position shown in (*b*) are practically the same as in (*a*); but in the right trouser leg in (*b*) there are more long wrinkles than in the right leg in (*a*), because in (*b*) the figure leans forwards farther and thus stretches the cloth of the trousers. As in

Fig. 44

the case of the coat sleeves, the wrinkles always diverge or radiate from the place having the greatest pull or strain.

73. In Fig. 44 (*a*) is shown the typical folding of the cloth of the ordinary trouser leg over the instep of a high shoe. In (*b*) are shown the wrinkles that occur in a rather loose coat when the arm is raised; the wrinkles appear not only across the upper part of the sleeve, but down the front of the coat to the coat buttons. Here the drawings of the trousers and coat are more fully rendered than those in Fig. 43.

74. Necessity for Observation and Making of Notes. Only a few examples can be given of how the laws of drapery are applied to men's clothing. The art student must keep

THE FIGURE IN ACTION

his eyes open as he goes about, on the street, in public places, street cars, etc., and must make note of just what are typical folds or wrinkles, for certain postures, in the clothes of the people he sees. These should be sketched in a notebook, on scrap pieces of paper, backs of envelopes, or anything else that may be convenient. These sketches will be of great value later.

FIGURE DRAWING EXERCISES

GENERAL INFORMATION

75. Required Work.—The required work in this Section will consist of the preparation of four plates of drawing exercises of uniform size, about $12\frac{1}{2}$ in. $\times 19$ in., as in previous cases, being prepared and submitted to the Schools for examination as before. Some of the plates will be arranged horizontally and will consist of two $9\frac{1}{2}'' \times 12\frac{1}{2}''$ exercises each, one exercise showing the blocked-in action lines and the other exercise the finished pictorial rendering of the figure or figures in action. The remaining plates will be arranged and contain exercises as listed in the text descriptions.

76. Preliminary Practice Work (Not To Be Sent In).—Although only four plates are required to be sent in to the Schools, it will be good practice for the student to draw (but not to send in) the other diagrams and illustrations of figures in action. In fact, throughout the Course, the student should do as much supplementary practice work as possible.

77. Character of the Plates.—Charcoal is to be used in preparing the drawings; line work is to be used for the blocking-in drawings to show action lines, and blended tones to portray the completed drawings. Methods of work, in rendering the plate exercises, should be employed as directed in the text. Any one who has faithfully done the practice work advised throughout this Section will have no difficulty with the drawing or the rendering of the plates.

THE FIGURE IN ACTION

PLATE 1-2

78. Exercise A, Plate 1-2.—Exercise A is to occupy the left $9\frac{1}{2}'' \times 12\frac{1}{2}''$ rectangle of Plate 1-2. To draw this exercise, make a time sketch, showing only the blocking-in lines and posture lines, direct from the living model, that is, from some one who will pose for several minutes, of a figure in arrested action. Prepare the drawing according to the method described in the text. Indicate at the bottom of the drawing the amount of time spent upon the sketch. Spray with fixatif and allow to dry.

79. Exercise B, Plate 1-2.—Exercise B is to occupy the right $9\frac{1}{2}'' \times 12\frac{1}{2}''$ rectangle of Plate 1-2. To draw this exercise, make a finished detail rendering, same size and position, of the blocked-in time sketch from life prepared for Exercise A, finishing it as described for previous plates. Spray with fixatif and allow to dry.

80. Final Work on Plate 1-2.—Letter or write at the top of the plate the title, Plate 1-2: The Figure in Action, and on the back of the sheet the class letters and number, name and address, and date. The sheet may then be rolled and mailed to the Schools in a tube, or if separate sketch-book pages have been pasted on the sheet it may be folded once and mailed flat to the Schools as before described. The work of Plate 3-4 may then be taken up.

PLATE 3-4

81. Exercise A, Plate 3-4.—Exercise A is to occupy the left $9\frac{1}{2}'' \times 12\frac{1}{2}''$ rectangle of Plate 3-4. To draw this exercise, make a blocking-in sketch, direct from a human figure in violent or rapid action, according to the method illustrated in Figs. 26, 27, and 28. Show with heavy block lines the action lines and block in the general contours of the rest of the figure. Make the figure about 8 inches or 10 inches high, and, if desired, make it on separate page of sketch book

THE FIGURE IN ACTION

and paste in proper rectangle. Spray with fixatif and allow to dry.

82. Exercise B, Plate 3-4.—Exercise B is to occupy the right $9\frac{1}{2}'' \times 12\frac{1}{2}''$ rectangle of Plate 3-4. To draw this exercise, with the blocked-in sketch of Exercise A as data, make a finished detail rendering of this same action study, same size and arrangement as in Exercise A. Render the drawing completely as has been done in the case of previous plates. Spray with fixatif and allow to dry.

It is important that these drawings of violent action should be made direct from life, and not in any other way. The student must not try to evade the requirements of this plate, for his later success in this work will depend on such practice in drawing direct from living models in action.

83. Final Work on Plate 3-4.—Letter or write at the top of the plate the title, Plate 3-4: The Figure in Action, and on the back of the sheet the class letters and number, name and address, and date. The sheet may then be rolled and mailed to the Schools in a tube, or if separate sketch-book pages have been pasted onto the sheet it may be folded once and mailed flat to the Schools as before described. The work of Plate 5-6 may then be taken up, unless there is work to be redrawn on previous plates.

PLATE 5-6

84. Drawing Exercises, Plate 5-6.—This plate is to be vertical, and divided into four $6\frac{1}{4}'' \times 9\frac{1}{2}''$ rectangles. It is to contain charcoal copies of the four charcoal studies of expressions shown in Figs. 29, 30, 31, and 32. Each head is to be made about three or four times the size shown in the illustration and the exercises are to be arranged on the sheet as follows:

Exercise A is to be drawn in the upper left-hand rectangle; this exercise is the face with features in repose.

Exercise B is to be drawn in the upper right-hand retangle; this exercise is the face smiling.

THE FIGURE IN ACTION

Exercise C is to be drawn in the lower left-hand corner; this exercise is the face expressing sorrow.

Exercise D is to be drawn in the lower right-hand corner; this exercise is the face expressing fear.

Spray all studies with fixatif and allow to dry.

85. Final Work on Plate 5-6.—Letter or write at the top of the plate the title, Plate 5-6: The Figure in Action, and on the back of the sheet the class letters and number, name and address, and date. Do not send this sheet to the Schools at this time, but hold it until Plate 7-8 has been finished. Proceed now with Plate 7-8, if all uncompleted work on previous plates has been finished.

PLATE 7-8

86. Drawing Exercises, Plate 7-8.—This plate is to be vertical, and divided into four $6\frac{1}{4}'' \times 9\frac{1}{2}''$ rectangles. It is to contain charcoal drawings of the four expressions of repose, smiling, sorrow, and fear; but, instead of being copied from other drawings, they are to be made direct from the face of some one who will pose. An excellent plan is to make the drawings from one's own face as seen in a mirror set up vertically before one as he works. The portrayals of these four expressions must be made from life. If possible, a photograph of the person whose face is being portrayed should be sent along with the drawing plate and fastened to it by pins or clips. Do not send photograph separately. The four studies are to be arranged on the sheet as follows:

Exercise A is to be drawn in the upper left-hand rectangle; this exercise is to be the face with features in repose.

Exercise B is to be drawn in the upper right-hand rectangle; this exercise is to be the face smiling.

Exercise C is to be drawn in the lower left-hand rectangle; this exercise is to be the face expressing sorrow.

Exercise D is to be drawn in the lower right-hand rectangle; this exercise is to be the face expressing fear.

Spray all studies with fixatif and allow to dry.

THE FIGURE IN ACTION

87. Final Work on Plate 7-8.—Letter or write at the top of the plate the title, Plate 7-8: The Figure in Action, and on the back of the sheet the class letters and number, name and address, and the date. Place Plates 5-6 and 7-8 in the mailing tube and send them together to the Schools in the usual way for examination. If the photograph sent with Plate 7-8 is mounted on a card, it will be necessary to send the plates flat, after folding them once to size $9\frac{1}{2}$ in. $\times 12\frac{1}{2}$ in.

If any redrawn work on any of the plates of this Section has been called for, and has not yet been completed, it should be satisfactorily finished at this time. Having completed all required work on the plates of this Section, the work of the next Section should be taken up at once.

OTHER BOOKS FROM CGR PUBLISHING AT CGRPUBLISHING.COM

1939 New York World's Fair: The World of Tomorrow in Photographs

San Francisco 1915 World's Fair: The Panama-Pacific International Expo.

1904 St. Louis World's Fair: The Louisiana Purchase Exposition in Photographs

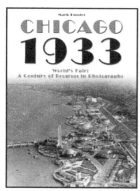
Chicago 1933 World's Fair: A Century of Progress in Photographs

19th Century New York: A Dramatic Collection of Images

The American Railway: The Trains, Railroads, and People Who Ran the Rails

The Aeroplane Speaks: Illustrated Historical Guide to Airplanes

The World's Fair of 1893 Ultra Massive Photographic Adventure Vol. 1

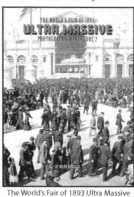
The World's Fair of 1893 Ultra Massive Photographic Adventure Vol. 2

The World's Fair of 1893 Ultra Massive Photographic Adventure Vol. 3

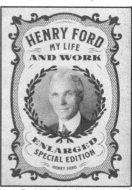
Henry Ford: My Life and Work - Enlarged Special Edition

Magnum Skywolf #1

Ethel the Cyborg Ninja Book 1

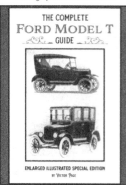
The Complete Ford Model T Guide: Enlarged Illustrated Special Edition

How To Draw Digital by Mark Bussler

Best of Gustave Doré Volume 1: Illustrations from History's Most Versatile...

OTHER BOOKS FROM CGR PUBLISHING AT CGRPUBLISHING.COM

Ultra Massive Video Game Console Guide Volume 1

Ultra Massive Video Game Console Guide Volume 2

Ultra Massive Video Game Console Guide Volume 3

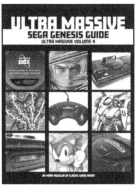
Ultra Massive Sega Genesis Guide

Antique Cars and Motor Vehicles: Illustrated Guide to Operation...

Chicago's White City Cookbook

The Clock Book: A Detailed Illustrated Collection of Classic Clocks

The Complete Book of Birds: Illustrated Enlarged Special Edition

1901 Buffalo World's Fair: The Pan-American Exposition in Photographs

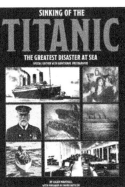
Sinking of the Titanic: The Greatest Disaster at Sea

Gustave Doré's London: A Pilgrimage: Retro Restored Special Edition

Milton's Paradise Lost: Gustave Doré Retro Restored Edition

The Art of World War 1

The Kaiser's Memoirs: Illustrated Enlarged Special Edition

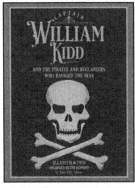
Captain William Kidd and the Pirates and Buccaneers Who Ravaged the Seas

The Complete Butterfly Book: Enlarged Illustrated Special Edition

- MAILING LIST -
JOIN FOR EXCLUSIVE OFFERS

www.CGRpublishing.com/subscribe

Made in the USA
Monee, IL
24 November 2021